What I Heard in the Silence

What I Heard in the Silence:

Role Reversal, Trauma, and Creativity in the Lives of Women

MARIA V. BERGMANN

INTERNATIONAL UNIVERSITIES PRESS, INC.
MADISON   CONNECTICUT

INTERNATIONAL UNIVERSITIES PRESS® and IUP (& design) ® are registered trademarks of International Universities Press, Inc.

Library of Congress Cataloging-in-Publication Data

Bergmann, Maria V.
    What I heard in the silence : role reversal, trauma, and creativity in the lives of women / Maria V. Bergmann.
       p. cm.
    Includes bibliographical references and indexes.
    ISBN 0-8236-6842-8
    1. Women—Mental health. 2. Psychoanalysis. 3. Psychoanalysis—Case studies. 4. Role reversal. 5. Psychic trauma. I. Title.

RC451.4.W6 B45   2000
616.89′0082—dc21   00-039572

Manufactured in the United States of America

To Martin
Ein Acher
and to
Michael, Meredith, and Daniel
with love.

Table of Contents

Acknowledgments   ix

Preface   xi

Introduction   1

Part I: *Women's Struggle to Experience Love, Sexuality, and Maternity*

1. Mother–Daughter Role Reversal, Delayed Marriage, and Maternity   9
2. Depression, the "Dead" Mother, and Role Reversal   29
3. The Psychoanalysis of Emma   41

Part II: *The Female Oedipus Complex: The Two Analyses of Maureen*

4. The Female Oedipus Complex: Antecedents and Evolution   67
5. Narcissistic and Phobic Character Formation in an Adult Patient: The First Analysis of Maureen   93
6. A Pathological Oedipal Constellation in a Female Patient: The Second Analysis of Maureen   113

Part III: *Trauma and Retraumatization in Clinical Work*

7. Thoughts on Superego Pathology in Survivors
    and Their Children   135
8. An Infantile Trauma and a Trauma during Analysis   161
9. Retraumatization Anxiety and the Defensive Function
    of the Negative Therapeutic Reaction   175

Part IV: *Creativity and Work Inhibition*

10. Creative Work, Work Inhibitions, and Their Relation
     to Internal Objects   195

References   213

Name Index   227

Subject Index   229

ACKNOWLEDGMENTS

To all those who have shaped my development as a person and as a psychoanalyst, I owe immense gratitude. My development as an analyst has spanned so many years that the list is very long. It includes my patients, my students, my colleagues, my teachers, and my analyst.

I want to express my very special thanks to Drs. Graciela Abelin and Ruth Lax for their enthusiastic and welcoming attitude toward my work. With them I have been able to test my ideas with complete freedom.

Friends and colleagues who have read an entire chapter or more of this book, and commented critically and generously on its content, include Drs. William Grossman, Otto Kernberg, Anton Kris, and Warren Poland.

The special capacities for insight as well as editorial skill of my son Michael were of great help to me. His poetic bent influenced my choice of a title for the book.

I want to express very special thanks to my most competent secretarial helpers, Donzelina Barroso and Erica Wylens, who gave their time and ceaseless efforts with warmth, enthusiasm, and friendship, even in my most difficult moments, to Catherine Ventura-Ward's editorial counsel, and to Michael Farrin, whose editorial skill helped me bring the book into final shape.

Versions of several of the chapters have been published previously, in whole or in part.

Chapter 1 is a revision of "The Effects of Role Reversal on Delayed Marriage and Maternity," which appeared in *The Psychoanalytic Study of the Child* (1985), 40:197–219. New Haven, CT: Yale University Press.

Chapter 4 is reprinted in revised form from *Early Female Development: Current Psychoanalytic Views,* edited by D. Mendell (1982). New York and London: SP Medical and Scientific Books, pp. 175–201.

Chapter 5 is a revision of "On the Genesis of Narcissistic and Phobic Character Formation in an Adult Patient: A Developmental View," which appeared in the *International Journal of Psycho-Analysis* (1980), 61:535–546.

Chapter 6 is a revised and expanded version of "The Nature and Function of a Pathological Oedipal Constellation in a Female Patient," which appeared in the *Psychoanalytic Quarterly* (1995), 64:517–532.

Chapter 7 is a considerably revised version of "Thoughts on Superego Pathology of Survivors and Their Children," which appeared in *Generations of the Holocaust,* edited by M. S. Bergmann and M. E. Jucovy (1982). New York: Basic Books, pp. 287–309.

Chapter 8 is a revision of "An Infantile Trauma, a Trauma during Analysis, and Their Connection," which appeared in the *International Journal of Psycho-Analysis* (1992), 73:447–454.

Chapter 9 consists of versions given at the Annual Meeting of the New York Freudian Society on April 18, 1998 and at the Spring Meeting of the American Psychoanalytic Association in Toronto, Canada on May 30, 1998.

Chapter 10 is a revision of "Creative Work, Work Inhibitions, and Their Relation to Internal Objects," which appeared in *Work and Its Inhibitions: Psychoanalytic Essays,* edited by C.W. Socarides and S. Kramer (1997). Madison, CT: International Universities Press, pp. 191–207. An earlier version appeared in *The Spectrum of Psychoanalysis, Essays in Honor of Martin S. Bergmann,* edited by A. K. Richards and A. D. Richards (1994). Madison, CT: International Universities Press, pp. 353–371.

Preface

Janine Chasseguet-Smirgel

There is something quite remarkable about this book and it may even be unique in its genre. It offers an unmistakable unity despite the fact that it consists in a collection of articles written over the past twenty years and updated into a current psychoanalytic framework. It thus constitutes an unequalled source of information about the evolution of psychoanalytic ideas, particularly those bearing on technique, in the United States during and following the "Hartmannian Era," that is in the period extending from the rise of ego psychology to its current decline. The book therefore represents an interesting contribution to the history of psychoanalysis in America.

Maria Bergmann seems to have been a follower of the ideas of Margaret Malher, something suggested by her numerous but always apposite references to this author's published writings as well as to her personal communications. In the depiction of her own technique in this work, she evokes certain instances of enactments, a subject currently receiving considerable attention in American psychoanalysis but which can be observed in the treatments conducted by many analysts, especially with more difficult patients. By this I mean patients who are difficult to reach through classical technique which is better suited to neurotic subjects who are more capable of symbolization.

xi

This brings us to another important aspect of this book. The patients that are so scrupulously and sensitively presented are essentially borderline, such as those have been described by Otto Kernberg. With the exception of one case (Mr. M), all the patients whose analyses are recounted here are women. Beyond their individual differences, they manifest striking similarities, making this work a valuable document on the problems of femininity that are encountered in clinical practice on both sides of the Atlantic. Eating disorders are presented in the cases of Emma, Anita, Maureen, and Laura as well as Mr. M, whose pathology was centered on uncertainties regarding his gender identity, a problem that was a common feature of almost all the patients discussed in this work. Experiencing themselves as neither men nor women, these patients were in a protracted fog, with pervasive feelings of unreality accompanied by episodes of depersonalization and twilight states. In varying degrees, they all demonstrated perverse trends.

These patients had all been severely traumatized, and the book thus also provides a clinical presentation of the effects of psychological trauma. Leaving aside the important question of real or imagined incest, there is an unequivocal "incest-like" atmosphere—to use the expression of the late French analyst Paul-Claude Racamier—that permeates many of these cases, and issues of abandonment are also in evidence to a greater or lesser extent, entailing feelings of aloneness and distress. One patient (Emma) had to endure, horribile dictu, the ligature of her Fallopian tubes and this invasive procedure was undertaken with the complicity of her mother. It can legitimately be wondered how it is that these patients did not come to irremediably give themselves over to unmitigated hatred, destructiveness and madness. It is probably due to the long, patient and reparative therapeutic efforts undertaken by Maria Bergmann. This allowed their artistic abilities to emerge and flower from within their chaotic and mutilated lives, restoring to them their creative gifts and capacities for love. Certainly the task was arduous, as is illustrated by "The Two Analyses of Maureen," the first of which addressed narcissistic pathology (in contrast to Kohut's work with Mr. Z), but this proved insufficient and necessitated further treatment oriented in another way.

In this book Maria Bergmann presents a theory of mother-daughter role reversal in which she takes pains to show the mother's contribution to this situation. A relationship might be drawn between this part of her work and an article by the French analyst

Pierre Bourdier (1972) who has described the "hyper-maturity of the children of mentally ill parents." In a certain manner, the parents of the patients discussed are themselves very gravely ill. They have made their children the repositories of their own pathology and have endeavored to transform them into mother-therapists. At the same time, haven't those patients sought solutions of self-sufficiency (autarkic solutions) for their distress, attempting to do without the frustrating and intrusive objects that have put them in the impossible role of being parents to their parents? Aren't the eating disorders, masturbation, addictions, and even perverse acts desperate attempts to achieve self-sufficiency? The encounter with analysis and the analyst has made it possible for these patients, through meticulous work in common, that is exemplary here, to regain the path to the object.

Introduction

> *The voice of the intellect is a soft one, but it does not rest till it has gained a hearing. Finally, after a countless succession of rebuffs, it succeeds. This is one of the few points on which one may be optimistic about the future of mankind. . . . And from it, one can derive yet other hopes. . . [Freud, 1925a, p. 53].*

A book is a journey. It goes over hillocks, bumps, valleys, and heights (trying to avoid an abyss). One retraverses one's life—one's inner life, one's self-analysis, and retravels through one's professional field, through one's external life, the events that were decisive in shaping one as a person.

When I undertook to write these papers, I started a new dialogue with myself, a journey which led to new discoveries I did not expect. Both what I rewrote and what I added contain new vistas of my psychoanalytic thought. More than ever before I became aware of the profound and still *current* relevance of Freud's discoveries, albeit in the context of the twentieth and twenty-first centuries. I also became aware of the extent to which I had changed as a clinician and needed to reformulate many of my views and rewrite even my most recently published thoughts.

1

I realized that having to make all these changes is a reflection of the enormous flux in our era and the rapidity with which new insights and consequent changes occur. For me this is a reflection not of a new eclecticism, for I stand by my Freudian orientation, but of a new relativism that permeates our time and that I consider relevant for our changing ideas: it all depends on who a particular patient is, and who the analyst is for that patient; how one assesses treatment issues with one individual may be quite unlike the assessment of comparable issues with another. Patient and analyst are two people in a room who hear each other in a certain way, which is difficult to register fully while in the midst of that dialogue.

As a student of psychoanalysis, I was steeped in a tradition in which Freud and his discoveries were idealized and a sense of certainty prevailed about what was known. "Know thyself," learn the truth, and you will be helped, even cured! During the Hartmann era, when I was a student, this attitude still permeated psychoanalytic thought. The idealization of Freud was interwoven with great excitement about his discovery of the unconscious and his ideas of psychic function. Many analysts who had been with Freud in Vienna immigrated to this country, bringing with them this enthusiastic spirit. Not averse to lay analysis (indeed, many of them were themselves nonmedical practitioners), they trained psychologists in psychoanalysis, provided such training remained "unofficial." Their idealism and optimism carried me and my contemporaries along, undaunted in our conviction of the relevance of psychoanalytic thought and treatment, if only one was able to apply Freud's teachings correctly.

Nevertheless, a beginner was not cushioned by the security and comfort of certainty. I was encouraged and deeply gratified when finally I discovered that a patient had made a change for the better in life because of our work together, but getting to that point, of course, took quite some time.

But the spirit of the post-Enlightenment period, which so permeated psychoanalysis, was a general characteristic of the zeitgeist with which I grew up. My father, a mathematician and logical positivist, believed in the power of reason as a means for understanding the phenomena of nature and the world in general. My mother, a psychoanalytically trained educator, believed that if only one understood how to do it, one could save children from developing severe neuroses and help them become educated at the same time.

It was not until I set out to write these lines that I realized how deeply I had been influenced by the post-Enlightenment idealism of our culture. I now understand why I once chose as a topic for an undergraduate paper, Condorcet's *Sketch for a Historical Picture of the Progress of the Human Spirit.* Condorcet, a leader of the Girondist faction in the French Revolution, wrote the essay in the final months of his life, which he spent in hiding from the Jacobins, who had condemned him to death. To the end, he remained convinced that the French Revolution would bring about the beginning of a better life for all humanity: he still had hope in progress based on reason.

I too still believe in the power of reason, and I admire the indomitable spirit that motivated Condorcet to write this essay. I know today that *l'esprit humain* is as important as reason, but often neither is dominant in the psychoanalytic situation. Myriad feelings, rather than reason emanating from the human spirit, are more powerful in determining motivation and subsequent action. Affect supersedes reason on the analytic couch; if it does not, we may be in as much trouble as when reason dominates and affect is absent.

Today we know a great deal more about the function of the human psyche and its motivations than did Freud. Our exploration of the world Freud opened up for us has taught us much about character formation, human conflict, and pathology, and about how a person's psychic reality and the multiple dimensions of transference color a patient's analytic experience during different periods of treatment. Knowledge of this latter sort compels us to make clinical choices about what we are going to say—unless it compels us to be silent. Above all, we have come to realize how overdetermined all human behavior is and that we are able to know only a fraction of the conscious and unconscious processes active at any given time, a fact that greatly complicates our assessment of the analytic situation and hampers our capacity for prediction. At the same time, our diagnostic and treatment evaluations are quicker and more likely to be accurate than was the case a generation ago. Although we are able to know only a small segment of the psychic life of another person, novel ideas are transmitted constantly by our coworkers, who share their experiences in an ever growing psychoanalytic dialogue.

This book has developed as a correction of some of my earlier views and as a document of my current ideas. However, each section deals with only a few aspects of each problem presented. These chapters are by no means intended as the last word on these questions. Together they give an overview of some current issues in our field as seen by one psychoanalytic clinician.

A major emphasis of this book is the growing awareness of female development as different in many respects from Freud's original assumptions regarding this "dark continent." This change required that I (along with many others) reconceptualize the history of women's sexual and psychic development. The major dislocations of traumatizing terrors during the twentieth century, starting with World War I, brought with them a gradual change in the traditional role of women as subordinate to men. Nineteenth-century goals for women rarely included a sense of purpose beyond the home, or a sense of being entitled to a unique personal life solution, a luxury hitherto restricted to men. As women became more active in the world outside the home, a new self-definition, which encompassed a changing feminine self-image, emerged with ever greater force. In our time, the traditional values of childrearing, motherhood, and life with a mate need to be integrated with a sense of femaleness and self-realization, which represent a woman's need to play a creative role in shaping her inner life, as well as influencing events in the outside world. As analysts, we must view these developments from the vantage point of helping women in treatment to carry out the many roles and life functions that must be integrated in the pursuit of greater self-realization.

The book begins with a chapter on what I call "role reversal." I first became alerted to this phenomenon by working on the pathology of Holocaust survivors and their children. There, in most of the cases studied, children grew up having to do their parents' bidding and shape their lives according to parental wishes in order to compensate for parental losses. I discovered that role reversal exists as a phenomenon in myriad family constellations. In the first chapter I have concentrated on illustrating instances of mother–daughter role reversal, their ensuing psychological problems and their treatment.

The issue of depression resulting from role reversal is discussed in Chapter 2. I found an interesting correlation between forms of depression discussed in André Green's book *On Private Madness* and depression in role reversal patients. Although the etiology in Green's cases and mine is different, the usefulness of Green's formulations and the similarities of pathology are compelling.

Chapter 3, the case of Emma, contains the complete analytic case history of an extreme case of the effects of role reversal.

I am indebted to many authors who have influenced and advanced my thinking, and to Dr. Dale Mendell for inviting me to

contribute to her first book on female development for which I
wrote an article on the female Oedipus complex. That was in 1982
and a much-updated version of that paper appears here as Chapter
4. I found I needed to rethink many issues, particularly those related
to a woman's developing psychic structure, the discovery of her
body image, her genitals, and their pleasure-giving functions, and
her concomitant anxieties—questions raised and discussed by many
authors in the intervening years. Among the many issues without
which a woman cannot be understood—let alone be treated by psychoanalysis or psychotherapy—are a woman's bisexuality, which
becomes reinforced by dependency on her mother, identification
with her, and feelings of guilt when she wants to differentiate and
separate from her, and even supersede her, and the ways in which
she internalizes her father's influence during each developmental
phase.

The first analysis of Maureen, recounted in Chapter 5, is of historical interest, as it was conducted twenty years ago and like many
analyses of the period, emphasized an ego psychology perspective
and the developmental hypotheses of Margaret Mahler. If conducted today, the analysis would likely place a stronger emphasis on
fantasy material and oedipal conflicts. Twenty years ago, "current
knowledge" held that perversion existed only in males, which exon-
erated Maureen and me from viewing any of her fantasies and
behavior from the point of view of that diagnostic entity.

When Maureen returned for her second analysis, described in
Chapter 6, she was in a different world, as was I. By this time perversion and character perversions were equally assignable to male
and female patients. How her second analysis was different from the
first is described in detail in order to demonstrate the changes in
our field and in my technique, particularly in understanding analytic work with complicated oppositional individuals such as
Maureen, who, once she came to realize that she needed to acknowledge herself as *only* female and was permitted to enjoy it, engaged in
a daunting and protracted negative therapeutic reaction.

The issue of trauma has become central in our era, as we witnessed the atrocities committed in our century, particularly during
World War II. When I became a member of the Study of Effects of
the Holocaust on the Second Generation (a study group sponsored
by the New York Psychoanalytic Association), an entirely new vista
was opened to me. The results of this work appear in *Generations of
the Holocaust* (Bergmann and Jucovy, 1982). The hitherto unknown

challenge of treating Holocaust victims and their children, as well as other severely traumatized individuals, led to a greater awareness of the nature of trauma and the challenges it imposes on the treatment situation. Our discoveries within the Holocaust Study Group constituted one of the most painful, but also one of the most enlightening experiences of my psychoanalytic journey. Chapter 7 of this book, "Thoughts on Superego Pathology in Survivors and their Children," grew out of this work and appears here in revised form.

Chapter 8 describes the analysis of a patient who suffered a trauma during the final stages of a successful analysis. As a result, a pervasive regression led to the lifting of an important aspect of the patient's infantile amnesia which ultimately brought about a greater therapeutic gain than would otherwise have been possible.

In Chapter 9 I deal with the patient's fear of reliving a trauma within the analytic transference, which I call fear of retraumatization. In one clinical example I discuss a case in which a patient manifested a severe negative therapeutic reaction as a defense against retraumatization. In another, a patient's debilitating reaction to an event in her current life led to the recovery and analysis of a repressed childhood trauma.

My psychoanalytic explorations into the nature of creativity, discussed in Chapter 10, began rather recently. It is still a puzzling and challenging field for psychoanalysts. Understanding how to help artists liberate their creativity by means of psychoanalytic work enables the analyst to contribute directly to a most vital aspect of our culture.

As one might expect, this book raises many more questions than it answers. I have attempted to document my ideas with clinical material in order to demonstrate the ever growing depth of psychoanalytic inquiry and the technical complexity of our work today.

Part I

Women's Struggle to Experience Love, Sexuality, and Maternity

1.

Mother–Daughter Role Reversal, Delayed Marriage, and Maternity

In recent years my patients have included an increasing number of women who came to me for psychoanalytic treatment near the end of their childbearing years. These were women who had postponed marriage and motherhood in favor of professional opportunities and social and sexual freedom. They all had advanced college degrees, secure professional status, and a life-style characterized by economic independence from men. They had been in intense relationships with men, usually older or younger than they, but rarely with those the same age. Most of these men did not want children, often, in the case of the older men, because they were already fathers. These women now found themselves childless and afraid to remain so. They came to treatment with a paralyzing internal conflict: how to be both lover to a mate and mother to a child.

A significant number of these patients had been in treatment previously with attractive male therapists. Attempts, however, to repeat the seductive aspects of the father–daughter relationship in an erotized transference (Blum, 1973) had gone unaddressed and therefore unresolved. Before coming to me, each woman had carefully "researched" her choice of a second analyst. It was imperative to each that this second analyst be a woman who had successfully combined marriage, motherhood, and a profession.

These patients shared certain fears and anxieties. They were unsure whether a woman could have both a child and a successful relationship with a man, and whether she could have a child and yet continue her professional career. A few of the women expressed a wish to have a child without a mate; others feared that maternity was a "trap." Some held the "conviction" that a woman who is successful professionally will be regarded as "masculine" and that no man will want her. In several women, unconscious doubts about their ability to produce a child had resulted in their "unintentionally" becoming pregnant: the majority of these patients had undergone one or several abortions prior to treatment.

Most of these women fully enjoyed their sexual experiences, but their unconscious conflicts prevented them from achieving motherhood; for others, maternity was desirable and imperative, but their experience of sexual pleasure and interactive relationships with men was inhibited. None had been able to reconcile the separate currents of maternity, sexuality, and professional activity. As regards the severity of their psychopathology, these patients were no more disturbed than a patient who marries in order to have a child, stays in an unhappy marriage, or settles for a lasting love relationship without children. What they suffered from was an essentially neurotic disturbance: an unresolved polarity between sexuality and motherhood.

These women presented similar characterological difficulties that led to conflict derivatives from various stages of development. Incestuous feelings toward their fathers, feelings that had not been repressed following the oedipal period, were prominent, along with a deep yearning for closeness with their mothers.

In this chapter, I draw on the analyses of six patients who differ in many respects, but who have a cluster of specific features in common. Their difficulties began during the preoedipal period, when their mothers, by clinging to them and not expressing joy in their daughters' growth and achievement, failed to let them outgrow the symbiotic phase. Narcissistic problems surfaced for both the mothers, who could not let their children separate, and for the daughters who were deprived of sharing joyful growth-promoting experiences with their mothers. These patients' object relationships were disturbed by problems that started early in life and led to a reversal of roles between mother and daughter. A seductive attitude toward the little girl was often apparent on the part of the father.

I suggest that this cluster of specific features constitutes a "central ⟵ psychic constellation," a term that Silverman, Rees, and Neubauer (1975) define as "a psychic organization possessing sufficient cohesion and stability to maintain a significant impact upon the course of further development" (p. 155). Silverman and his coauthors attempted to isolate phase-specific elements of character development related to affects, choice of defenses, and the role of a given environment that have developed by the time a child is $3^1/2$ years old. They viewed the Oedipus complex within a developmental continuum.[1]

In this chapter, material related to developmental lines (A. Freud, 1963) and to the central psychic constellation were obtained through reconstruction. Solnit (1982), Escoll (1983), and others have observed the reappearance of early object relationship themes in the transference and their significance for genetic reconstruction. In my patients, the central psychic constellation comprised a number of early psychic characteristics that together became a predictable motivational system in adulthood and aided in the understanding of recurrent problems related to marriage and maternity.

Freud believed that becoming a wife and mother was a complementary process; the wish for a child stemmed from the earlier wish for a penis, and marriage and motherhood supplied a woman with her mature sexual identity and fulfillment. It is my impression, however, that the wish for a penis and the wish for a child stem from different motivational sources. The wish for a penis, for instance, can lead to a wish for a penis in heterosexual love or in any other form of a woman's love life, but without the integration of other adult goals.

In the following examination of the analyses of six women, I use the concept of the central psychic constellation as a tool of reconstruction. In view of the similarity of some decisive specific data, it could become valuable as a tool of prediction within carefully specified limits in the treatment of adults who have certain related problems.

---

[1] In their essay, data related to developmental lines and to the central psychic constellation were obtained through transference analysis and reconstruction.

THE WISH FOR A SYMBIOTIC RELATIONSHIP

As my patients approached the end of their childbearing years, the wish for a child surfaced with particular urgency, reviving lifelong dormant wishes for closeness with their mothers. This yearning included symbiotic and, later, restitutional wishes in relation to their mothers. The symbiotic wishes were preconscious: the patients hoped for an intimate relationship with their own wished-for infants, one that would provide this yearned-for feeling they had lost too soon or never fully experienced with their own mothers. The wishes surfaced as transference fantasies early in treatment, or when a love relationship had ended. Family romance fantasies sometimes disguised underlying symbiotic yearnings; several patients expressed the wish to be my only child and exclusive love object.

These childless women had erected strong defenses against fears of reengulfment by their mothers (Mahler and Gosliner, 1955), and against fears of abandonment by either parent. These anxieties also appeared in the transference, as strong ambivalent swings and difficulties in regulating closeness and distance vis-à-vis the analyst. At the same time, the women expressed yearnings for a father who would exclude the mother from father–daughter intimacies, suggesting that a need for exclusive dyadic object relationships had become firmly anchored during the preoedipal period (Mahler, 1971; Abelin, 1980), though it might have found full expression either then or in the oedipal period.

Triadic relationships were tolerated only at the cost of internal conflicts and sometimes ended in divorce following the birth of a child. Even after achieving the capacity for experiencing motherhood, patients who had not yet resolved their oedipal triangular conflicts manifested a tendency to exclude the husband and engage in symbiotic relationships with their child.

THE EMERGENCE OF ROLE REVERSAL
AS A GENETIC TURNING POINT

In the course of normal development, most children reverse the roles of mother and child in both fantasy and play activities. In the women described here, however, the reversal of roles occurred in reality. Their mothers' neediness forced these girls to alleviate their mothers' distress by attempting to mother their own mothers.

Each of these patients was the oldest child in her family. She found herself mothering younger siblings as well as her mother. This was poignantly relived in the transference neurosis: if I suffered from a minor, visible injury, these patients would become oversolicitous and compete with my family, particularly my husband, in their caretaking fantasies. It became apparent from dreams and fantasies that in childhood (and to this very day), whenever their mothers had been ill, troubled, or unavailable, these patients as little girls had become helping caregivers in the family, a role encouraged by their fathers, who frequently were absent—physically, emotionally, or both (many of the fathers had served in the military and were away for long periods).

Each little girl, perceiving her mother's neediness, had become a mother to her own mother and siblings before she could experience the protection, security, and pleasures enjoyed by children with adequate mothering. In turn, the mothers, by making demands on them, made these girls part of their narcissistic, anxiety-laden world. Memories of being the "child-mother" were relived with painful affect and vivid imagery.

In states of anxiety or stress, the mothers had difficulties with impulse control. Discharge of stressful feelings often led to a loss of personal communication with the child "as a child," as if the mother had lost sight of their respective roles. Each child felt compelled to take care of her mother. In reliving, in the transference, early longings for the mother's emotional presence, the patients described feeling *unrecognized, ignored,* and *overlooked;* one patient described her feeling as being "*emotionally disconfirmed.*"

Inability to communicate rage in reaction to being overlooked led in these women to a structural regression with weakened self-esteem and a transitory loss of differentiation from the mother as caregiver. Withdrawal of the mother's object cathexis from the child "as a child" led to a disruption of self-constancy, with an accompanying fantasy of role reversal shared by mother and child.

This fantasy creates a temporary hiatus in the *real* relationship between mother and child, and the child's self-cathexis is temporarily weakened in the service of maintaining the tie to her mother. This disturbance in the cohesiveness of the child's developing self representation and self-constancy leads to fragmentation of the child's developing self-image. A diminished self-cathexis will prevail until the child's inner representation of self corresponds again to the conscious experience of herself as a child or, seen from the object's point of view, until the mother regains her maternal role. Role reversal serves to prevent the loss of relatedness between mother and child and thereby preserves some continuity within the child's self representation. Thus, in spite of its damaging effects, role reversal is a defensive operation in that it preserves the cohesiveness of the child's self. The child, rescued by a move toward lesser differentiation from the object but still unsure of its "staying power," may begin to experience separation anxiety and become phobia prone.

Reversal of the role of mother and child, in reality or in fantasy, interferes with identification with the mother as a predictable child-caring object. In many instances, these girls exhibited a "quasi-parental precocity" that circumvented the emergence of sibling rivalry and led characterologically to precocious altruism and surrender toward anyone younger or needier (A. Freud, 1936, pp. 140-142).

One patient said:

> When I remembered, in my last session, that I saw my younger sister being nursed, I also remembered for the first time that my mother was home. It was after my sister was born. I had a nurse's outfit, and my doll was injured and bandaged all over and needed special attention. I felt that my mother had never been there for me *alone* because she didn't stay home until the younger children came. She taught me how to be a mother, and how to take care of all the things she had to do, and of the younger children. As long as I can remember, I tried to make life easier for her. Yet she feels like a victim to this very day! I was always an adult and by the time I was grown up, I had had it with being with children.

One may speculate to what extent the nurse's outfit and the injured doll may have been an unconscious shared fantasy, by my patient and her mother, about an "injured, bandaged, doll-child"— the mother (a victim to this very day), still in need of special care by her older daughter; or the daughter, now in need of mothering, having been "injured" by the birth of the new baby.

This patient had picked lovers according to the model of taking care of helpless younger children. Her relationships had ended badly, however, because each time she had hoped in vain for reciprocity and protection from her mate, as she had originally from her preoccupied mother.

When the mother experiences the child as a distant part of herself, what is "left out" of the relationship is never fully cathected, nor is it repressed (Burlingham, 1935). Thus, self-perception, self-constancy, internalization, and identification with the mother remain underdeveloped. Fear of abandonment assumes a central role (Brodey, 1965). *What is left out* will be left out again in the transference relationship, whether the analyst is in the role of parent or child. Instead, feelings (often accurate) of not being understood will be expressed, until words for what was "left out" have been found jointly by analyst and patient. In the transference, role reversal fantasies may appear as fears of complete abandonment, if the patient would not comply by first taking care of the analyst-mother (Fleming, 1975).

Most of my patients remembered not being allowed to be enraged or needy. One patient said, "No wonder I don't want a baby. *She* is my baby. She is either a child or a queen." From early childhood, whenever the mothers abdicated their roles, these patients took care of their younger siblings. One patient commented, at various times, "I feel like a child or like a mother but not as me with a continuing feeling of me"; "My mother loves me when I am her mother, but I want a mother too; I thought of you as my mother"; and, later, "I feel so rejected when my mother can't cope, and during these moments I hate the idea of having a child."

I was particularly struck by another characteristic that these women shared: in all six cases there had been interference with their ability, as children, to engage in doll play. In normal development this activity provides opportunities for testing a variety of roles in fantasy: the child can play at being father or mother, sibling or baby. My patients, however, having actually been a "little mother" to their siblings and to their own mothers, showed significant disturbances in doll play. They recall playing with the toys of siblings, or treating younger siblings as their "doll children," for whom they often created toys and games. They envied girls whose mothers gave them lovely dolls and children they visited whose mothers participated in doll play.

Almost without exception, memories predominated in which dolls were taken apart or destroyed. Because younger siblings were their play objects, these girls had little emotional space for dolls on whom they could bestow love, about whom they could fantasize, and whom they could endow with unique features they did not have to explain to anyone. The disturbance resulting from the reversal of the roles of mother and child in reality seemed to have eliminated the desire to give fantasies free reign in doll play. I wondered whether this was a sign of disturbance in mother–child intimacy that prevented these patients from experiencing first their mothers as unique, and later a man as unique and irreplaceable.

The disturbances in doll play had other repercussions as well. Doll play is basic to development of the female body image, including internal vaginal body cathexis (Kestenberg, 1968, 1971), and is crucial in overcoming fears of object loss, particularly in relation to the mother (Blum, 1977a). The lack of doll play clearly interfered with these developments.

While parental attitudes had created difficulties for these patients, they also seemed to have created specific strengths. Both parents had considered these women to be special children, and had imbued them with high hopes for future achievement. As children they became "exceptions" (Jacobson, 1959), and role reversal became a source of gratification. Yet these girls also felt helpless and weighed down by the emotional burdens placed upon them. They lost the sense of a carefree childhood too quickly: feeling both special and helpless created an oscillating self-cathexis. Symbolically, by reversing roles, these little girls became the mothers they had never had. Role reversal served as a defensive substitute for separation-individuation, in that these children acted precociously as "independent adult helpers," thereby creating a fantasied identity. But role reversal also defined their places in the family: they could feel secure because they were needed.

These children grew up to become caregiving women, task-oriented and responsible in their object relationships. Their capacity to "take it" and the praise they received for being "special" had promoted the development of initiative, courage, and a sense of adventure. The ability to fight for something in spite of pain was a conscious motivational asset in solving inner conflict.

The role reversal I have described here constitutes a specific variant on a theme of narcissistic pathology (see chapter 5). As Brodey (1965) observed, if a patient's mother has not resolved her earliest fear of abandonment, the patient is unable to cathect the child as a separate libidinal object. The child must therefore "conform to expectation to prevent severe psychological decompensation in the parents" (p. 183). Kernberg (1975) has described narcissistic patients who adopt a stance of coolness or self-preoccupied distance toward people they feel close to in order to control hostile feelings. This attitude enables them to maintain a self-cathexis and avoid fragmentation of the self. These disturbances bring to mind Bach's description (1980) of adults who cannot maintain subjective and objective self-awareness simultaneously, an incapacity that would preclude a mother's expressing her own narcissistic needs while tending to a child's. By transforming an older child into a mother to care for them, mothers so afflicted may then be able to treat their younger children more appropriately.

What I have called role reversal formed another, particularly important strand in these women's central psychic constellation, which made them prone to subsequent disturbances in self and object constancy. For them, separation carried with it the threat of total abandonment. Because internalization and identification vis-à-vis the mother's *maternal* aspects was deficient, premature self-sufficiency was frequently produced at the cost of narcissistic well-being. Another important strand in their central psychic constellations resulted from a precociously sexualized father–daughter relationship.

THE FATHER'S ROLE

As the end of their childbearing capacity loomed, these patients each experienced a turning point in their life cycle. Heightened incestuous guilt, which emanated from their unmarried state and unconsciously affirmed the tie to the father, surfaced at this time and added to inner pressures.

Inconsistent protectiveness by an emotionally unpredictable mother had led to an intensification of the relationship between the little girl and her father. In most cases, the patients had early memories of being close to their father whenever he was home, memories that probably preceded their first discovery of him as a toddler's delightful companion following differentiation.

In these patients, the preoedipal tie to the father was characterized by a surge of wishes that he provide security and protection, while he in turn took on a maternal role when the mother abdicated her functions. The intense mutual love between father and daughter and the aura of seductive fantasies and, frequently, seductive behavior that characterized their relationship from early on led to omnipotent feelings, created a sexual precocity, and made it difficult for the girl to delineate her realistic place in the family. Early love for the father, along with increased ambivalence toward the mother, interfered with resolution of the rapprochement crisis and intensified separation problems (Mahler, 1966, 1975b; Abelin, 1980). Identification with the father was based on a need for security and nurturing, which strengthened the incestuous tie. It also intensified a need for sustenance that sometimes assumed an addictive quality in adulthood. In analysis this need appeared concurrently with oral wishes and phase-specific penis envy, connected to a pervasive sense of deprivation and, later, sexualized oedipal wishes.

The sexualized tie to the father consolidated oedipal precocity and, in combination with role reversal, concretized the fantasy of having *had* babies with the father. Upon the mother's emotional withdrawal, externalization and role play assumed a concreteness and an aura of reality. Thus incestuous guilt became a permanent source of internal conflict, paid for by childlessness. When identification with the maternal father produced the wish, "I want a child," it represented a bisexual and narcissistic wish for self-completion. In adulthood an independent wish for a baby increased separation anxiety and fears of abandonment. Identification with the mother did not include the wish for a baby, but identification with the maternal and oedipal father did.

The mother was recognized as being the father's sexual mate, and identification with this *role* carried the girl into heterosexuality during adolescence. The mother, however, was also devalued as "the child." At times of parental marital tensions these patients felt the need to protect their mothers, but secretly sided with their fathers. This conflict concretized and externalized the oedipal fantasy of being the father's "other woman," a role that seemed much more desirable than that of the married mother, who was in danger of being abandoned. The mistress fantasy represented both an oedipal victory over the mother and a "preoedipal victory"—that of remaining Daddy's little girl at the same time.

Some of the women did not progress developmentally beyond the "mistress phase" without analysis, much as they wanted to be married. Their experience of sexual closeness with a mate was intertwined with feelings of revenge and narcissistic triumph over their mothers. Oedipal feelings for the father were relived in analysis, sometimes with an unusual amount of pain, which stemmed both from the concreteness of the tie and from disappointment in the childhood "love life" that had ended by his becoming the girl's "lost lover." The father remained an idealized object of love and identification; frequently, there was much less ambivalence toward him than toward the mother. However, there frequently was a guilt-laden fantasy that professional prominence based on cognitive or intellectual capacities would make a woman "masculine" and cause infertility. One sided identification with the mother and the girl's depth of preference for her father reinforced bisexual wishes, making it difficult to reach a stable sense of feminine identity. In adulthood this led to anxiety about marital commitment.

The early sexualization of the patients' relationships with their fathers and their impaired capacity to separate from him formed another strand in the central psychic constellation. The oedipal father fixation produced the fantasy that the little girl *had indeed had* a baby with him and that she *had* been his "other woman." Unconscious themes of oedipal and maternal victory over the mother interfered with postadolescent capacity for the transfer of love feelings and the desire for a child to a man of her own who was her age.

THE NEGATIVE OEDIPAL CONSTELLATION

In these patients, the negative oedipal phase seemed short-circuited. As I have mentioned, symbiotic wishes early in the treatment either surfaced directly in fantasies or were vigorously defended against, so that the mother, as the patient's "girl baby," was cared for lovingly or rejected with frustration and rage.

The girl's identity formation was inhibited. Mahler (1968) describes two pivotal stages of identity formation: the separation–individuation phase and the phase of resolution of bisexual identification. The integration of body-image representations with pregenital experience depends on successful identification with the parent of the same sex. In addition, "affirming emotional attitudes of both parents to the child's sexual identity" are of paramount importance for "distinct feelings of self-identity" and the solution of the oedipal conflict (p. 138).

Blos (1974) makes the point that the negative oedipal conflict survives in a repressed state until adolescence. My patients seemed never to fully experience the negative oedipal conflict and therefore did not repress it in Blos' sense. It remained in a developmentally rudimentary form, amalgamated with revived symbiotic longings, seemingly from the time of its appearance until its reappearance in the transference. The negative oedipal conflict had remained characterologically alive in feeling states of unfulfilled yearnings and unrealized idealizations.

I believe that a girl's love for her mother is normally not affected by the discovery of sexual differences. In instances where it is, the impact is mitigated, and their love relationship safeguarded, if the mother allows her little girl to be a "little woman" (and can accept her phase-specific penis envy at the same time). The little girl who is allowed to apply her mother's cosmetics and strut about in mother's high heels, while laughing with impish delight, is engaging in phallic–exhibitionistic self-expression. Permission to express her need to show off her body, to perform, to be a tomboy without having to forfeit her simultaneous feminine development, and to play the mother's role helps the girl to feel physically loved as a female child. This approval counteracts her lowered self-esteem, which may be developmentally phase-specific, transitory, and expressed in female genital anxieties (Lax, 1997; Richards, 1996), penis envy, or sibling rivalry. When the girl feels physically loved, oedipal rather than pseudo-oedipal relationships will develop toward each parent. This promotes the girl's acceptance of her clitoris and vagina as adequate organs and sources of pleasure. When her feminine body image becomes anchored as lovable, the little girl feels able to reach the oedipal phase with her mother's permission. Identifying with her mother, she can value both her mother and herself as female.

The mother's affirmation of the girl's femininity promotes this identification, as well as an idealization of the mother. The girl child needs this affirmation. Preoedipal or oedipal, she needs to experience mother–girl intimacy, which grows out of sharing and loving "feminine things" and "women's concerns," which is itself fostered by their mutual acceptance of the female body as lovable. If the mother allows participation in her world and the girl can *play* at being an adult woman, the girl feels she is permitted to remain a child. Insufficient consolidation of the love tie to the mother during the negative oedipal period will preclude the repression of incestuous feelings toward the father during and following the oedipal phase, and they will continue into latency; a struggle for exclusive possession of the mother will thus be avoided. Under more favorable conditions, the incest barrier is maintained because the oedipal mother is recognized as belonging to the father. In my cases, however, that barrier was not sufficiently affirmed: the mother always seemed too childlike to be experienced fully as a mother, and the father was too available as an incestuous love object, so that far-reaching characterological adaptation against threatening bisexual wishes and incestuous stirrings became urgent.

Many of my patients' mothers preferred to share personal feelings with their daughters rather than their husbands, thereby exposing the latter to the daughters' seductive wishes and behavior, and leading to precocious oedipalized intimacies. During the negative oedipal phase, the reemerging symbiotic wishes that had been directed toward the mother were sexualized, and wishes for separation from the mother failed once more.

Concrete wishes and fantasies about the analyst became central early in the transference: they apparently filled a gap left by disturbances of identification with the patients' mothers. There was an unstated transference pressure on me to help them overcome narcissistic self-devaluation stemming from their childless, unmarried states.

The unresponsiveness of these mothers toward their daughters' feminine and bisexual tendencies had not allowed a flowering of the negative oedipal love tie and its subsequent repression. This was one more trend forming the central psychic constellation. The girls' sense of feminine identity was infirm, and they were unprotected against sexualization and overstimulation in the oedipal father–girl relationship.

SPECIFIC PROBLEMS IN LATENCY AND ADOLESCENCE

Normal oedipal experiences strengthen the incest barrier and induce the growing child to differentiate identification from love. Internalization of the parents as oedipal objects promotes superego structuring and, later, oedipal mourning. Loewald (1973, p. 15) has observed that under favorable conditions oedipal relationships are transformed into internalized, intrapsychic, depersonified relationships. Internalization as an ongoing process fosters emancipation from the original parental objects. In the women 1 have described, this process did not take place. New objects, therefore, were experienced as incestuous. Analysis had to bring out the extent to which both love and idealization were still attached to mother and father. The intrusiveness of both parents in their relationship with the role reversal child continued into latency and puberty, interfering with adolescent needs for separation and autonomy.

The fathers tended to supervise their adolescent daughters' appearance and attire, not in the interest of greater modesty, and often in ways that would enhance the girls' seductiveness and sexual appeal. Hairdos were discussed, for instance, or sweaters that would make growing breasts protrude. The mothers, for their part, tended to share the girls' excitement about their dates but were also excessively inquisitive. In analysis we discovered again and again that the parents' excessive interest in the girls' dates confirmed once more the strength of the unconscious incestuous tie and their fear of losing their daughters. This interfered with the girls' growing attempts to find a love object who was a peer.

It is more difficult to describe the positive results of role reversal as they emerged in postadolescent sublimations, because they did not appear as complaints. The patients assumed adult responsibilities for their parents, particularly for the mother, a pattern that was consolidated in latency but became even more apparent in adolescence. Characterologically, this strong sense of responsibility disposed them toward a certain asceticism and fostered the capacity, from adolescence on, to delay gratification and yield to others. These girls often became confidantes and advisors to *other* girls in matters of the heart. Frequently they became interested in the helping professions or in caring for other women's children. As adults, for instance, they tended to become ideal mothers to the children of divorced boyfriends.

Jacobson (1964, p. 206) has pointed out how instability of the superego interferes with identity formation and self-constancy. She describes persons whose sense of identity alters when object relationships change from positive to negative affects and back again, vacillating between love and hate. Object constancy and reality testing are interdependent, but the constant object implies a firm libidinal cathexis of the object representation, a realistic perception of the object, and a resultant capacity to sustain love (Bak, 1971).

In these patients, unfulfilled incestuous wishes surfaced again during adolescence and interfered with peer relationships and the choice of a mate. Relations to men showed the imprint of their failure to resolve oedipal issues. Typically, initial idealization of a man was followed by disappointment. This pattern became embedded in character structure and resurfaced in adult relationships with men. Alternating idealization and disillusionment also characterized the transference neurosis.

In masturbation fantasies, dreams, and the transference, two topics predominated: primal scene fantasies in which the patient would replace the analyst's husband; and torture fantasies attesting to sexual overstimulation during childhood. The torture fantasies also indicated masochistic submission to both parents, particularly the mother, which had its inception in the preoedipal period under the aegis of role reversal. These fantasies were narrated with excruciating pain, an irrevocable sense of exclusion from the parental couple, and intense narcissistic injury.

ADULTHOOD

When core infantile conflict formations remain intact, there is only partial separation from the original objects of adulthood. Adult love relations can be sustained only as long as their unconscious connection to the ambivalently loved oedipal objects is maintained and as long as revenge fantasies can remain dissociated or repressed.

In the case of my patients, because the unconscious incestuous tie to the father was maintained, adult love relationships were playful and seductive; they were not, however, nourishing, except in the beginning, for either partner. Before analysis, some of the women were either frigid or could reach clitoral orgasm only by prolonged direct stimulation. The vagina remained excluded, sometimes unconsciously "saved" for mother or father. There were typical fantasies that prevented orgasm: the women, though suspecting that the men were primarily interested in themselves, at the same time felt obliged to satisfy their mates, often at the expense of their own sexual needs. Lack of communication with their mates regarding these needs was another way in which role reversal in childhood interfered with orgasm in the adult woman.

It was as if in adult love relationships, oedipal themes had become actualized, thereby burdening adult love life with incestuous guilt. On an unconscious level, these women often had difficulty differentiating lovers from their mothers or fathers, and their own sexual role or that of a mate from the relationship roles of their mother and father.

Adult love relationships repeated the pattern of the oedipal conflict. Initially, these relationships drew their strength from the narcissistic triumph of circumventing the incest taboo: infantile grandiosity and narcissistic strivings found satisfaction in the love relationship. During the early phases, parental idealizations were displaced onto the lover. A web of fantasy was spun around him, with unconscious hopes for assuaging childhood injuries and conscious wishes of realizing adult life goals.

Unconsciously, the patient needed the lover to become the seductive parent, required to commit incest, which lent the love tie an addictive quality (Blum, 1973) and made it "very special." Uniqueness, which was not experienced with the mother early in life, was thus temporarily found in some of these relationships via the unconscious incestuous fantasy that held the relationship together. It was this living out of incestuous oedipal wishes that gave the relationship its special "magic." During the incestuous and narcissistically gratifying phase the woman remained the child, actively seeking good mothering but able to accept it only from a member of the opposite sex with whom she identified (see chapter 4).

An intensive search for a husband or permanent lover took place only ostensibly and concealed a wish to find "the good mother of symbiosis" in the union with the lover. These women's love relationships lacked the depth of postoedipal commitment. The lovers alternately played the roles of parent and child, at times giving the analyst the impression that they were "playing house."

When parents have been prematurely disappointing, narcissistic gratification cannot be obtained later in life without the assistance of another person. These patients therefore needed to keep their lovers in the role of a narcissistically gratifying parent. At the same time, the initial success in the adult relationship revived fears of losing the incestuous ties to parents and so led to overt anxiety. Separation from the mother seemed impossible: it meant not only forfeiting forever any hope of reaching a meaningful closeness to her maternal aspect, but also being saddled with feelings of guilt about leaving the mother, who needed the daughter as a permanent emotional caregiver. It was easier to divide commitment and love between an adult lover and the father of unconscious fantasy.

For a time the women succeeded in staving off separation anxiety and incestuous guilt, but anxiety about separating from their *real* parents and the fear of making a commitment to marriage and motherhood brought the unconscious conflict to the fore. In fact, analysis revealed time and again that the adult women unconsciously preferred their fathers to their lovers or husbands. Because unconsciously these women had already had a child with their fathers, the wish for a baby was pushed into the background.

In the second phase of their relationships, idealizations gave way to disappointment because of unrequited childhood fantasies. Symbiotic and incestuous longings that had nurtured the love tie were transferred from the parents to the lover or husband only temporarily, and disappointment brought the relationships to an end.

MARRIAGE

The achievement of marriage and maternity depends on coming to terms with childhood losses. Some women do not feel compelled to marry and have children; for a variety of reasons, they settle for an older or younger permanent mate, or perhaps a series of partners. My patients, however, *wanted* marriage and motherhood, both of which were felt needs. Having been "special" and idealized children, they wanted to build a family of their own to experience parenthood and represent themselves as part of an ideal couple that truly cared for a child. Such deeply held conscious ideals aided the analytic process.

Nonetheless, marriage was unconsciously equated with losing a part of the self that in fantasy represented part of a parent. One patient presented a telling dream: "I am marching down the aisle to get married and my future husband waits for me. I become frozen and cannot walk. I wake up." Unconsciously, the frozen stiffness represented a "traumatic freezing," a reliving of an incapacity to hold on or move away. It represented also an unconscious link to the father's penis as representing nourishment not obtained from the mother: the patient could not marry lest she lose the nourishing tie to the father by not remaining his phallic extension. The fact that the patient herself personified the paternal phallus by becoming frozen emerged as a reconstruction once a memory from her adolescence made the connection clear to both of us (see Lewin, 1933). Anxiety over object loss may have caused the patient to awaken.

Another patient viewed marriage and motherhood as a "prison or trap." Her commitment to her lovers was tenuous and marred by overwhelming anxieties, while at the same time the tie to her parents remained a strong and active force. She commented that marriage was "the worst fear of my life."

As a rule it took several years of intensive analytic work for these women to relinquish incestuous, ambivalent ties to the parents, to feel free to fall in love with a peer, and to get married. Typically, after becoming comfortable in their marriage, these patients proceeded to plan for a child. This fact demonstrated that they had at least partially forgiven their mothers.

MATERNITY

Unconscious needs to repeat the early family constellation, and the unconscious guilt these needs stir up, prevented these patients from being able to tolerate triangular relationships without fears of abandonment that in turn interfered with the wish to have a baby. Blos (1974) stresses that adult mothering is possible only if the young woman attains a postambivalent relationship with her mother. I do not believe that such a relationship, however desirable, is ever completely attainable.

It became apparent in analysis that just as the mother and the patient as prospective mother were not differentiated, so the patient recalling her childhood could not differentiate herself from a fantasied prospective child. In both prospect and retrospect, mother and child were merged; the lover became the "good mother" of symbiosis, while the "bad mother" image was displaced onto the real mother, onto her substitutes (e.g., the lover's wife), or onto a prospective child. The patients were fearful that the baby would replace them once again by being considered first. Unconsciously the prospective child was identified with a parental sibling or oedipal rival.

At times the child also represented the paternal phallus, and childbirth then became linked to early narcissistic disillusionments or to a fantasy of being hurt or ripped apart (Lax, 1997; Richards, 1996). Feelings of revenge for not having been allowed to remain a child were sometimes displaced in fantasy onto the prospective child; these feelings might also merge with jealousy toward a sibling, usually male.

One patient said, "I can't have a baby because then I would have to lose my mother. To keep my child out of her life would kill her. It is as if I had kept her alive by letting *her* be my baby. If I had a real baby, I would have to give up my mother. I have such guilt toward her that I have to keep her alive." Another woman said, "When I think of getting married, I have the image of a little girl holding the hand of a big man. I idealize a man I don't love as an adult woman. I obviously don't want to have a baby. It seems as though I had always been waiting for Daddy."

When contemplating having a child, many of these women demonstrated an incapacity to rely and trust on the baby's father. One patient said, "I have a fantasy of being alone; a cold wind is blowing, I am isolated and poor. I have no job and I am alone with a baby. If I get married and have a child, I shall be a wife and mother without a career and without money." This was a frequently recurring image. Another patient said, "I imagine having a baby and there's just nobody out there who cares. I have no parents and no husband—I am trapped! How am I going to rear this child alone and ever get back to my profession? Who is going to pay the bills? I feel all alone. It is a nightmare." Abandonment appeared to be a punishment for having abandoned the "child-mother."

Some of these women passed the end of their childbearing years without having achieved motherhood. They then went through a period of intense mourning for not having been able to produce a child. The lost child represented the patient herself, as well as the loss of a sense of deep closeness with her own mother during childhood.

SUMMARY

Role reversal is a phenomenon that appears not only in the interactions discussed here but in other types of relationship. The conflicts I focus on here have previously been assigned to pregenital and incestuous oedipal fixations. When the wish for a child is too conflict-laden because of a fixation on the fantasy of a libidinally nourishing father and by the hope of finding the *real* mother, the establishment of an independent adult self leads to deep internal conflict. Role reversal, if present, adds the dimension of narcissistic pathology, conflicts related to self-constancy, and the continuation of conflictual object relations from childhood into adulthood.

Pursuing a profession and being lover to a mate and a mother to children requires, as does analytic work itself, the giving up of a considerable number of infantile gratifications. This process is encumbered by the weight of parental models who themselves strove for infantile and narcissistic gratification, thereby leaving the child insufficient room in which to express and fulfill phase-specific infantile needs. When patients have faced such encumbrances, new identifications must be created in adulthood.

In my patients, a central psychic constellation, with role reversal its most prominent feature, remained active throughout the life cycle. They had intense symbiotic longings that propelled them on toward a lifelong search for finding the symbiotic mother in lover, husband, and baby. Only by achieving this could they forgive their own mothers for abandoning them emotionally.

The fantasy "once there was a baby that no one would take care of . . ." had its roots in memories of childhood role reversal and in unconscious incestuous ties that did not permit separation from the mother without superego punishment. The central experience of emotional abandonment led to unstable self and object constancy.

Reversing roles, the daughter became her mother's mother and identified with her father. A preference for dyadic over triadic relationships characterized unconscious conflicts. Role reversal lent conviction to the sense of having already *had* a baby with the father and of being his "other woman," thereby intensifying an incestuous fixation.

The alternating currents of the oedipal conflict persisted in these women's adult love relationships, in which they lived out an incestuous fantasy. These fantasies, though sometimes addictive in character, eventuated in heightened separation anxiety, whether the lover represented the patient's mother, father, or self. Insufficient repression and superego structuring prevented these relationships from lasting.

These women could be described as "prisoners of childhood." Many of the clinical features they presented could be subsumed under "fate neurosis" (Deutsch, 1930). Psychoanalytic treatment enabled them to overcome some of the effects of role reversal. The giving up of erotized relationships via the analysis of the erotized transference (Freud, 1915b; Blum, 1973) was the most decisive step that led these women from living out the unconscious tie to mother and father as a "mistress" to achieving independent womanhood.

2.

Depression, The "Dead" Mother, and Role Reversal

In 1980, André Green introduced to psychoanalysis the concept of the "dead" mother, a concept I have found to be clinically relevant to the psychological origins of role reversal. Green uses the concept descriptively, in relation to a biographical chapter in the history of some of his analysands. The "dead" mother is a mother who, fully alive to the child during a certain period of early childhood, has suffered a traumatic loss (e.g., the death of her father, her husband, or a sibling) before consolidation of the child's ego. As a result the mother can no longer offer the libidinal supplies the child needs to preserve its own vitality and aliveness. Along with the sense of loss following her withdrawal, the child carries within itself a double image of the mother: the "good" mother who was fully alive before her bereavement, and the mother who has become "dead" as a result of her bereavement. Such children, then, are not chronically depressed but instead fluctuate in their feeling states, depending on which of these images is in ascendancy. The "dead" mother is not a "bad" mother, but rather, because of her emotional unavailability, is like a mother who is physically absent.

Green's concept of the dead mother is that of an intrapsychic event wherein certain patients have internalized a double registry of the mother, before and after her bereavement. They differ from children whose mothers were chronically depressed, because the mothers he describes have become depressed only as a result of trauma. A discernible difference between the mother before and after remains in the child's intrapsychic maternal representation.

The mother's trauma becomes internalized in one way by her and in another by her child. Green's observations relate to a historical event in the history of the depressed patient, and to the fate of the mother's intrapsychic representation within the child. His emphasis is not on the object relationship between mother and child per se. Green suggests that the patient's identification with the "dead" mother recathects traces of the trauma that remain unconscious. The mother's withdrawal is not retaliatory but, according to Green, comes about against the child's will. The child attempts to "repair" the mother, who is absorbed in her bereavement, but does so in vain (Green, 1980, p. 150). The child then tries to become like her (p. 151), which results in identification with the dead mother. In this, Green's formulations follow Freud's thinking in "Mourning and Melancholia" (1917) about internalization and bereavement: the mourner internalizes and identifies with certain aspects of the person being mourned. In this situation, the mother is bereaved by object loss and the child identifies with the bereaved mother. In Green's thinking, the mother's libidinal withdrawal leads to depression in the child.

There is a striking similarity between some of the depressive reactions of the patients and their mothers described by Green and the affective reactions and behavior of my patients following role reversal. In the six cases discussed in chapter 1, and in cases I have since analyzed where role reversal was prominent, I discovered that each patient who developed this defensive constellation had been exposed to some maternal withdrawal and depression from early childhood through her formative years, and often until the patient left home as an adult. In these cases, depression in the mother was fluctuating, and typically manifested itself in an inability to cope: as a result, care of the child became too much for her to handle. In some cases, the mother became depressed after the birth of the patient's younger sibling and therefore was even less accessible in her caretaking functions. Although external traumatic circumstances at times exacerbated the maternal depression, mothers can in such situations find comfort and consolation in the love they bestow upon and receive from their children even while mourning a loss. In the cases I have described, however, there was no bereavement and no mourning. In my experience, bereavement can lead to mourning or myriad other psychological reactions, but true mourning does not lead to depression. Here, the mothers' depression was due to a narcissistic disturbance that led ultimately to role reversal.

Despite the different causes of maternal withdrawal, bereavement, or depression seen in these cases, my observations parallel Green's (1980) description in that the child whose mother has withdrawn interest develops a wish to reanimate her, to revitalize her, and the child "remains prisoner to [her] economy of survival" (p. 156). I believe that a deficiency in the daughter's libidinal reservoir is created by narcissistic hurt and disillusionment, built up by repeated episodes of rejection, and in turn creates a cumulative or strain trauma: no matter how much the child attempts to bring the mother back as a cheerful, life-affirming presence, the relationship between mother and child remains one-sided and, in my observation, contingent on role reversal.

In such cases, the daughter experiences the mother as "dead" when the latter is depressed, but as "good" once the daughter adapts by relating to the mother in a way that allows her to become "the child." The mother's affective states then fluctuate between depression and childlike narcissistic pleasure. These mothers become good objects when they feel cared for and loved by husband and daughter. What the daughters sacrifice, or what they submit to with regard to their mothers' needs, promotes a narcissistic adaptation in both: it is in order to be lovable that the daughter subordinates her own needs to those of the mother. Frequently this adaptation constitutes the foundation for a sadomasochistic object relationship between them.

Role reversal of the sort we are discussing is not a defense mechanism, but an early defensive characterological stance. It starts as a survival mechanism vis-à-vis the mother, but develops into traits within the character structure. Narcissistic rage is defended against by a masochistic and self-deprecatory self-image: the girl may feel that "something is wrong" with her. Nevertheless, this structure manifests a high degree of adaptation to maternal narcissistic and depressive pathology, and to whatever "life with father" develops for the child as a result. Role reversal is a strain trauma; against a reservoir of unconscious rage directed at the parents, the child must make an adaptive effort in order not to feel abandoned.

Object loss, as Green points out, occasions a restructuring of psychic reality that leads to a transformation of relationships in actual reality. The loss experienced by the child in the cases I am describing relates to a mother's need to withdraw. This lessening of maternal interest is the obverse of a preoccupation with self, brought on by internal conflicts. Role reversal is deployed here to deal with a specific type of object loss—an internal loss due to a mother's narcissistic and depressive pathology, which causes her withdrawal from the child as a lovable, important presence (see chapter 1). The mothers of the patients I have described were never physically absent from home, but they withdrew emotionally from their children. The little daughters, by contrast, invariably tried to reach their mothers. By going affectively to "where the mother is," they would try to recreate the bond with her. This shows similarities to Green's description of the child's wish to "reanimate her mother." I have learned from my patients' descriptions of their feelings that the little girl will attempt to comfort her mother, cheer her up, and make her smile, laugh, and behave like a mother who is life-affirming. The striking and understandable result is that the mother, when she is able to respond at all, accepts her child's offerings on a narcissistic level. She allows the child to nurture her, to "feed" her, to do things for her, and to take care of her. *It is thus that role reversal comes about.*

In the process, as a result of this mutual adaptation, the daughter becomes dependent on variations in the mother's mood, which the child henceforth will attempt to anticipate. The little daughter must strive to master a traumatic situation that has come about in the mother–child interaction. The trauma is now the child's, by virtue of the narcissistic loss she has sustained through the mother's own narcissistic pathology. In my experience, the daughter of a depressed mother does everything possible to find *a bridge* to her mother's feelings and reestablish contact. Role reversal enables her to do this, though at cost.

The mothers of my role reversal patients, I note again, had not experienced bereavement during my patients' childhoods; nonetheless, they fit Green's description in that their depression occasioned in their daughters a measure of helplessness, consequent on experiencing a loss of the mother's love. (Green notes that insomnia and nocturnal terrors are often the result of such an experience, and I have found this to be the case with my patients.) We know from Freud's work that bereavement leads to mourning and that the mourning process has a natural end. The mothers I am describing, however, demonstrated depressive moods and traits that *permanently* affected their ability to mother. The children experienced in their mothers a narcissistic sense of loss and disillusionment, which they frequently turned against themselves. The children felt a measure of hope, however, when the role reversal adaptation succeeded. When the mothers felt loved and cared for by their daughters, they became "good" objects. These children, of course, had intermittently to give up their own childhood by becoming their mother's mother.

I believe that in the process of internalizing the mother's depression and narcissistic needs, the child may not simply identify with the mother's feelings but may struggle against them and succeed in preserving the core of an independent self, aided by the father, if at an emotional cost. In role reversal, the extent of the mother's "deadness" or depression is denied, and the child does not give up trying to reach her. To cope with this disbelief in the mother's lack of interest, a split in the maternal representation is likely to develop. The fluctuating internal representations of the image of the mother and the unpredictability of her affective response affect self-constancy, object constancy, and the capacity to trust. Green (1980) notes that this affective split creates "a hole in the texture of object relations with the mother"; though she continues a relationship with the child, "her heart is not in it" (p. 151).

The child's role reversal begins as a survival mechanism but later becomes a sense of pride, omnipotence, and narcissistic well-being that is not readily relinquished. The patient, reluctant to give it up, questions the viability of more recently acquired capacities. In role reversal the child becomes the active, preoedipal mother (Brunswick, 1940) toward her own mother (see chapter 4 on the female Oedipus complex).

When this conflict is revived at termination, the danger of a negative therapeutic reaction becomes prominent. The reaction can be avoided in its most severe form by interpreting the cost of renunciation, which goes back to a period very early in life that may have been relived in subsequent developmental stages, and now once more comes into view in the transference at the end of the analysis.[1]

---

[1]As Green notes: "The patient spends his life nourishing his dead, as though he alone has charge of it. Keeper of the tomb, sole possessor of the key of the vault, he fulfills his function of foster parent in secret. He keeps the dead mother prisoner and she remains his personal property. The mother has become the infant of the child. It is [for the child] to repair her narcissistic wound. . . . The subject is caught between two losses, presence in death or absence in life. Hence the extreme ambivalence to bring the dead mother back to life" (p. 164).

THE RELATIONSHIP WITH THE FATHER

In situations where role reversal produced difficulties in the relationship between mother and daughter, it is crucial to know how the girl child finds access to a love relationship with her father. It may be that love for the father will be converted into unfulfilled yearnings as well, because the girl fears the loss of her mother's love. Alternatively, the father can become a substitute maternal object, caring, holding, serving as a mirror for accomplishments and as an object of identification, and providing relief from the weight of the mother's depression (see chapter 3). In the patients described in chapter 1, taking care of the mother was often associated with feelings of oedipal victory—the mother became "the child" of father and daughter. When the mother became depressed, father and daughter took care of her, giving her a "second chance" to be a child, presumably under more favorable circumstances. This "mutual aid syndrome" may become a shared unconscious fantasy between mother and daughter and may extend to the family unit. During the oedipal period, "leaving" the mother for the father can create a conflict of allegiance: as the mother needs the child's attention and care, the girl's wish to become closer to her father becomes connected with conflicts of abandonment and guilt toward her mother, beyond phase-specific oedipal needs. The strong incestuous tie to the preoedipal mother, the premature, precocious "adulthood" that has resulted from the girl's caretaking functions, and her oedipal rivalry for her father frequently create excessive anxiety. Primal scene fantasies may become connected to feelings of narcissistic injury and loss. Likely to arise at this time are sexual conflicts related to incestuous feelings heightened when the girl's love for her father is in ascendancy. Sometimes father and daughter establish a special bond of warmth and friendship, answering their shared need to escape periodically from the depressed mother. This in turn seems to strengthen the daughter's fantasy of being the father's "other woman." The heightened oedipal guilt that results makes the shift from her father to a man of her own much more difficult when the daughter reaches adulthood (see chapter 1). The primary source of oedipal guilt stems from the fact that the mother unconsciously becomes the incestuous child of father and daughter in a shared fantasy concretized in joint father–daughter caretaking activities aimed at rescuing the mother and restoring her to the family as a maternal presence (see chapter 3).

ROLE REVERSAL IN THE TRANSFERENCE

Green (1980) observed that in the patients he describes depression appears in the transference: the "dead" mother is relived when the patient adopts her characteristics or projects them onto the analyst. That depression is triggered by a narcissistic wound and by object loss: "The shadow of the mother is profiled in object relationships henceforth" (p. 154). I have also found in cases of role reversal that the mother's depression and her relationship with the patient appears in the transference even in the early stages of treatment. While the cause for a transference depression is not always reducible to bereavement or role reversal, when the reversal is rooted in the patient's negative and positive oedipal periods, it can be reconstructed from the transference relationship. Although the pathology ensuing from a depressed mother's handling of her young child goes back to the preoedipal period, reconstruction is deepened and clarified when current adult object relationships are traceable to the conflicts of both the negative and the positive oedipal periods.

Both Green's patients, who experienced bereavement of the mother, and my patients, who experienced a mother prone to depression, relived the depression in the transference, permitting reconstruction of the early mother–child relationship and ensuing affective disturbances. Green (1980) has stressed the *loss of meaning* following premature disillusionment and the patient's *quest for meaning* initiated by the experience of the emotionally absent mother (p. 152). The reliving of such a disillusioning relationship may cause a transference depression. When meaning cannot be derived from a mother–child object relationship anchored in reality, the experience of absence will create either a fantasy formation (e.g., a pathological idealization, or a "fantasy mother"), or a premature turning away from the relationship. Loss of meaning is relived when the female patient who had a depressed mother repeatedly asks "Why?!" Why was it not possible for the mother to smile, to take initiative, to touch the child, to play with the child, to develop joint projects? Why could the mother not express satisfaction with the little girl so that she could know that she was lovable? Why could the mother not find her beautiful, or bright, and why could the mother not recognize the extent to which the child contributed to the mother's emotional nourishment? Finally, why could the mother not praise the child for her accomplishments? As the patient I quoted in chapter 1 (p. 13) said, "I felt emotionally disconfirmed." This patient, attuned to a high degree of adaptation in a nonreceptive environment, found herself many years later teaching mathematics to fairly unmotivated students. Their lack of interest in the subject was due, to a large extent, to external circumstances. "If I find *one* student in the whole group who pays close attention to my lecture and I can see interest and comprehension in the expression of the face," the patient said, "I am all right. I need *one person* who can understand what I am saying." This illustrates the need to have meaning reaffirmed. Unconsciously, the *one* person to whom a link is made in fantasy is likely to be an idealized parental representation who *is not* involved in role reversal with the daughter.

The female patient with a history of role reversal with her mother will be searching, in the transference relationship with her female analyst, for the mother she never found in childhood. The analyst will be alternately idealized as having become the mother the patient never had and who has now been found, or devalued because the transference relationship has left the patient wanting fulfillment of a primary need it has revived but cannot gratify. The narcissistic wound left by having been "disconfirmed" in early life will be relived in all its ferocity, but this time with expressions of protest, hostility, and a need to fight for change. An affective storm delayed since childhood because the "child-mother" had to be protected from hostility can now be expressed in the transference relationship. Object loss in the analytic relationship can be feared less as a result and can now be talked about. An intense narcissistic rage suppressed in childhood in favor of an early adaptation to the mother's needs as well as to the girl's need, to prevent feelings of abandonment, may now be expressed and brought into the open in the transference. The minutiae of the mother–child relationship now have a chance to be understood and used to discover a new inner vitality in relationships with others.

A striking feature in the transference relationships of my role reversal patients has been a failure of separation from the mother because they needed to continue taking care of her. The mother had become the child who would never grow up and who must never be left. Relations to her were fraught with too much conflict for these patients to dare genuine separation and complete psychic differentiation. Ties to her, both libidinal and hostile, were expressed in the transference in various ways: by regressive needs for love; by sexualization of the transference on a preoedipal or oedipal level, where the analyst became the needy mother or the sexual father; or by barely concealed masturbation fantasies of a libidinal, hostile, or sadomasochistic nature in which the analyst was assigned a role. Under these circumstances, the establishment of internal freedom and individuation became an analytic task that could be addressed only by achieving differentiation from the mother. This was accomplished in psychoanalytic treatment by mourning the early loss of an affectionate, growth-promoting relationship with the mother; by analysis of survival mechanisms needed for coping; and by analysis of the need for narcissistic affirmation from others. Issues of affirmation had become clarified by the time the treatment process was culminating in work toward termination.

In the analysis of patients whose depressed mothers could be reached primarily via role reversal, the memories of these mothers are reexperienced in myriad ways. Because the mother's impact on character development is so incisive, the patient may develop a lack of spontaneity in overcoming feelings of distance from others without first obtaining narcissistic affirmation. A fear of object loss or a sense of emptiness may remain that hides a well of hostility toward the mother. Frequently these deficits will be bridged by choosing a profession where serving or healing others provides the affirmation withheld by the primary object. As a result of treatment, narcissistic depletion and feelings of emptiness and depression may be overcome.

Cognitive capacities and intellectual achievements will be used by some patients in the service of bridging the gap left by affective deficit. Sublimations will frequently not be stable, and the patient may remain vulnerable in her intellectual achievements and object relations unless there is affirmation of emotional and intellectual capacity by the outside world. Lasting object relations with deep personal involvement and concern for the other person may be in jeopardy. A narcissistic wound, reawakened from childhood, will enhance a masochistic stance or other forms of vulnerability in adult relationships, particularly when such a relationship threatens to end in a traumatic way.

Early disillusionment as a result of narcissistic pathology experienced in relation to one or both parents has a profound influence on the psychic development of the individual and, later, on the girl's ego ideal formation as a woman, a mother, and a mate, and on her personal life goals and their realization. Role reversal makes the daughter prone to fantasies of idealization and wish fulfillment, of making the mother "alive" through caregiving behavior and working toward healing her so that she can become an idealizable object. There is also a wish that the daughter might revert to the role of being the child of a caregiving mother. The failure of this realization in reality in turn influences the creation of the feminine ego ideal, which builds on relatively stable internalizations of primary objects, on realizable internal goals, on positive active relations with the outside world, and on achievement of the manifold potentials of a woman in her love life and intellectual development. The woman who has experienced role reversal is handicapped by her early shared fantasies with her parents. The analyst who is aware of this can be attuned to the delicate balance needed to facilitate individuation so that self-realization based on real achievements may become a reality for the adult woman who can draw on new sources of narcissistic gratification and sublimation.

My conceptualizations of children who form a role reversal relationship with their mothers stem from a two-person psychology, whereas Green moves on a one-person psychological plane. My work deals only with mother–daughter relationships in which the former is open to role reversal and the latter responds, that is, where a mutual adaptation takes place. This mutual adaptation gives both mother and child a measure of hope.

My female patients, once freed from the defensive constellation of role reversal, achieved a capacity for reality orientation on their own, related to their own destiny and not that of the role reversal mother or the role reversal preoedipal or oedipal family. Once the patient felt convinced she was liberated to lead an independent life, the oedipal conflict as both an internal and an existential problem could be reappraised in the analysis.

The striking similarity between Green's depressed patients and my role reversal patients becomes apparent in the transference where their early suffering is relived in analysis. Although the mothers Green describes withdrew from the child as a result of bereavement, whereas role reversal mothers suffered from narcissistic pathology and depression that was characterologically anchored, the similarities are significant. Both Green's patients and mine attempt to reanimate the mother, though the role reversal child does so by taking on maternal functions toward her, thereby establishing a relationship that was not possible so long as the mother remained withdrawn and unresponsive.

The specific importance of Green's ideas for role reversal lies in his finding that the internal representation of the withdrawn, depressed mother, who has been internalized by the child as "dead," has led to depression in the child. The "dead" mother confronts a young child by being "absent," unable to relate with appropriate affect to the growing child's needs. She is "there but not there." The extent to which such withdrawal on the part of the mother will lead to pathology in her young child depends, in role reversal cases, on the mother's neediness, on the degree of her narcissistic pathology, and on the pair's capacity for mutual adaptation. It will depend also on the extent to which the father acts with appropriate affect toward his little girl. An example of the analysis of an adult patient who was the role reversal child of a depressed, "absent," and "dead" mother is presented in the next chapter.

* Idealisierungskapazitäten werden überschnitten

3.

The Psychoanalysis of Emma

The analysis of Emma revealed role reversal in the extreme: her mother was depressed and unconsciously needed to become the role reversal child of both Emma and Emma's father. Emma's adaptation, based on a shared fantasy between mother and child, delayed her intrapsychic capacity for intimacy and marriage, and led to an inability to have children.

Emma came to analysis at the age of 31. She was tall, with very short platinum-dyed hair and heavily made-up eyes. At first glance it was hard to tell from her attire of boots, blazers, knapsack, and personally designed T-shirts depicting clean-shaven male heads, whether she was male or female. She wore slacks or very short skirts and had a collection of androgynous-looking watches that were her only jewelry. The total effect of her appearance, unexpectedly, was quite elegant.

Emma suffered from severe mood swings and intermittent states of depression. She had been bulimic and anorexic since age 13 and had frequent anxiety attacks accompanied by light-headedness (a feeling she did not "have both feet on the ground"), tachycardia, and a fear of dying. She was prone to rashes, which worsened when she would pick at her face, "trying to get rid of impurities."

Episodes of bulimia and anorexia were more frequent when she was lonely or angry. Overeating felt comforting, but as soon as she felt excessively full she had to get rid of the feeling by vomiting.

Afterward she felt purified and her depression lifted; feeling cleansed and in a good mood, she could start life anew, as if the entire episode had never happened. She wished that her body would look neither feminine nor masculine, but "in between." She did not want her breasts to protrude. She enjoyed oral, anal, and vaginal intercourse equally, and in her masturbation fantasies three men pleasured her at her three orifices simultaneously. An additional symptom was a severe work inhibition accompanied by pervasive feelings of emptiness. Emma had consulted an analyst in her native country following an exacerbation of her symptoms upon her decision to move to New York. When Emma came to analysis with me, she was a graphic designer, and while in analysis she became a fashion photographer and discovered her true artistic talent.

LIFE HISTORY

Emma was the only child of an architect father and a mother who didn't work. Emma was between 4 and 5 years old when her parents, together with two other families from their city, built a home on "barren land" (Emma's words) on the outskirts of a village. The local residents disliked this "foreign" invasion, and Emma felt like an outsider with the village children even after they took her in as one of them. She played mostly with boys and never lost the feeling that she didn't belong.

The family ate their main meal at noon. From the time Emma was 4 or 5, her mother had left coldcuts, cheese, and fruit in the refrigerator for her daughter's evening meal, which the little girl would eat after her parents went to the city for the evening. Emma ate alone and put herself to sleep. She was allowed to call their neighbor "when something was wrong," but she never did. Sometimes there were noises or a storm outside, and she would be frightened when the shades rattled. On such nights it was hard for her to fall asleep. All this made her extremely lonely and initiated the inception of a ritual in which dependency on food substituted for a nurturing mother. While in analysis, she still occasionally suffered from insomnia and anxiety attacks at night.

Emma's mother, until adopted at age 3, had lived in an orphanage. The maternal grandmother, who had adopted her mother, was the most nurturing woman in Emma's life. I wondered whether she had adopted the girl because she was unable to have children of her own; the patient did not know. In the third year of Emma's analysis, she flew home to say good-bye to her grandmother, who was dying. Emma felt as if it were she who had been her grandmother's adopted child: when she was little, her grandmother comforted her and was with her when she was sick. When Emma felt hurt, she and her grandmother "could think about it together so it wouldn't hurt so much."

Emma's mother had never experienced being nurtured by her birth mother, whose children had been taken away from her because she suffered from "a religious delirium," and was placed in an institution. As a small child, Emma visited the institution with her mother twice a year. She remembered the terrible smell and the unattractive surroundings in which this grandmother lived and her lack of human contact with her visitors. The lack of love shown by Emma's mother for her birth mother impressed the young girl deeply, and filled her with dread.

Emma's mother's lack of maternal feelings, her distance and sadness, made her daughter a lonely child. Emma was often bored. Her mother, though at home, frequently did not talk. She never played with Emma, who subsequently could not connect to her toys and games, and tended to look at them from a distance.

She remembered pushing in the eyes of her dolls. Though she was interested in building things, like her architect father, no one showed her how to play or to build. When she was 6, she played boys' games with a 4-year-old neighbor boy, her only playmate at the time. They would play card games and play in the mud.

When Emma was 8, the 10-year-old son of a family friend visited weekly. Emma remembered her mother saying, "Now we can bathe them together." She remembered that they played with each other's genitals in the bathtub. He then became her closest friend. Until the age of 10, she had no close girl friends.

When Emma was reaching latency age, she rejected the feminine role. She wore blue jeans, rebelled against female clichés, and identified with boys. Indeed, she was told that she looked like her father, and was more like him. She did not want to look like "a little woman." She did not play housewife, wear clothes with ruffles, try to be attractive, or avoid getting dirty, as most little girls did. She was not one of them. Emma began to reject femininity, just as her own mother had rejected maternity.

She went to a girls' high school and remained friends with two girls she met there. Their views were similar to hers: they did not want to marry and did not want children. Emma's high school was in a nearby city, and the walk to the bus was a lonely one through barren countryside. When Emma was 13, she and a girl friend were left alone for two weeks while their parents took a trip together. In protest, the two girls decided to diet, and each lost over ten pounds. When the parents returned, they were shocked and thought the girls had been ill. After that, Emma developed a secret pride in her figure. She began to overeat when alone, but immediately vomited when she felt too full. Thus began her bulimia–anorexia cycle.

Emma described her father, whom she adored, as an aesthetic, artistic, and rational man, with a great sense of humor. He played acrobatic games with Emma and threw her up in the air from the time she was little. Her father represented a "reality correction" for her mother's unending unhappiness and depressed distance. Emma reached the oedipal level with difficulty. There was little evidence of jealousy of her parents as a couple. A wish for a child with her father never surfaced. Emma loved her mother erotically (during her negative oedipal phase) and wished to be embraced by her, to reach a closeness with her, but at the same time her mother's depressions terrified her and she feared becoming like her. Her mother was never a genuine rival for the father's affections.

When Emma was about 20, her mother confided to Emma that the father had a woman friend with whom he spent time away from home and on vacations. This made Emma feel very sorry for her mother. The more independent Emma tried to become, the more clinging her mother became. She was depressed and clung to her daughter, particularly after Emma left home to live on her own in a nearby city. Emma felt threatened by her mother's possessiveness and dependency. Later she left her native country and came to New York, largely to get away from her mother. Thus, Emma's oedipal rival was her father's "other woman," an unknown person. Emma met this woman only after her father's death, four years into her analysis. She described the woman as warm and outgoing, and felt she understood her father's need for her.

From early childhood on, Emma remembered, her home life was disturbed by violent fights between her parents, which usually ended with her mother crying inconsolably. At times her parents did not speak to each other for several days. During those periods Emma's mother was particularly withdrawn. She remembered fearing, during her parents' violent fights at the dinner table, that if they separated she would lose one of them. Perhaps her father would kill her mother in a fight. Or perhaps she would be forced to stay with her mother and lose her father. She thought sometimes that her mother's love for her was based on the belief that Emma would choose to stay with *her*. She would then become her mother's exclusive possession.

As a small child, Emma was terrified during these fights. In adolescence and young adulthood, she was disturbed that she could not feel for her mother during these fights, and that she could not identify with her. She needed to be as different from her mother as possible. Early in the analysis, Emma would avoid contact with people, manifesting shyness like her mother, who rejected anything unfamiliar or new. Her identification with her father, however, made it possible for her to shift away from her anxiety about being like her mother. As a result, she became more like her father, who traveled, had a love life outside the home, and enjoyed conquering new areas of life. Emma's move to New York attested to that identification. Her symptoms, however, indicated that she was not entirely prepared for the separation from her mother. The somatic symptoms and fear of death stemmed from guilt feelings about abandoning her mother, who felt her daughter was "all she had."

Until she came to New York, Emma had never moved very far from home. Her parents never asked what she was planning to do with her life. "They were not indifferent, but fatalistic," Emma said. They did not seem to care what she studied. She felt unprotected and felt that their attitude accounted for her lack of orientation in the world. She had had to figure out everything about life by herself. Her parents did not ask about her life, only about her financial needs; they did not seem interested in what she did.

As a teenager in school Emma had become less shy and more social; she had her first sexual experiences with men when she was 16. At 20, she began a serious relationship with a man in his forties. He was a painter and had been her graphic design teacher. They fell in love and he divorced his wife. He lived with Emma for seven years.

During this love affair Emma became a sexual woman. She also learned about the art world and the world in general. She met other artists and was fascinated by the intellectual and artistic ambiance in which she found herself. After several years, however, her lover became increasingly jealous and fearful that she would leave him for another man. After each fight they had Emma had to overeat and vomit in secret. Her lover would then find the refrigerator empty, and think another man had been there. In these fights, whereby

Emma relived the scenes she had witnessed between her parents, she cast her lover in the role of her overpossessive mother.

Emma had her fallopian tubes tied when she was 22. Her mother was not only fully aware of this surgery, but actively involved; it was she who had found a surgeon for her daughter. Emma's father declared his neutrality; he did not participate in the medical consultation that preceded the operation, nor did he prevent the surgery.

THE ANALYTIC PROCESS

When Emma began treatment with me, she rationalized the sterilization as a decision in favor of a career. She was convinced that motherhood and professional interests were incompatible. As analysis progressed, it became evident that one of the advantages of her sterilization was that Emma did not worry about unwanted pregnancies. Thus, a wished-for license for promiscuity was implicit in her choice to have the operation. As we reached deeper levels, it emerged that the operation was an unconscious reproach to her mother: Emma was telling her that her mothering had been so inadequate that she wished to have nothing to do with becoming a mother herself. At the same time, the surgery was unconsciously an act of loyalty toward her mother, who could now forever remain "Emma's only child."

The sterilization, then, had the significance of a symptom through which two contradictory sets of wishes find expression in the same act: it was an act of hostility toward her mother, as well as an act of loyalty. Through it, she gave her mother what she unconsciously most wanted. In the analysis it emerged that Emma and her mother had a shared fantasy that the latter would be the only "child" in the family. Later it became clear that Emma's mother (unconsciously the child) became the *incestuous* child of father and daughter.

Emma's conflict between professional goals and motherhood surfaced for the first time in analysis. She wanted to be sure she could have a career without leaving her own child as she had been left by her mother; she felt she would have protected her own child much better than her mother had protected her. Apparently her sterilization removed enough of the disturbing aspects of her femininity to allow her to enjoy her sexual life as a woman. "I did not want to be dependent on a husband and do housework like my mother," she said. She added:

> I wanted to study and have my own work. I had no role models of people raising children in an admirable way until I came to this country, where women have both children and a profession. Before the operation we used condoms. When I was 16, I used the pill, but my parents were against it. (My parents cared about the pill but not about my ovaries!) Between the ages of 18 and 20 it became clear that I did not want a child. My mother talked to the gynecologist. The operation had to be unofficial because of my age and had to be performed in a private hospital. I was glad to be rid of the worry. I could avoid abortions and have less anxiety. I didn't want to have a heavy body like a pregnant woman. The bulimia and anorexia had become regular after I began having intercourse. I was afraid to carry something in my body which couldn't come out, "like a foreign body."

Unconsciously the eating disorder was equated with the fact that Emma's mother had aided her in removing part of her female insides, to "empty it out." Emma seemed to have unconsciously received her mother's message that she wanted to be her daughter's only child.

When Emma's love affair broke up after seven years, she began a brief affair with her roommate, a woman, who had been a maternal friend, washing her clothing and cooking for her. She discovered while in the analysis, however, that her friend was psychopathic and on drugs. She borrowed large sums of money from Emma that she did not repay. After Emma left for New York, she failed to pay the rent on their apartment and made off with some of Emma's furniture. Emma was extremely hurt by this behavior and was totally unprepared for it, having loved and idealized her friend. This was not an isolated incident; Emma had a tendency to be overly trusting, to lend money that was never repaid, and there were several incidents in which her belongings were stolen, including expensive camera equipment.

In New York Emma got a loft and her first good job through a man with whom she had a brief affair. She shared the loft space, usually with male roommates. Increasingly confident socially, she began to go out to discotheques. Such evenings sometimes ended in short-lived sexual relationships with men, which she reported as pleasurable or "very beautiful." None of these encounters, however, led to committed relationships.

TRANSFERENCE

Initially, Emma was frightened of a committed relationship and of analytic regression. Her negative transference dealt entirely with fears of love and closeness, and she was afraid of feelings of attachment toward me. She needed to confirm in reality that she was free to travel around the world, wherever she could find work, and that I would not be clinging like her mother or doctrinaire like her father. She needed tangible evidence that she could get away and return whenever she chose. Once she was able to identify her fear of closeness as a lifelong fear of her mother's possessiveness and depression, and understood her identification with her father's need to get away from home, her departures stopped being characterized by a restless, anxiety-driven need; now simply work-related absences, they were planned as much as possible to coincide with my vacations. The compulsion to get away gradually abated as I became differentiated from her parents.

In Emma's initial treatment relationship there was a wish to use me as a support in her rebellion against her parents. It was clear from the start that she had tried all her life to understand her parents, in spite of great anxiety that she might lose them. The analysis of this anxiety via her transference relationship had served an organizing function: it freed her sense of self from the threatening and unreliable parental representations and thereby allowed deeper transference development. This in turn improved her capacity to differentiate psychic from social reality. Initially, differentiation from her parents meant only that she would lose them. Unconsciously she had welded them into a single internal fused object representation that led to an androgynous self representation: to conjoin them was to keep them together. This unconscious wishful fantasy formed the basis of her bisexual self representation.

While Emma was terrified of engulfment by her mother and feared identifying with her, she needed to know she could return "home" to see me, much like a child in the rapprochement subphase (Mahler, 1966, 1971). This was most evident in treatment. While away, she frequently called, faxed, and wrote long letters. She had an inordinate anxiety about expressing neediness and therefore had to put a distance between us whenever she felt hostile, a repetition of her behavior during childhood and adolescence. It took a long time for her to be able to tolerate her own ambivalence without self-condemnation and to experience me as a new object, someone who would not be possessive or demanding, and who would welcome the spontaneous expression of her feelings, even hostility. Eventually she was able to confront her anxiety about her mother's depressed possessiveness, which had always frightened and angered her. As she was reliving this in the transference, she could understand how, given her mother's extreme emotional fragility, she had never dared express hostility toward her.

In the second year of analysis, Emma began to be interested in her conflicts related to bisexuality. For a long time she attempted to present in her appearance an externalized combination of mother and father. She told me she thought she was "rather androgynous." One aspect of Emma's bisexuality related to the mixture of deprivation and indulgence perpetuated during her childhood, which had become characterologically embedded because of her conflictual identifications. Her mother (feminine but weak) had needed constant reassurance and gratification, which she freely demanded of Emma, whereas her father was independent, dominating, masculine, and strong (and hence desirable to emulate).

During this period Emma brought in a dream: "I am visiting a male friend to say good-bye before driving home. I have a Volkswagen packed and stuffed with my belongings I am attached to, and all my expensive camera equipment. I hesitate to leave it in the street, thinking I might be inviting theft. I returned to the street after a brief visit. My car and everything in it has disappeared. I woke up in shock and great anxiety."

After telling the dream, Emma was silent a long time. I said to her it strikes me that she has often reported that her things have been stolen, or taken away from her, or that she has lost something she is fond of. She agreed and said she constantly got too many things from her mother, who was compelled to buy her things she did not like. They had different tastes: Emma liked to keep her living space empty, while her parents' house was very crowded: art works from different periods were thrown together, and her father had glass-enclosed collections of insects, plants, and butterflies.

With the help of this dream we were able to understand that Emma unconsciously needed to "stuff herself" with her "good fantasy (feminine) mother" (who presumably could have encouraged Emma's motherhood). It also became clear that taking command of her own hostility toward her mother by vomiting food and emitting an ejaculative jet of vomit into the toilet, became a way she could identify with her masculine father. This

bulimic enactment represented her split self and object representations and her embedded androgynous character pattern. The
enactment magically made her feel good, yet simultaneously
assured her that she could symbolically "empty out" the internal
image of her mother that most threatened her. The excessive
ingestion stood for her identification with her needy child-
mother, toward whom she felt highly ambivalent; the vomiting
represented her "masculine" independence, her identification
with her father, which had been her way to experience freedom
from her engulfing mother. Her split identity was her way of
defending against deep anxieties: her conflict between her fear of
engulfment by her helpless and depressed mother and her unconscious wish to experience her as loving and to be fused with her.
At the same time, there was a fear that her engulfing mother
would become powerful enough to obliterate Emma's self-image
and that she might then become like her. Had not the mother
already, by actively helping her become sterilized, communicated
to her, in the most concrete manner imaginable, her own disdain
for motherhood? Having been an adoptive child, having lost her
birth mother to psychotic delusions, and having spent the first
three years of her life in an orphanage, Emma's mother apparently had never recovered enough from these traumata to feel
maternal, despite the fact that her adoptive mother (Emma's
"good" grandmother) had been a maternal and loving woman. By
aiding her daughter's sterilization, Emma's mother also unconsciously encouraged her promiscuity, thereby paving the way for a
further identification with her father.

Further analysis of Emma's dream revealed that "being overstuffed" was also a representation of her masturbation fantasy of
having all three of her orifices filled up by men. Unconsciously, the
Volkswagen also represented a wishful fantasy about having a child,
as well as being overfed and enjoying it. I asked her: "Was the overstuffed car also an overstuffed belly you had to get rid of, a baby
perhaps?" After that question, Emma had a dream that related to
her core trauma: "My mother and I were in a car. We went to buy a
melon. We got a whole melon, but it was peeled already. There was
something wrong: the melon was whole but it was peeled—the
melon symbolizes pain, something is exposed that is inside." Emma
associated that the melon relates to pregnancy (getting a fat
stomach): "Without the outside skin it is only the inside. The melon
is a baby. *It doesn't get born.* I also wanted a baby. When I was little,

Mother said to me, let's have one more child, and I wanted that too. In reality neither parent wanted to have one more child. They never thought child care was simple." Emma's baby would have been that "one more child."

This second dream created a great deal of anxiety. It emerged that Emma unconsciously wanted to have a baby by her mother. Yet she also asserted, "It has always been important for me to be slender when I am with men." Then she said, "I was never in a situation when I could think something over before I did it. I can't think it over again about having babies. I didn't want to adopt a child, I was afraid of that—my mother was adopted. I could not have taken responsibility for the child—yet I could not have given the child away. My mother was no role model of a mother. She was tied to my father and totally dependent on him (more a child than I was). She had no special skills. I wanted to be sure I could live my *own* life. My mother was always in an inferior position, mistreated and the weaker in the fights with my father. This was decisive in my decision not to have a child." Unconsciously, Emma felt responsible for her mother, who had become her "adopted child."

During her growing years, Emma had experienced as a rejection of herself her mother's rejection of motherhood. In analysis she came to understand how this rejection had driven her to be sterilized. Although she consciously struggled to free herself from all dependency needs, she admitted longing for her mother's love and craving a closeness she never experienced. Emma attempted, by destroying her reproductive capacity, to expiate her guilt for having taken revenge against her mother. By rejecting the possibility of having children, Emma avoided feeling rejected by her mother, as well as any unconscious pressure she might have felt to reject her own child. And, of course, her sacrifice of motherhood allowed her to make her mother her only child. This was a most poignant role reversal. As a result of her sterilization, Emma apparently experienced an even greater need to identify with her father, which contributed to the development of her bisexual self-image and femininity–masculinity conflict. Both the pain of feeling rejected by her nonmaternal mother but loved and accepted by her volatile father, who spent much time away from home, contributed to Emma's bulimia–anorexia cycle: beginning at puberty, she had increasingly sought control through denying her loneliness by eating, and through trying to strengthen the masculine image of her body by vomiting.

In her third year of analysis, we were able to understand how Emma's conflict over feeling rejected by her mother and in turn rejecting motherhood had resulted in her developing a phobic anxiety about carrying something in her body she could not eject at will: a baby, a penis, or food. She realized in analysis why the bulimia–anorexia cycle had become more frequent after she began to have sexual relations: she was terrified of a possible pregnancy and also needed to feel that she could free herself from the man she was involved with at any time. Emma had the fantasy that had she become pregnant, she could not have "chosen" how female or male—how "in-between"—she could be at any given time.

Through analysis it emerged that while she was growing up there had been no way for her to experience her female body and female internal organs as valuable. By enabling to arrange her sterilization, actively (or in her father's case) passively, both of her parents helped her create within herself a concrete emptiness, that paralleled the vacuity of personal relationships within the family unit. Emma had difficulty in analysis verbalizing her regrets about not being able to conceive a child, and was afraid of deep mourning for what had happened. Unconsciously she had become her mother's substitute husband. It was her answer to her mother's saying, "You are all I have in life."

Toward the end of the third year of her analysis and into the fourth, Emma relived in the transference neurosis the long periods of lonely silence that during her childhood had pervaded the atmosphere between herself and her mother in the father's absence. I thought that during such periods Emma may at times have become dissociated. Her analytic hours were characterized by long periods of silence. Sometimes nothing came from Emma: she felt not "all there," but confused, absent, or wanting. At other times she felt a pressure to talk, but could not. She was lonely. She could not associate. She said she could not "find herself." She felt so alone, she seemed temporarily unable to do analytic work.

WORKING THROUGH AND COUNTERTRANSFERENCE

At the end of some hours Emma's silences and withdrawals left me "starving," wishing for more contact with her than she could gratify. I felt her loneliness. Even after the bulimia–anorexia symptom had been cured, the underlying characterological problem remained. At times, as she relived being emotionally distant, her psychoanalytic "intake" seemed in jeopardy. All this made it even more difficult to assess the extent to which Emma could internalize analytic interpretations—already she suffered periodically from a pervasive feeling of inner emptiness. Her difficulty in associating was a sign of this emptiness. It was as if I had to "feed her something" before she could continue. Our joint reconstructions led her to characterize her emptiness as her "contact problem," which was related to anger or rage with people. In states of emptiness Emma also experienced a feeling of boredom and was afraid she would have no more creative ideas.

We spoke about the fact that when she feels "overstuffed" she has difficulty associating. I said, referring to the Volkswagen dream, that perhaps when she feels "overstuffed" by what I say to her, the meaning of my words can be "stolen" and she might *not* miss that— might even feel relieved! She laughed and said she never felt that consciously. I addressed her shifting reality sense, which resulted in her being temporarily disconnected from me in transference: I interpreted that in such situations she unconsciously liked to change from her overstuffing mother to her father, who never overstuffed her and who fled the home when he needed to. She confirmed this and said that her father fixed things aesthetically in their home, a capacity she associated with his profession. I said, "Perhaps you are disappointed that we cannot do this in analysis" (I could not make her into a man or grant her wish for the freedom to be "more masculine or feminine" at will). Such exchanges broke the impasse of her detached feeling state: Emma then felt neither stuffed nor excessively empty or lonely and could again do analytic work.

It now became possible for Emma and myself to reconstruct long periods of lonely childhood feelings, during which food had been her only companion, and she had had difficulty playing and occupying her time. Her mother, during her own disturbed and lonely childhood, had not learned how to play until well after she was adopted and therefore did not know very well how to play with the younger Emma. Emma felt there had always been something missing in her relationship with her mother. We reconstructed that during Emma's childhood her mother must have transmitted a nonverbalizable, desolate feeling-state from her own early childhood in the orphanage. She probably, unconsciously, made Emma experience some of what she must have felt. In situations of acute loneliness and anxiety, Emma lost contact with a part of herself that she recovered through her bulimia ritual. Once she had recovered from this symptom, she could gradually internalize our work, and differentiation from her parents became possible. The realization that she neither resembled her mother nor her father created a process analogous to normal separation-individuation. This, however, did not occur until the second and third years of her treatment.

In her third year of analysis, Emma became anxious to tackle both her bulimia–anorexia, and her work inhibition, and actively fought against them in reality. As she began to master the eating disorder, she was able to stop bingeing and vomiting as long as we were meeting regularly; she would relapse, however, as soon as I would leave for a vacation, however brief. It was not until after her fourth year of analysis that she was able to stop completely, even when I was absent, and she felt a sense of triumph having rid herself of this addictive, hostile, and self-destructive behavior.

Emma's work inhibition was interconnected with conflicts related to the bulimia–anorexia. "To put off work is a ritual," she said. "It's being alone eating and vomiting. After the ritual, I'm ready to start working." (Here the ritual seems to be an addictive and masturbatory equivalent.) "Sometimes," she went on, "the bulimia also happens after a positive excitement, such as a new project. I go in front of the mirror and poke around on my face; afterwards I vomit. It has also happened when I have a sense of internal upheaval. There is a self-hatred when I buy everything in order to eat it all up and vomit it out afterwards. While it is taking place I feel a sense of excitement (the ritual is sexualized). At home it used to be worse and it used to take longer; there was more time to kill."

The lack of contact between Emma and her mother had led to Emma's eating disorder. Her identification with her father and her need to get away from her mother had led to her promiscuity, which her surgery, abetted by both, had facilitated. She needed to feel that "someone is always there," but at the same time she needed to know that she could get away. The bulimia–anorexia had represented a symbolic ingestion of what she had lacked in love and caring from her mother, and in protective understanding from her father: she had been prematurely left on her own and had needed to occupy herself in a loveless, lonely house and neighborhood. I believe that her identification with her father saved her from a permanent deep depression. Emma's identification with her father became part of a characterological defense, which made it possible for her to feel less bound and committed to her mother.

CREATIVITY

Our work on the bulimia–anorexia symptom and its relation to her fluctuating gender identification freed Emma for a new spurt of creativity in which she was able to invent new ways of portraying the body: there was greater freedom, more movement in her work, and in it gender identity was more readily apparent. She eventually acquired an impressive position in her new field, and her work, increasingly original, began appearing in magazines throughout the world.

While in analysis, Emma had changed from working as a graphic designer to working as a fashion photographer. While getting started in her new field, she set up fashion shoots using volunteer models, hairdressers, and makeup artists. They wanted publicity and so worked for nothing, but were unreliable. Sometimes they did not show up and had to be replaced at the last moment. This was extremely difficult for Emma, who herself lacked self-constancy and had difficulty making demands on others. She easily became distressed, felt completely lost, and feared she would run out of creative ideas. I pointed out that she temporarily lost her capacity to be creative when she felt angry about being precipitously abandoned. I raised the question of how she might cope with such a situation without becoming desperate and depressed, and feeling *empty*. I interpreted that upon being faced with unreliability she felt injured in her self-esteem, withdrew from people, and became preoccupied with herself. Since in childhood she had been used to getting things instead of getting love, her social skills had remained undeveloped. Emma needed help in bridging the gap between her unfulfilled narcissistic needs and her reality-based need to get along with others on a team. Through gaining this insight into her behavior, she was able to empathize with her volunteers' lives and to relate better to her working group.

Emma possessed an unusual ability to recognize physiognomic types. She could match them up with deceased personalities from stage or screen to create photographic impersonations so convincing they were accepted for important exhibitions. This helped her to maintain a fantasy that denied her fear of death, which stemmed from the perverse aspects of her character formation. Interestingly, Arlow (1991), in an article on character perversion, notes that this fear is frequently found among people with this characterological defense, as is a tendency to choose a profession such as "fashion designer, interior decorator...there are many references, especially humorous ones to the 'deceptive quality of female adornment and embellishment'" (p. 185). Emma, because of her unconscious fantasy of fluctuating gender identity, had little difficulty using disguises, poses, and costumes to impersonate personality types. In a birthday album for her father, Emma appeared in one picture in a long green velvet evening gown, looking exquisitely feminine. One might say she wore a "femininity costume" for him.

For her fashion photography she developed a sense of the dramatic and unusual. Through her use of extreme color combinations and unusual postures, her female figures frequently exhibit a regal phallic stance; for instance, a very high hairdo that on closer inspection achieves its height and shape from being interwoven with a cactus.

Emma also worked for men's fashion magazines. She photographed her male models in precarious acrobatic positions, exhibiting a magical ability to defy gravity and perform great physical feats (reminiscent of the sexually exciting acrobatic games with her father in childhood). She knew how to appeal to the homosexual component in fashion-conscious heterosexual men, as well as to homosexual men themselves. Her bisexuality and fluctuating gender identity were used in the service of creativity and original artistic self-expression.

Her creativity seemed to flow from a greater understanding of herself and her enjoyment of shifting impersonations based on unconscious fantasies: the impersonation of famous women represented an unconscious wish to transform her depressed mother into an alive, beautiful, and feminine woman with whom Emma could have identified. Like other characterologically perverse individuals, Emma exhibited a denial of temporal dimensions that muted her fear of death, and fear of gender differences. She could enjoy equally the female and male impersonations she created in her photographic work, with its highly original ideas of costuming.

Like Chaplin, Emma had the ability to capture in a nonverbal way the essence of an hilarious scene between two people. Emma's work is successful because her photographic fantasies express the fantasies of many people, less endowed, and by so doing, lend support to the intermediary realm between fantasy and reality, for both herself and her audience.

For Emma, who could not bear children, creativity was in part a substitute for procreation. As she had turned hostility toward her mother against herself by having herself sterilized, the question arises of the extent to which this fact may have stunted her capacity for sublimation. Emma's creativity rested on transforming her handicaps into something positive. Her lack of gender differentiation was expressed in the strikingly original way in which the men and women in her photographs are dressed. Her difficulty in consistently using secondary process thinking aided the original manner in which she used three-dimensionality in her work, the manner in which she makes people interact with each other, and the way she places people in an original and often amusing landscape or cityscape with surrealist touches.

LOVE, WORK, AND CREATIVITY

In the fourth year of Emma's analysis, her father died of a sudden heart attack and Emma flew home. After the funeral she wrote me a letter I shall quote in part:

> Some time has passed since I talked to you on the phone. There have been many ups and downs. Everything *sometimes becomes very abstract for me* (emphasis added). But I allow myself my feelings when I am alone, and I cry when I feel like it. On the other hand, I am concentrating on "catching my mother in midair." My role with her now is that of a close friend—a child, a mother, a life-partner, a priest, an income tax advisor, and a household helper. [Role reversal at its fullest!] Therefore, I don't have much time to think. Of course there were some signs and symptoms after forty years of megastress. My father was "invincible" according to his own words, and he felt he would live forever. I think he played with many serious risks, but, of course, he did not know how close he was to getting a heart attack. My mother and I talk a lot and we get to know each other better. She says that she has lived *his* life for almost forty years, and now it is very difficult for her to live her own life all of a sudden. However, I have the feeling that I have at least gotten her to the point where she considers her own life worth living. In the beginning she was so very lost—she was like the child who was lost and forlorn, left in the orphanage, who was waiting for someone to come and visit. She talked about that and cried in a way that was heartbreaking. I sensed the depth of her *anxiety about not being loved and being left, a package which she has fully transmitted to me* [emphasis added]. We talked about that as well. I am trying to talk to her as much as I can, which helps, and we are getting closer. There are so many puzzles about my father. I have always felt so close to him, but

then there are so many gaps like large white blotches since he died, which I know I shall never be able to know about. I shall have a lot to talk about when I return, and I am very glad that I am at the point where I am in my analysis, so that I feel strong.

Later that year Emma enacted another surgical change of her body. She had a second nose operation, because the first, two years earlier, had not satisfied her. She also began a new period of promiscuity, and said, "It seems to me that I am sexually freer. I am enjoying that tremendously. Of course, I ask myself, why I enjoy these one-nighters so much. Perhaps because it is the exact opposite of the relationship between my parents: after a certain point their relationship was not physical any more, but very committed—my affairs are intensive and physically passionate, but without commitment."

Later that year the patient met an old friend she had known since early childhood. They had always been very close, but there had been no sexual relationship, because Emma had thought he was gay. When he casually mentioned that he had to renew his passport, she learned he was an American citizen. She said spontaneously, "Oh, then you can marry me and I can get a green card." Her friend agreed.

A wedding was arranged with great pomp and circumstance. Emma wore a black glittering dress with white stars. She wrote me a letter just after the wedding:

So, now I am married. A great deal has happened. It was a tremendous blast. I was neither excited nor nervous. The whole thing was *a little abstract* for me, but positive [emphasis added]. It was a fantastic celebration. Everything was perfect the whole day. First, the whole crowd of guests went with us for our marriage ceremony, about fifteen people with cameras, and there was a constant blinking of lights. After that, there was the traditional kiss and a lot of rice throwing and then we went for lunch, which took place in a garden, decorated in a sentimental, kitschy, but beautiful way. There was a lot more photography. I am going to have a wedding album consisting of twenty volumes. What made me feel strange was the whole situation. Only W's mother and a few friends and relatives thought that the entire wedding was a matter of love and romance. W's mother gave me a ring, which she received fifty years ago from her husband. I thought, who knows where this is going? And what did I let myself in for? This way or that way it is a commitment. My husband and I didn't have much time to talk about what we had thought about the whole thing. He is going back

to his home town with his mother and I am going with a close friend
to X where I have a little job and many more possibilities, also in magazines. As far as work is concerned it is all very positive. When we came
back to my home town I was able to relax and have some rest. With my
husband I have a great feeling of inner security. It is a friendship and
I know that I can rely on him. . . .

Somewhat later, she wrote:

My private life has become extremely mixed up: I have started a
sexual relationship with my husband. Already on the first night after
my arrival somehow it simply happened—he took the first step and I
went along, and I enjoyed it enormously. We continued into the next
day. The following evening I got a panic attack. I suddenly had the
feeling I got myself into something, or rather, through this wedding
and by sleeping with my husband, I had maneuvered myself into a situation in which I did not want to be. I suddenly was not sure how he
sees the situation, what he expects. But what I was most afraid of is
that I would land in a typical husband–wife relationship. And then,
on top of it, I am married. I felt horrible, I felt sick, I had the feeling
that I was choking and couldn't get air. I suddenly did not know the
way out anymore and I felt as closed in as I did with my mother before
I decided I had to leave and come to New York. During the night I
hardly slept and I left the house early in the morning. I went to the
cemetery, which incidentally is beautiful, and I really cried for my
father for the first time. The rest of the day, I remained rather silent.
I wasn't able to speak. I couldn't speak about that until the evening.
My husband noticed something was wrong and I told him about my
feelings about being committed and about my anxiety and that I feel
very insecure, and that almost all people during the marriage ceremony thought that we are an ordinary married couple. He said he
had told everybody he was getting married so that he can belong to
someone, which is true; this is true for me also to a certain extent. I
told him that I am not anxious that we are married and are having
sex, as long as our friendship remains the way it is, uncomplicated,
full of trust, openness, and humor, and I don't have to have anxiety
that everything is going to change, and I don't have to be afraid of
jealousy. He quieted me down and said that for him the whole thing
is also very new. The longest relationship he had had with a woman
was twenty-five years ago. Then his last sexual relationship with a
woman five years ago was short-lived and after that he thought he was
gay. He has had many friendships with men, but few sexual activities
with men or women. He also feels that I can leave any time I want. He
would not try to hold me or be jealous. I believed him; this is how I

know him. After this conversation, the rest of the week was very beautiful. I thought a great deal about why I suddenly had been so anxious and what it meant. I had been so afraid to lose my independence. I wanted someone to be close to me but not too close. I don't have the experience how to do something like that properly. I was left alone so much by my mother who had no time for me, or she was there too much, particularly when my father was with his woman friend. She said to me: "You are everything I have in life." Now that I am away from my husband and my mother, I get the feeling that we are a good team and our sexual life was a great and a wonderful surprise for me. We have so much in common as we have been friends for so long, and we can always talk about things. I also realized that when I am at home with my mother I have no privacy. When I get up in the morning I am still half asleep, she tells me a lot of things, she asks questions and talks. I get homesick for New York, for my own room, my own things, and my own friends. So much is happening, particularly in my work.

Thereafter, when Emma visited her mother with her husband, her mother was quarrelsome, dissatisfied, and seemed unhappy her daughter was married. It became clear to Emma that she had to be *the lost mother's presence (what the mother always missed) to her mother;* she had to be what her mother had always been missing (the pivotal role reversal). This insight once again revived Emma's fears of commitment, her difficulty in coping with her mother, and her inability to mourn her father.

Nevertheless, Emma began to make an increasingly feminine adjustment, and she and her husband made plans to live together. The patient's work inhibition seemed mastered, and her creativity afforded new levels of gratification. She had gone from a masturbation fantasy of men pleasuring her in her three orifices simultaneously, to living with one man whom she loved, with whom she was sexually happy, and to whom she was married.

TERMINATION PHASE

During Emma's termination phase, her anxiety attacks, her original physical symptoms, and fear of dying associated with separation, this time from me, recurred. Bulimia and anorexia did not recur, nor did her work inhibition. Emma's hostility and resentment toward her parents and others when she was unable to master a task became more accessible in treatment. In this process, renewed feelings of disillusionment with her parents and with her analysis as not having given her complete mastery over some of her anxieties became prominent. These anxieties related to her capacity to take new steps in life and in creative work, and to master these on her own. Emma's physical symptoms, anxieties, and fear of dying receded after we worked through her guilt about leaving her mother for her husband. Emma became increasingly able to enjoy her analytic gains without feeling that she "owed something" to her mother. She was then ready for termination.

REFLECTIONS ON EMMA'S ANALYSIS

Analytic work with Emma revolved around three areas: her sense of self and her image of her body, which she perceived as damaged; the unfolding of her sexual awareness and behavior; and the unfolding of her imaginativeness and creativity. At the end of Emma's treatment, an equilibrium was established in her marriage. The fact that she married within a year of her father's death is reminiscent of Bak's description (1973) of people who fall in love after the death of a love object. After her father's death, Emma was reexposed to the danger of engulfment by her mother. In her original adaptation to her family, Emma had attempted to stave off engulfment and depression by role reversal. Such a defensive constellation, however, may be in danger of collapse: it needs continuous reenactment to affirm its successful operation. Emma's role reversal was not a defense mechanism in Anna Freud's sense (1936); rather, it was a type of object relationship that burdens the child unable to protect itself from the dangers role reversal poses to a burgeoning sense of self (see chapter 1). While Emma's sterilization was unconsciously meant to settle her relationship with her mother, in actuality her conflicts were intensified as she sacrificed the possibility of having children. She gained, however, the necessary freedom to find a partner. Emma's mother (unconsciously the child) became the incestuous child of father and daughter in reality—not just in Emma's fantasy life. This conflict became so powerful that Emma's wish to become a wife and mother went underground. Emma's sterilization precluded the possibility of pregnancy, but gave her the chance to obtain sexual freedom. Through her sterilization, she gave up a unique aspect of her femininity. Feeling that she would never be a complete woman enhanced her masculine identification with her father, who also could not bear a child. Emma's sterilization represented a split between her wish to take care of her mother and her wish to escape from her. At the same time, Emma's wishes for motherhood became repressed. They resurfaced in analysis, however, and her childhood identification with her father was now in conflict with her feminine identification.

Emma's relationship with the man she married was based on a precarious emotional balance. Her characterologically embedded need to flee from engulfment was probably still present. That she did find this man and could marry him was one of the positive results of her analysis; it is difficult to know whether her conflicts regarding her fluctuating gender identity and active and passive tendencies are sufficiently in balance for the marriage to hold. Her relationship with her husband could still be undermined. This could occur if, in feeling-states of depression, she fears being or becoming too much like her mother and has to flee; or, if, in her eyes, her husband begins to appear more like her mother. Emma's newly developed capacity to fall in love and get married is evidence that she has to a great extent worked through her fluctuating gender identity. Her bisexual anlage can now serve her creativity and fuel her identification with her father, her one viable parent, without apparent intrapsychic conflict.

In view of the one-sided nature of her model for identification, Emma continues to exhibit a "characterological hunger" for such models. The fragmentation of models for identification was manifested in the emotional vacuity within the family. As Emma became more creative, she was able to produce both masculine and feminine models in a pictorial manner, an achievement of a new sublimation.

Conscious idealization could be based only on her father: Emma wanted to lead a "man's life" and yet feel like a woman. Her need for "mobility and humor" to counteract her phobic anxieties about being stuck in one place and being helpless and depressed, like her mother, constantly recurred. Because Emma consciously loved being a woman, her fashion photography was relatively uncomplicated and without conflict. As long as she could live in total freedom, Emma felt like a female and was feminine.

Emma's bisexuality reflected her mother's lack of feminine sexual identity and was an attempt at integration of the best features of each gender within herself. Her promiscuity represented an identification with her father, who periodically needed to flee from the possessive atmosphere of their home.

Emma's fluctuating gender identity exemplified her shifting identifications and her difficulty in identifying with her mother, as did the bulimia–anorexia cycle. She feared possessiveness, jealousy, and lack of freedom, as well as her own dependency on objects. She felt she needed to be alone, but was afraid of being abandoned. Her fear of death related to an abandonment theme, as well as to her hostile aggression against her parents, particularly her mother.

During analysis, Emma relived the fear of being abandoned by her mother, as well as the wish to abandon her mother before she would become totally engulfed by her. It became clear that Emma's internal representation of her mother as abandoning and destroying was stronger than her representation of her mother as nurturing. I believe that this internal representation of the menacing mother made Emma phobic about carrying a child: the bulimia was associated with the threat of being pregnant. The baby who was a "persecutor," who threatens the mother's life, unconsciously also represented Emma's mother as Emma's baby. It was the concretized act of sterilization that helped Emma differentiate herself from her mother. The collusion of her parents in this act facilitated Emma's "killing her future babies" and allowed her unconsciously to become "male," like her father. The need to disidentify with her traumatized mother also made it more difficult for Emma to become a parent herself.

The self-sterilization facilitated role reversal: Emma's relationship with her mother, who was unconsciously the incestuous child of father and daughter, and who continuously needed the emotional help of both in order not to become excessively depressed, made Emma's capacity to reach the oedipal level extremely difficult. This fact pervaded Emma's home life in her growing years. Emma's need to mother her own mother, whose needs overshadowed or obliterated her daughter's, created a powerful conflict because it clashed with Emma's narcissistic wishes for self-expression. Emma's relationship with her mother became traumatic. Her mother was distant and overbearing at the same time, and her father was more seductive than loving. The fact that the mother, who had to remain the child in reality, nonetheless aided and abetted the sterilization procedure as an active participant, was traumatic for Emma.

The sustaining transference relationship, which permitted Emma to understand contradictory issues without feeling con-

demned, enabled her to mourn the loss of her fertility. She was, at
the same time, able to work through her phobia toward her
engulfing mother, and became a caring and sheltering adult for her,
modeled on her experience of me as a maternal transference object.
As a result of her analysis, Emma was able to have a creative and productive life, and this achievement enhanced her internal sense of
freedom without anxiety or guilt.

Part II

The Female Oedipus Complex: The Two Analyses of Maureen

Part III

4.

The Female Oedipus Complex: Antecedents and Evolution

> [T]here has been a general refusal to recognize that
> psycho-analytic research could not, like a
> philosophical system, produce a complete and ready-
> made theoretical structure, but had to find its way
> step by step along the path towards understanding
> the intricacies of the mind by making an analytic
> dissection of both normal and abnormal
> phenomena [Freud, 1923, pp. 35–36]

In the female child's early relationship with her parents there occur decisive developments that influence the psychic experience of her Oedipus complex. I shall discuss, in terms of development, psychic structure, and object relations, the developments that culminate in a girl's Oedipus complex and shape this universal constellation.

The history of a girl's femininity has already begun before she is born; her emotional destiny is affected not only by her mother's attitude toward her own femininity, but by the reliving of her mother's relationship toward her own mother when she was little. Awareness of gender identity thus provides unconscious historical and dynamic generational links that are set in motion with

67

each birth, and the nature of these links sets a precedent for the girl's later oedipal role.

In order for the first self and object representations to be firmly rooted in the psychic structure, the girl must feel welcomed into the world by a mother who accepts her child's femaleness without major psychic conflict. The child can then start her life with a primary acceptance of herself as a girl.

As the girl develops, her mother experiences certain reactions: maternal, fostering her child's capacity for identification; restitutional, representing the realization of an earlier wished-for self-image; or narcissistic, competitive, or clinging, oriented toward intrapsychic conflicts revived from her own childhood. The girl perceives how her mother experiences her *own* female body and whether or not she values it as a healthy and lovable narcissistic possession. If gender difference is established and accepted without too much hostility toward her mother, the disillusionment and loss of self-esteem which even under normal circumstances may occur in the phallic phase will be overcome, enabling the girl to reach the oedipal level. Under pathological conditions, however, fixation may result. Separation processes, particularly those of the rapprochement subphase, and object relationship conflicts with one or both parents or parent substitutes may lead to developmental disturbances, short-circuiting the girl's attainment of her negative and/or positive oedipal levels. Ambivalent feelings toward one or both parents will therefore further prevent separation at the oedipal level.

FREUD'S VIEWS ON FEMALE SEXUALITY

For Freud the Oedipus complex was the nuclear childhood event and the kernel of future neurosis. His concepts originally derived from reports from female patients of actual seductions by their fathers during childhood, though he soon discovered that these seductions were fantasies rather than facts.

In 1897 Freud wrote to Fliess that "sexual phantasy *invariably* seizes upon the theme of the parents" (p. 260; emphasis added); "I have found in my own case too, falling in love with the mother and jealousy of the father, and I now regard it as a universal event of early childhood" (p. 265). In 1900 he wrote: "a girl's first affection is for her father and a boy's first childish desires are for his mother.

Accordingly, the father becomes a disturbing rival to the boy and the mother to the girl" (p. 257). In 1900 Freud had not yet recognized the existence of a girl's affectionate relationship with her mother before or during the onset of her love for her father. Freud's concepts were essentially phallocentric. He believed that boys and girls at a young age thought that all human beings have a penis, that girls believed the clitoris would grow into one, and that children of both sexes ignored the existence of the vagina until puberty. He believed (Freud, 1905) that universal oedipal wishes in children (and later in adults) underwent repression and remained unconscious, and that the origin of these repressions was both phylo- and ontogenetic. He also believed that castration anxiety and the incest taboo were the major determinants of the oedipal fantasy.

In 1931, Freud's theoretical expansion included the preoedipal phase, in which the mother was recognized as the first love object for both boys and girls. But while Freud postulated that boys are able to sustain an ambivalent relationship with their fathers and keep their mothers as their primary love objects into the oedipal phase, he suggested that girls proceed along different developmental lines. For boys the Oedipus complex was considered a primary formation, for girls a secondary one. Achievement of the positive oedipal phase for girls could come only after completion of the negative phase (love for mother and hatred for father). Compared to the development of the boy, who keeps the mother as his primary preoedipal love object, Freud believed that the girl's transfer of libido from mother to father constitutes an extra step.

Freud (1925b) considered penis envy to be the leading cause for a girl's shift from mother to father: "She has seen it and knows that she is without it and wants to have it" (p. 252). He thought that penis envy and fantasies of castration propel girls into the oedipal phase. The girl's desire for a penis is transformed into a desire to have a child (preferably a boy) from her father. Her mother not only becomes a rival, but is unconsciously reproached for her lack of a penis, as well as for having "seduced her" with loving care and attention. When the girl realizes that her desire for a baby with her father cannot be fulfilled, she abandons her wish (Freud, 1924a) and turns away from him. Freud (1905) believed that for the girl to "grow out of" the Oedipus complex she needs to give up clitoral masturbation at puberty. This in turn enables her as a young adult to achieve a mature sexual state with a sexually cathected vagina, capable of true pleasure.

Freud postulated that the girl, because she need not fear castration, is under less pressure than a boy to form a superego. This led Freud to consider the girl's superego development deficient. He believed that the demands of domesticity and motherhood limit a woman's life goals, which in turn fosters cultural approval of female dependency. The oedipal situation for the girl becomes a "haven of refuge" (Freud, 1933) from her penis envy, from which she emerges only gradually. The boy's superego, by contrast, molded out of the need to achieve an oedipal victory over the father, has to overcome castration anxiety, unconscious guilt, and the need for punishment.

Although Freud admitted the existence of early vaginal sensations, observing that "it is true that recently an increasing number of observers report that vaginal impulses are present even in these early years," he nonetheless insisted that "the main genital occurrences of childhood must take place in relation to the clitoris" (1931, p. 228). He certainly did not include these impulses in his theory of female sexuality, or as part of the female Oedipus complex.

In Freud's views, the girl upon reaching womanhood must effect a triple change in order to reach and resolve her oedipal conflict: from active to passive, from mother to father, from clitoris to vagina as primary locus of her feminine sexuality.

Freud continually strove for a clear distinction between biological and psychic phenomena and considered primary femininity a psychological issue. Despite this, he was charged with reductionism by some critics, because he believed that the ultimate answers to psychological problems of femininity would be resolved through discoveries in physiology and biochemistry.

Freud assumed that the child is born with a certain sexual identity and a bisexual potential. He wanted to discover how the child develops a *psychic* sexual identity. Freud considered this not a biological, psychophysical, or cultural question but a psychological one that grew out of the active interplay of developmental processes. His inquiry centered on how the psychological experience becomes synthesized into a definite body- and self-image (Freud, 1905). Although he constructed a purely psychological theory of feminine development, he conceded its tentativeness and candidly admitted that female sexuality continued to baffle him. Thus, despite Freud's awareness of the significance of his presentation, he continued to regard female sexuality as an unsolved psychological mystery.

Several of Freud's disciples took issue with his model of female sexuality. Melanie Klein (1928), Karen Horney (1926, 1932, 1933), and Ernest Jones (1935) did not regard penis envy as the result of the girl's fear of castration or of something having been taken away or lost. Instead they viewed penis envy as related to hostile fantasies toward the parents, such as fantasies of incorporation and destruction of the penis (actually, a part-object fantasy), derived from conflict-laden experiences and interfering with later parental identifications. Jones (1933) believed the ultimate question to be whether a woman is born or made. Jones (1935) asserted that he did not regard a woman as *"un homme manqué,* a permanently disappointed creature struggling to console herself with secondary substitutes alien to her nature" (p. 273).

For Horney, primary femininity preceded the phallic phase and was based on both biological and cultural factors. She believed that there was an innate sense of human femaleness and that the assumption that "half of humanity" thought of itself as anatomically inferior was ill-founded. Horney believed that before the phallic phase girls repress vaginal sensations. "Behind the 'failure to discover' the vagina is a denial of its existence" (Horney, 1933, p. 69): it is denied by boys because of fear and hostile wishes projected onto the mother (or her body), and by girls because of castration wishes toward the father, which turn into fears of internal bodily injury. Horney, and with her Klein and Jones, stressed that revenge fantasies result in fears of bodily harm, the intention to inflict, which is projected onto parents by *children of either sex.* This may of course have an effect on the child's capacity for identification.

DEVELOPMENTAL PRECURSORS

The first self is a body self. Body image formation is dependent on the child's successful emergence from the symbiotic phase. During the subphase of differentiation, the body is gradually experienced as separate from that of the mother.

The integration of the body self, its differentiation from objects, and the capacity to distinguish inside from outside involve the mother's need-satisfying activity and her regulation of pleasurable and painful affects. If the rhythm of satisfaction and frustration is disrupted, an interference will be seen in the development of reality testing, perceptual and cognitive development, motor activity, the beginnings of anticipation, and the signal function (Tolpin, 1971; Lichtenberg, 1978). Unless the child is traumatized, however, body awareness will remain constant and body experiences will become autonomous, even under stress (Hartmann, 1939). Loss of self-cohesion may arise from severe developmental disturbances that lead to fragmentation of the self-structure, and to disturbances in the differentiation of inner from outer reality.

As growth proceeds, and as inner body needs are perceived, the child learns to verbalize its needs and takes preventive and adaptive measures for self-protection. Identity formation begins at the same time as psychic structure formation. A mother's positive attitude during the various psychosexual phases helps ensure that feminine developmental determinants will not become involved in permanent intrapsychic conflict. If the girl experiences her symbiotic period as being "good enough," she will reach and successfully negotiate the subphase of differentiation with a gradually consolidating sense of gender identity. Libidinal and aggressive drive derivatives will tend toward fusion, leading to body enjoyment and exploration.

THE ORAL PHASE AS PRIMARY BODY CATHEXIS

For Freud (1905) the oral phase marked the dawning of psychic body experience: the mouth was the first erotogenic zone to be cathected and served as a model for affective experiences related to other body openings. Jones (1911) observed that the vagina derives an oral representation from the mouth and that all early stimulation relates to body openings. Oral, anal, and vaginal sensations, he noted, all date from infancy: "The anus is evidently identified with the vagina to begin with, and the differentiation of the two is an extremely obscure process, more so perhaps than any other in female development. . . [and] . . . it takes place at an earlier age than is generally supposed" (p. 443). Hoffer (1949, 1950) described how infants use their mouths and hands to explore and cathect body surfaces with pleasure, and Kris (1951) observed that infants from loving homes cathect their bodies libidinally and experience autoerotic pleasures much earlier than children from broken homes or institutions. In 1955, Spitz discussed the significance of the oral cavity in terms of its function as the first boundary between inside and outside.

Kestenberg (1968) stated that it was rare for a girl to cathect her genitalia as early as a boy would, particularly "in the first two years of life . . . A cloacal concept of the genitalia pervades a girl's anal stage of development" (p. 459; see also Bonaparte, 1953; Kestenberg, 1968). Today we are aware that it is not only the cathexis of the erotogenic zones that has a direct bearing on body image formation (Greenacre, 1950) but, even more important, the mother's attitude toward the female aspect of her young daughter's body. This plays an important role in the girl's ability to obtain pleasure from her body and from her mother's acceptance of it.

The term *primary femininity* (Stoller, 1977) connotes the pleasurable sexual sensations that constitute a "core feeling," including the beginnings of body cathexis before there is an awareness of sexual differences. Early vaginal sensations affect body schematization and differentiation of self from non-self at the earliest level of psychic structure formation (Greenacre, 1950; Kleeman, 1976).

The hypothesis that self-stimulation of the vaginal introitus and labia having never been conscious is subject to primary repression of the vagina as an erotogenic zone was advanced by Barnett (1966). She suggested that voluntary muscular control over mouth and anus leads to a sense of mastery over these organs, as the child learns to control—one might say—what comes in and what goes out. The incapacity to experience control over the vaginal cavity, however, may threaten the girl's developing body image and lead to early repression of vaginal sensations; clitoral hypercathexis emerges to further promote vaginal repression. Although this hypothesis is descriptively convincing, there is today still no evidence, from infant observation or work with patients of any age, that the girl's early body image formation and the repression of vaginal sensations are related; nor can we say with certainty that the clitoris as a source of stimulation during infancy or early childhood is a factor in vaginal repression.

Pleasurable sensations arise during the first year of life, with an increase in excitement between the 15th and the 27th month involving penile erections in boys, and vaginal lubrication and self-stimulation of the lower vaginal canal, the clitoris, the labia, and the introitus in girls (Kleeman, 1976). Vaginal sensations during infancy may also serve the purpose of discharging psychological stress (Greenacre, 1950; Kestenberg, 1956). The girl, though capable of strong self-stimulation between the 18th and the 24th month, was once thought to know less about her genitalia than does the boy about his. Recently, many authors have concurred that little girls seem to be aware early in life that there is an inside space and openings (mouth, anus, and possibly vagina) and that early masturbatory activity includes awareness of inner space and body openings (Fast, 1984, 1990; Mayer, 1985; Laufer, 1993; Elise, 1998; Lax, 1997).

It is unclear how vaginal sensations are registered before the psychic structure is sufficiently established. Baby girls enjoy masturbation, but the psychological role of such early sensations is difficult to assess before there is a psychic structure. It is difficult to visualize how these early sensations are registered and to know whether they find their way into later female body image formation. I believe that early sensations become significant only when they emerge from repression in a phase-specific context. When parents enjoy their child as a girl, the girl's sense of herself, her "core gender identity" (Stoller, 1968), will be facilitated. The dawning of a girl's pleasurable experience of her body in the first two years of life precedes penis envy—if present—during that developmental phase. Discovery of gender identity is later reinforced by cognitive developments and affective responses that confirm body cathexis and aid in the development of body narcissism.[1]

Direct observations indicate that children become aware of their gender identity, from the 15th month on, long before the inception of penis envy in girls, which may accompany the inception of oedipal rivalry. Although girls before the age of 2 have been observed to experience a "low-keyed" emotional response upon discovery of the boy's penis (Mahler and McDevitt, 1968), this appears to affect unduly neither the girl's core gender identity, nor her ability to cathect her exterior and interior genital representation (Roiphe and Galenson, 1971, 1973). Roiphe and Galenson suggest that between the 15th and the 19th month, a girl's perception of her lack of a penis becomes associated with fantasies of the mother's absence, and a sense of loss experienced as part of the separation from the pleasure-giving mother.[1]

Doll play provides a means for discharging and mastering vaginal tensions by projecting them to the outside (Kestenberg, 1968). Blum (1977a) has pointed out that the doll helps the child during periods of fear of object loss and fears related to a lack of self-definition. Doll play is especially important between the ages of 2 and 4, when the girl's discovery of her vagina and the beginnings of genital masturba-

---

[1]Dianne Elise (1998) has eloquently described the relation between a girl's feeling of absence of her nurturing mother and a sense of loss or insufficiency related to a girl's experience of her genitalia as adequate and pleasure-giving.

tion normally occur. The doll represents various aspects of the self and helps a girl to consolidate her inner feminine core and to achieve thereby a permanent cathexis of her vagina in preparation for the development of her self-image (Kestenberg, 1971).

The role of the father is significant in both preoedipal and oedipal phases (Abelin, 1971). Although parental attitudes vary with each child and each phase (Coleman, Kris, and Provence, 1953; Benedek, 1973), the ability of the father to complement the pre-oedipal developmental needs of a girl, should the mother fail in her maternal function, may save the girl from severe pathology. However, this may make the differentiation of the preoedipal from the oedipal father more difficult for her later on.

Gender identity is based on a correct perception of self and others. If the child is exposed to anxiety-arousing interactions, ego functions that promote play and speech may suffer distortions. Perceptual denial of gender differences interferes with symbolization and thinking processes (Roiphe and Galenson, 1971). Indeed, there is a reciprocal relation between gender identity and the development of symbolization, and thinking as an ego function. If the mother–child interaction permits internalization, the child's process of symbolization and thinking will be facilitated.

Thus, early vaginal sensations and preoedipal psychosexual experiences aid in the consolidation of preoedipal body cathexis and promote the development of body narcissism. Before the onset of the phallic phase, internalized parent–child interaction facilitates the development of specific ego functions that prepare the girl for her oedipal experience.

THE RAPPROCHEMENT SUBPHASE

The rapprochement subphase marks a crisis of separation-individuation and is a critical period in the establishment of gender identity. Anxiety regarding object loss and loss of love emerges as the child follows a new spurt in attempting to separate from the mother. The first definite wishes to separate from the mother but not lose her, emerge at this time. If because of her own anxiety, a mother cannot permit her child to establish the independent space the child needs, or if she cannot tolerate the child's oscillation between independence and clinging, the rapprochement crisis will not be resolved.

This phase is difficult for the mother, as she must struggle with inner conflict over relinquishing the dyad, her symbiotic tie to the child—a tie that for many women represents the height of bliss.

During this phase the child betrays an unconscious need to merge with the "good mother of symbiosis" and to avoid the "bad mother of reengulfment." However, separation can be achieved only from the former. If the mother, because there is too much hostile interaction, cannot foster the successful completion of this phase, the child may resort to splitting the maternal representation into good and bad. It is not possible to separate effectively from an inner maternal representation that is split, or too ambivalently cathected.

The child who remains fixated at the rapprochement crisis will manifest pervasive separation anxiety and leave the conflicts of the subphase unresolved. Transient neurotic symptoms may ensue, or the beginnings of intrapsychic conflict, such as a phobia signifying unmastered separation anxiety (Freud, 1926; Mahler, 1975b).

Manifest separation anxiety in the relationship between the girl and her mother will surface during the inception of the oedipal phase. Frequent fluctuations between the girl's positive oedipal feelings and her negative oedipal conflicts will continue for a time and may postpone integration of a feminine self-image. Under normal conditions, resolution of the rapprochement crisis prepares the girl to enter the positive Oedipus complex (Mahler, 1966, 1975b).

THE NEGATIVE OEDIPAL PHASE

Freud saw penis envy as the "bedrock" of feminine sexuality (1937, p. 252). The girl resents her mother for having "made her" a girl. Freud (1933) believed that penis envy (resulting from feelings of castration) could lead to certain characterological predispositions, such as female masochism, jealousy, frigidity, depression, and other symptoms referred to as the "masculinity complex." He believed that the girl, by giving up phallic wishes, preserves an essential aspect of her narcissism. He thought that she may sustain a "narcissistic blow" on becoming aware of anatomical differences, and that this narcissistic wound influences positive and negative oedipal wishes. I believe that if the girl has been able to develop female narcissistic body feelings, she will be able to value her genitalia and will not feel she must pretend or wish to be a boy. Bisexual elements will gradually be integrated into the character structure as a normal aspect of her "core feeling."

Identification with her mother as a female person will make penis envy a transitory experience, phase-specific for the phallic period that precedes, or develops concomitantly with, the positive Oedipus complex.

Anna Freud designated the early dyadic period of the phallic phase as the "phallic–narcissistic phase," and reserved the term *phallic–oedipal phase* for the later, triangular segment of phallic-oedipal relationships (Edgcumbe and Burgner, 1975). If, during the phallic–narcissistic phase, the girl becomes fixated on the penis as a part object, she will experience feelings of rejection and unconsciously believe that she is not lovable because she is a girl. When the early relationship between mother and child has been excessively hostile, the girl will be unable to internalize a good image of her. A fantasy image will then be formed to sustain the girl's inner representation of the "good mother" (see chapters 1 and 5). The hostile interaction between the girl and her mother will be overdetermined, and the missing penis may become the issue on which their relationship revolves. Possession of the penis will then symbolize the fantasized good relationship with the "good mother," which in reality has been lacking. Unconsciously, the part-object penis then stands for the whole object relationship. The girl will fantasize that she might have been loved by the "good mother" if only she had been a boy.

During the phallic–oedipal phase, the girl's internalization processes may have led to the symbolization of feelings of deficiency, and penis envy may have become a metaphor for other traumata. Penis envy may then have functioned as a screen or "shorthand" for childhood disappointments, and as an expression of unmet needs stemming from the mother–child dyad (Grossman and Stewart, 1976). Unmet needs are conducive to narcissistic rage against the love-denying mother, and to unconscious fantasies against her that can be transformed into penis envy. Clinically it is important to differentiate between women who demonstrate penis envy and those who wish to destroy the male genitalia. Only the unconsciously "castrating" woman wishes to destroy the man or his penis. The envious girl or woman does no more than envy; she is capable of object relationships and of symbolization. She wishes to feel "whole," but not to destroy. The unconsciously "castrating" woman wishes to destroy an object or body part. Penis envy undergoes phase-specific transformations at different developmental phases: it is reactive to object relationship problems in early development, but does not play a primary role in regard to female gender identity.

Clinical observation has not eliminated the ambiguities inherent in the concept of the negative Oedipus complex as originally conceived: "No writer actually gives evidence . . . of a clearly negative oedipal phase in the girl in which she is active and masculine in her oedipal relationships with her parents, without awareness of her lack of a penis and without feelings of being different from boys. . . . They are more likely to formulate their material in terms of negative and positive aspects of oedipal development, if they use the concept at all" (Edgcumbe et al., 1975, p. 40).

During the phallic phase proper, the girl's experience becomes increasingly object directed. When envy toward her father develops, her unconscious masculine wishes are enhanced, which leads to a wish to "replace" him in order to achieve a new physical and loving closeness with the mother. The phallic phase thus culminates in the girl's entering her negative Oedipus complex and in a sharper, more object-directed masturbation fantasy. Current clinical experience suggests that this fantasy is triangular in character and not pre-oedipal, as was previously assumed. Such fantasies, whether directed toward the mother or, later, the father as primary objects, are usually triangular and alternate during the girl's oedipal phase. It is particularly in the transference reliving of oedipal relationships that evidence is found to suggest that the negative oedipal phase is indeed primarily oedipal in character.

When oedipal progression is short-circuited and the father fails to become a primary object, a fixation at the negative oedipal phase may result. At such times, penis envy and breast envy may become unconsciously fused and substitute for each other. Exhibitionistic and scopophilic activities may propel the girl into developing penis envy in rivalries with boys, feelings of castration, and dissatisfaction with her body. Lowered self-esteem may thus interfere with the development of female sexual identifications. The girl may unconsciously substitute her body for the missing penis and strive for a narcissistic identification with her father as a means of feeling closer to him. The wish to be like the father instead of having his baby, is expressed in the body-phallus equation (Lewin, 1933) and is a substitute for the loss of self-esteem.

When identity formation has organized the boundaries of the self, early genital play paves the way for acceptance of the vagina in adulthood. If identification with the mother is disturbed, however, and the girl is disillusioned, there may be a loss of cathexis of the internal genitalia and a subsequent loss of self-esteem. The girl may then turn to the idealized father, wishing to be like him and, unconsciously, to possess his penis. Revenge fantasies against both mother and father may result, leading to preoedipal fixations, possibly on a wish to possess the mother exclusively and exclude the father.

Clinical observation suggests that there is a constant oscillation between positive and negative oedipal feelings in children of either sex; for that reason, if for no other, the phenomena that characterize the negative oedipal conflict cannot on some alternate account be viewed as exclusively preoedipal. Negative oedipal feelings from their inception and amalgamation into the oedipal phase proper undergo developmental stages that include various adaptations to objects, even during later stages, as when reawakened in puberty or adolescence.

Preoedipal fantasies may become so conflictual as to occasion, as a defense, a precocious move toward oedipal fantasies. The term *oedipalization* has been used (Kernberg, 1977) to refer to such seemingly oedipal conflicts that defend against the more dangerous preoedipal conflicts they cover. Phallic–narcissistic object relations are usually pseudo-oedipal and differ radically from genuine oedipal conflicts.

Mastery of the negative oedipal phase leads to the girl's stable identification with her mother. In that identification, libidinal feelings dominate over hostile ones and render penis envy, if present, an expression of a transitory feeling of deficiency, rather than of femaleness. Thus, the unconscious wishes of the negative oedipal phase express a phase-specific step without which the girl's identification with the mother as a woman is not possible. This includes an awareness and acceptance of their female bodies and the girl's erotic interest in the body of the mother. These steps play a pivotal role in the development of the girl's body image and help her to enter the positive oedipal phase.

Freud's views about the girl's development of femininity have not been clinically verified. He believed that the girl stops masturbating when she becomes disappointed in the performance of her clitoris; she feels inferior because she views her lack of a penis as a deficiency (Freud, 1925b). He also believed that girls would turn into frigid women unless they stopped masturbating before puberty. It is now believed that the clitoris is the focal point of masturbation for girls from the preoedipal and oedipal periods into maturity (Clower, 1977).

In my view, masturbation, during any psychosexual period, may express loneliness, ambivalent feelings, or destructive fantasies and wishes. The masturbation fantasy may comfort a child who has experienced narcissistic injury. A polarization between vaginal and clitoral impulses may develop, leading to difficulty in integrating body cathexis into a unified genital representation. The clitoris, possibly because of its accessibility and because it is an immediate source of pleasure, acquires an inner representation and body cathexis more easily than do other parts of the female genitalia. A lack of harmony between clitoral and vaginal representations may lead to confusion in identity formation, reality testing, and thinking.

The oedipal girl tends to masturbate actively and to have masturbation fantasies in which the clitoris functions as a fantasy penis. Oedipal wishes, both active and passive, remain unconscious. The fantasy phallus represented by the clitoris becomes heir to unconscious communications with the mother; in such fantasies the phallus may represent the baby, the breast, or the activity of the primal scene.

Girls generally experience greater masturbation guilt than do boys. During phallic-oedipal development hostility toward both parents, but particularly the mother, is sometimes based on the shattered hope that masturbation will produce a penis. Idealization of the penis frequently leads to depression, self-devaluation, and rage toward both mother and father. In adulthood the ability to integrate clitoris and vagina into a unified inner genital representation is the most important factor in genital maturation. If the mother forbids masturbation during the preoedipal or oedipal period, oedipal hatred may become intensified. In fact, for the girl to move from the preoedipal to the oedipal phase, her ambivalence conflict with her mother must be balanced; an excess of love or hatred may keep the girl fixated at the negative oedipal phase, in a search for the good and active preoedipal mother (Brunswick, 1940). If this search for love from her mother leads to fixation, she may be in conflict about expressing deeply passionate love feelings for her father during the oedipal period.

A CONTEMPORARY VIEW

How is the Oedipus complex, particularly the female Oedipus complex, viewed today? The oedipal stage is linked developmentally to pregenital and genital psychic precursors. Psychic structure and function develop during ever changing object relationships involving internal and environmental pressures affecting mother, father, and child. It appears that in psychoanalytic thought we have moved from Freud's hydraulic model of the psychic structure to one more closely resembling a Calder mobile, a tentacled structure balanced or unbalanced by the quality and weight of its parts.

Freud saw the Oedipus complex as a polarization of instinctual derivatives expressed in feelings of love and hatred toward the parents. Feelings of love tied to the parent of the opposite sex and feelings of hate toward the parent of the same sex were characteristic of the positive Oedipus complex. These conceptualizations are still considered valid today, but contemporary psychoanalytic thought sees these feelings as being in a state of flux and the Oedipus complex as an organizer of all psychic life, before and after the latency period, and indeed throughout life.

Freud regarded the Oedipus complex as the nucleus of neurosis, which was understood as a failure to outgrow or resolve it. In his paper on the dissolution of the complex, Freud (1924a) attempted to differentiate its repression from its dissolution. The word *Untergang* (literally, "a going under" in German) is traditionally associated with the setting sun, and is less final than the English term *dissolution*. Freud believed that the normal person resolves, or dissolves, the Oedipus complex, in contrast to the neurotic, who succeeds only in repressing it. Thus, in Freud's view, in later life derivatives of the Oedipus complex can reemerge from repression. Today, the distinction between dissolution and repression appears less valid than it did for Freud: a person who has absolutely dissolved his or her oedipal conflict would, after all, be incapable of developing a transference relationship, or of falling in love (M. S. Bergmann, 1971).

A number of authors have been concerned with the concept of dissolution and the fate of oedipal fantasies. Loewald (1973), for instance, suggested that repression narrows and limits human choices. As an alternative to repression, he postulated a developmental process of internalization. His formulations suggest that repression is not the only psychic force at the disposal of the oedipal child. Ever changing internalizations of the parental representations provide building blocks for an ever changing psychic structure, keeping developmental avenues open. Repression by itself tends to freeze psychic structure, whereas "internalization as a completed process implies emancipation and individuation from the object" (p. 16).

In the 1930s, and since, repeatedly emphasis was placed on the events of the preoedipal period and their influence on the Oedipus complex—specifically on a core conflict being manifest in the girl's preoedipal relationship with her mother (Lampl-De Groot, 1965; M. V. Bergmann, 1995; Halberstadt-Freud, 1998). As soon as the mother is recognized or loved as a separate person, a fear arises of losing her or at least her love. Ambivalence and anxiety over hostile wishes toward her set in. The child's ambivalence is directed not only toward the "sexual" mother, but also to the survival of the pre-oedipal mother. In analysis, we often find that preoedipal problems need to be worked out before patients can fully experience their oedipal wishes. The question has arisen whether pathology can orig-inate in the oedipal phase itself, in the absence of preoedipal antecedents. There is also controversy over the genetic origins of pathology regarding the fate of the Oedipus complex. The question is repeatedly raised whether "the psychic events of the preoedipal phase *influence* those of the oedipal phase (but do not) . . . *determine* them" (Brenner, 1979, p. 193; emphasis added), or whether they determine the psychic *structure* within which the Oedipus complex is experienced.

Although Freud viewed oedipal object relations as shifting from mother to father (or vice versa), they instead can be conceptualized as simultaneous identifications, of varying relative strengths, with both parents, or as identificatory disturbances weighted with shifting valences at different periods of intrapsychic struggle and growth. At any given time, from the phallic phase onward, either dyadic or triadic pressures determine oedipal object relationships (on the model suggested by Anna Freud and discussed earlier in this chapter). However, even during preponderantly dyadic periods, tri-angulation plays a role.

The Oedipus complex has been described as an example "par excellence, of an individual's unconscious view of the world" (Shapiro, 1977, p. 563). As a universal human fantasy, it encom-passes unconscious affect-laden ideas about parental objects related to good and bad, active and passive, male and female. The uncon-scious organization of the female Oedipus complex, although ema-nating from a combination of drive derivatives, environmental influences, and organizing functions of the ego, will probably be determined primarily by the fate of a girl's identification processes. At first, the girl will experience her own body in relation to her mother's. Later, in my view, a more encompassing identification with the mother will be the most important influence on the devel-opment of her psychic structure and her experience of herself first as a girl and later as a woman.

Oedipal development is viewed in terms of separation–individuation issues and ego functions, as well as psychosexual phenomena, drive manifestations, and defense. The extent of separation-individuation achieved in the child will determine his or her capacity to negotiate the positive Oedipus complex. The need to revert to the negative oedipal phase may be viewed as an attempt on the part of the child to cling to a parent. Omnipotent fantasies sometimes stemming from the practicing subphases may reemerge when oedipal pressures keep the child fixated at the negative oedipal level and do not permit separation. Clinical experience has taught us that oedipal issues reemerge in all important developmental phases in life—adolescence, marriage, parenthood, menopause, senescence. We no longer assume, therefore, that an individual is finished with oedipal issues once he or she passes through the oedipal phase in childhood. Further, we believe now that the success of this passage, which is a relative matter in any case, need not occur at that time. It may instead be achieved during puberty or adolescence, when oedipal issues are revived, or when a crisis erupts later in life (say, divorce or the premature death of a parent) that stirs them up once again.

The oedipal phase, then, is currently viewed as a nodal point of conflictual identifications, whose fate will be determined at various emotional crossroads later in life. The child's capacity to move from dyadic to triadic object relationships remains puzzling. In spite of the psychic structure the child has acquired by the time of this transition, it is extremely difficult to construct, from the analysis of adults, the precise nature of an individual's internalizations during this crucial phase of childhood. In our clinical work we have become increasingly aware that negative and positive oedipal themes arise simultaneously in a patient's treatment.

It would appear that if the girl can remain identified with her mother, both during oedipal rivalry and during experiences of the primal scene—the birth of siblings and other traumatic internal and external events which are unconsciously registered as being "the mother's fault"—she will be able to enter a triadic phase without fear of object loss. But if identification with the mother is only partial, because her mental representation in the child is vested with a predominance not of libido but of hostile aggression, a segment of the Oedipus complex will not be resolved; it will fall prey to fixation or regression. The girl's capacity to integrate her genitality depends not only on reaching the oedipal phase, but on its phase-specific resolution.

Individuation from parental representations comes gradually with the capacity for internalization, and it is with this capacity that inner representations of parents and self begin to be consolidated in the ego and the superego. This is possible only if channels for internalization are opened by new developmental spurts of separation-individuation and are not closed off by the intrusion of object relationship themes that have blocked development in earlier periods. As a psychic organizer, the Oedipus complex represents a culmination or new synthesis of ongoing psychic processes (Rangell, 1972; Mahler, 1975b). We think of the oedipal phase as one of transition, gradually reached and gradually resolved in phase-specific terms *only*. Indeed, in the narrowest sense, the Oedipus complex may have no final resolution in either sex (Ticho, 1977). Phases of relative stability (and tranquility) may alternate with revivals of oedipal conflicts later in life, requiring a new psychic integration. A woman's conflict concerning her femininity, her feminine ego ideal, or her autonomous strivings for self-realization, may continue throughout her lifetime (Blum, 1977a).

Since the Oedipus complex is regarded as a structure of ongoing object relationships, its history and the manner and quality of its internalization are considered more crucial than isolated traumatic occurrences during childhood. Preverbal experiences, affective changes, and early ego functions have a direct bearing on later psychic organizers, which in turn are significant for oedipal development (A. Freud, 1971).

An important clinical problem involves the question whether (or to what extent) a person has reached the Oedipus phase, or has reached it and retreated from it. The Oedipus complex is not merely an unconscious cluster of wish-fulfilling fantasies, nor do love and hate wishes within triangular relationships with the parents necessarily mean that structure formation has attained the oedipal level.

Clinically, the passionate love of the little girl for her father is abandoned because of a conflict of allegiances she cannot resolve: "Mother won't allow it"—a fear of the mother and her punishment—a preoedipal reason; "Father doesn't respond"—because he prefers the mother or other siblings—an oedipal rejection proper. This conflict may congeal into an unconscious prohibition: "My superego doesn't allow it." Only in relation to this last reason does the incest taboo play a central role. Patients differ with regard to which of these alternatives is the most crucial to psychic development.

Freud (1919) noted that the Oedipus complex, if not properly resolved, leaves a pervasive sense of inferiority throughout life. Its resolution and the building of self-regulating and autonomous structures depend on the capacity to cathect oedipal objects as separate. Ferenczi called the resolution of the Oedipus complex the most important experience of separation during childhood (Gedo and Goldberg, 1973, p. 78). Only if objects are considered as separate and not as part of an earlier narcissistic self structure is triangulation possible, and only then can the oedipal experience be organized on a more mature level.

The Oedipus complex energizes all human activity. It is the source of both creativity and pathology. In creative persons bisexual wishes undergo a further transformation into creative activity itself. I believe that successful creative endeavor is achieved by the utilization of integrated bisexual wishes. While much of the suffering imposed by neurotic illness is derived from the Oedipus complex, so too is much of the creativity and richness of cultural life, including appreciation of the arts. In novels, poetry, painting, and opera, for instance, oedipal themes abound, ending in oedipal tragedy or oedipal triumph.

CONCURRENT DEVELOPMENTS INFLUENCED BY THE OEDIPUS COMPLEX

The positive Oedipus complex, with its focus on triangulation, implies a new interest in the primal scene and fantasies about sexual relations between the parents. The role of the child as an intruder occasions a high degree of sexual excitement, including fantasies of exposure, which contributes significantly to the shaping of the oedipal constellation.

Does a cathexis of motility and perception achieved within a primarily libidinal atmosphere with the *real* parents make primal scene experiences or fantasies easier to bear? Will looking, which becomes part of a libidinally cathected exploration leading to organized perception or motility—cathected with pleasure as the child seeks out the wonders of the environment—influence the extent to which parental lovemaking is tolerated by the girl during her oedipal phase? A less favorable environment may lead to a greater sense of isolation, or to narcissistic injury due to hostile fantasies connected to curtailed motility, distorted perception, and a sense of exclusion. These developing ego functions then influence the child's superego precursors.

In discussions of pavor nocturnus, the excessive overstimulation, sexual excitement, and infantile traumata of children have been noted where there has been close physical proximity to parental intercourse (Greenacre, 1967). Children whose parents have created a hostile atmosphere during the day fantasize a more sadistic version of intercourse and so are more frightened. The child's internal resources and cognitive functions play a major role in fantasies and adaptive capacities related to primal scene experiences (Esman, 1973).

Freud was aware that masochism exists in both men and women: "it is easily verifiable . . . that . . . men often display a masochistic attitude—a state that amounts to bondage—toward women. What they reject is not passivity in general, but passivity toward a male" (1937, p. 252n). However, there is no biological or psychological evidence that boys or girls, or adults of either sex, wish to experience pain in conjunction with pleasure, unless they are suffering from a perversion. Freud's position that a woman is not fulfilled in her self-feelings unless she has suffered the pain of childbirth is not borne out by women patients.

The sexualization of pain as an adaptive mechanism was first mentioned by Freud (1924b), who called it "an economic problem" that may bind anxiety or hostility toward the object held responsible (consciously or unconsciously) for the pain, whether fantasized or actually experienced by the child.

Freud spoke of a typical "female" masochism. He knew that masochism beginning in childhood transcends gender differentiation and stems from excessive ambivalence toward introjected parental objects. Hostility not discharged against the object is turned against the self. Freud illustrated this clearly in "A Child Is Being Beaten" (1919). The role of the mother in relation to the fantasy of being beaten must be added to Freud's original ideas on this subject. Analysis provides abundant evidence that a girl in particular can experience pleasure only after she has rid herself of guilt feelings toward her mother: the more hostile the relationship between mother and child, the more relentless and severe the beating fantasy will be (see also Lax, 1997).

Sadomasochistic fantasies from the preoedipal phase color the masturbation fantasies of the oedipal phase, and the girl's oedipal wishes include a wished-for penetration, even though she may consider this dangerous. Masochism has been observed to appear frequently when narcissistic rage is not properly discharged, as part of a syndrome related to yet unverbalizable traumatic events (e.g., the pain of surgery that has become sexualized in a girl's love for her surgeon).

SUPEREGO DEVELOPMENT

Freud (1923) postulated that the superego is formed through a "precipitate" of previous object choices, and that it represents a "gradient within the ego" that manifests itself after internalization of the parental figures following the oedipal phase. When there have been difficulties in the internalization of parental representations, there will be a corresponding problem in impulse control. This will affect the nature of the oedipal experience. Sexual and hostile impulses and incestuous fantasies may then be acted out in adulthood, thereby affecting object choices. If the oedipal phase has been negotiated successfully, and internalization of oedipal conflicts has given way to more lasting identifications and character development, the superego will develop into a consolidated part of the psychic structure, aiding in the selection of objects in adulthood.

We know that the beginnings of psychic structure formation are formed out of the capacity to delay gratification, which is facilitated when the infant begins to internalize a loving maternal object. Although weaning, toilet training, separation problems, resolution of the rapprochement subphase, and the struggle to achieve object constancy all influence psychic structure formation and thereby the superego, it is the oedipal development, more than any other phase, that demands massive renunciation of unconscious sexual and hostile fantasies on the part of the growing child. Both idealizing and critical attitudes toward parental objects help in forming the superego; its structuralization binds hostility, which would otherwise be turned against the self, and helps to establish a firmer sense of identity in the child.

Although there are differences between boys and girls in the development of the superego, the evidence does not corroborate, as Freud maintained, that the female superego is more lenient or deficient, or that superego development is primarily related to castration anxiety. In fact, the prevalence of depression in women, in part an outcome of frustrated ideals and aspirations, is considered an important indicator of the existence of a *severe* female superego (Jacobson, 1937). Referring to her 1937 article on the development of the superego under conditions of early disappointment, Jacobson (1964) stated that she believed that because of the early onset of her castration conflict the little girl develops the nucleus of a true ego ideal even earlier than the little boy. Today we would cast some doubt on this statement and give greater emphasis to the nature of the early mother–daughter relationship as determining ego ideal formation in a girl.

In the negative oedipal phase there is an idealization of the mother and an identification with the father, whereas in the positive phase we find an idealization of the father and an identification with the mother; both are instrumental in the formation of ego ideal and superego. This, of course, is an oversimplification. Many of these developments overlap, and at times an identification may be experienced with the father more freely than with the mother, or vice versa; the same can be said for the development of idealizations in either the positive or the negative oedipal phase. As we have seen, narcissistic injury and parental devaluation may heighten penis envy and lead to identification with the father. Such a constellation often results in a fixation in the negative Oedipus complex. When objects are devalued, idealizations break down and lead to narcissistic character pathology (Chasseguet-Smirgel, 1970; Kernberg, 1975). If the ego ideal and superego have not yet been completely formed, the child is unable to tolerate hostility-evoking experiences, and disillusionment and hostile devaluation of the parents will cause her to suffer. Whether the female ego ideal will be part of a normal narcissistic self structure depends on the girl's capacity to overcome narcissistic injuries, and her ability to identify with each parent in a positive, life-affirming way. If narcissistic problems have become focused on the developmental idea of the "missing phallus," this may permit an idealization of the mother in fantasy but will impede an identification with the real mother and any enduring relationship with her. If the girl succeeds in creating a stable identification with her mother, an integration of her bisexual needs will follow. This will strengthen normal superego formation and will help in the formation of oedipal and postoedipal internalizations.

The postoedipal superego loses some of the grandiosity and wishful fantasies of the preoedipal and oedipal periods and becomes protective toward the self. Identifications are divested of the "preoedipal vicissitudes of aggression" (Hartmann, 1939). The superego helps the ego to control id derivatives and narcissistic strivings, and in general aids impulse control. It also helps to build autonomous ego functions and reality testing (Stein, 1966). It is only after the superego has been formed that love, identification, and hostility can be directed toward one and the same object (Jacobson, 1964).

The experience of motherhood, which consolidates individuation, depends on the girl's ability to loosen her preoedipal fixation on her mother. The struggle for liberation from the mother will fail if the girl's split between good and bad internalizations has not healed. Blos (1980) pointed out that a preoedipal girl may take flight into heterosexuality to cover up her yearning for the preoedipal mother, toward whom there has been too much ambivalence; hostility toward the mother may be deflected onto penis envy covered by an unconvincing heterosexuality. (This, incidentally, is a good example of "oedipalization.")

Oedipal development may remain partial and thereby create an internal conflict. Oedipal failure will consolidate during development when a move from mother to father occurs without sufficient previous identification with the former. This will happen when the girl's relationship with her mother has been lacking in aliveness and closeness, and when hostile interaction between them supersedes the libidinal aspects of the relationship—or when an excessively maternal father or nonmaternal mother causes confusion of parental roles and thereby influences the child's subsequent identifications. The question regarding female development has been raised: "does the girl change her love object from her mother to her father? Or does she add a heterosexual object choice to a homosexual one?" (Halberstadt-Freud, 1998, p. 42).

A girl who is disappointed in her mother may nevertheless identify with her as a sexual person—"the sexual vagina" (Kestenberg, 1980) but be unable to identify with her maternal functions ("the non-sexual vagina"). The mother may appear either as an independent, heterosexual woman loving the father (an image with which the patient can identify, even if as an excluded oedipal onlooker), or as the threatening preoedipal mother "forcing" the patient into an unwanted role.

Thus, if identifications with parents remain incomplete or confused, resulting in incomplete internalizations of the parents as a couple and of parent–child interactions, the oedipal experience will be fragmented. (Not only hostile behavior on the part of parents toward the child, but seductive behavior as well, will fragment identification processes.) Such experiences in childhood will influence the woman's choice of a mate and the strength of her wish to have a child. Failure in oedipal development may become manifest when a young woman contemplating motherhood turns from a dyadic relationship with her mate toward a triadic one including a child; conflicting identifications regarding representations of parents and self, and a conflict between wishing to remain a child and having a child, will influence her sense of feminine identity. On the conscious level this conflict may be expressed as a fear that having children will make intellectual or professional development impossible, or that professional success will increase the danger of not having a child. Conflicts from the negative and positive oedipal periods exist simultaneously. These coexisting conflicts exert a lasting influence on the girl's psychic reality. Oscillations of contradictory unconscious needs and wishes that affect her growth will reflect her later destiny as a young woman.

CONCLUDING REMARKS

To some analysts, clinical work suggests that the girl has a more difficult task in overcoming competitive wishes and hostility toward the mother than has the boy. I do not believe this to be a clinical fact. I believe that "female" masochism toward parents or other love objects is experienced by both boys and girls, and often appears in masturbation fantasies, particularly fantasies of being beaten, in which sadomasochistic object relationships between child and either parent play a prominent role.

A type of modern woman not described in the early analytic literature has emerged, a woman who can identify with her mother's sexuality but not her mother's maternal role, or vice versa. A split maternal identification, or high degree of ambivalence, as well as extensive bisexual conflicts too difficult to integrate into a coherent character structure, may characterize her internal conflicts. Crucial decisions related to her adult role, her attitudes toward her career, her maternal role, and her future object choices are determined by the nature of her preoedipal and oedipal identifications (see chapter 1).

An incapacity to move from dyadic to triangular object relationships can prevent the resolution of oedipal rivalry in childhood or adolescence. Thus, preparation and motivation toward finding a lover and toward motherhood are disturbed. When love relationships with peers are embarked on in adolescence and young adulthood, there may be a strong oscillation between excessive closeness and wishes for merging with lovers, as well as separation anxiety and conflicts related to difficulties of individuation. As a result, the Oedipus complex appears as a permanent organization that fluctuates with character development. Triangular relationships may became revived and dissolved again. Because phase-specific changes within the intrapsychic organization determine methods of conflict resolution at any given time, modes of oedipal resolution may fluctuate and change over time. Recent psychoanalytic literature seems to confirm that neither negative nor positive oedipal conflicts are ever truly "resolved." Rather, they attain a phase-specific quiescent state of adaptation, only to surge up again in situations of inner conflict during pivotal developmental phases later in life (Laufer, 1993; Lax, 1994, 1997).

5.

Narcissistic and Phobic Character Formation in an Adult Patient: The First Analysis of Maureen

Reconstruction has played an important role in psychoanalytic technique from the very beginning. Freud and his early followers constructed events which by themselves could not be recalled by patients during the analysis, but which appeared in associations, transference, dream fragments, and acting out. Greenacre (1975) proposed the idea of reconstruction in relation to a "basic transference" that recapitulates the early child–mother relationship and includes feeling states from the preverbal period (p. 704).

Margaret Mahler's work on the developmental subphases shed new light on reconstruction.[1] While early psychoanalytic writers attempted to reconstruct traumatic events that had resulted in pathological developments, Mahler provided a paradigm of mother–child interaction that serves as a frame for evaluating a patient's early life history; the comparison between normal and

---

[1] I am especially grateful to Dr. Mahler, whose interest in this paper led me to develop my thoughts in this area.

93

pathological variations can be used as a basis for reconstructing events during the preverbal years within a phase- or subphase-specific framework (Blum, 1974, 1977b). Blum (1977b) stresses that these reconstructions "are particularly relevant to the origins of structuralization, to preoedipal patterns and their later reactivation or persisting influence" (p. 758). Blum also emphasizes that data about the initial structure formations are not, as a rule, accessible to psychoanalysis, but that analyst and patient may create "preliminary models of past development and pathogenesis" (p. 757).

Many analysts, foremost among them Brenner (1975), maintain against this view that the complexity of the oedipal phase so reorganizes early psychic structure that subphase characteristics formulated from direct infant observation cannot be used in understanding adult patients. The opposing view does not imply, however, that in some patients, primarily those who fail to reach the oedipal phase, the archaic structure is reasonably intact and sufficiently cathected to force its derivatives into the treatment directly. While it is certainly true that there is no royal road from Mahler's findings to the understanding of the intrapsychic structure of adults I do believe that in analysis, when the transference deepens, feelings that could never have been verbalized in early childhood can be put into words for the first time. When adaptations to stress are traversed successfully in early development, they leave no discernible traces, but maladaptations or arrests can appear in the transference as a demand on the analyst. As the adult patient, who now commands the requisite cognitive structure he or she lacked as a young child, finds words for the stressful interactions of infancy, the analyst's interpretations and reconstructions can help the patient to develop psychic representations of these traumatic events, thereby permitting a more successful adaptation. I have come to believe that transference experience may include affective responses from the preverbal period, when strong affect became integrated with a conflictual theme during the formation of psychic structure. This affect becomes a *core affect* that appears again and again in conflict formation and thereby becomes accessible to transference analysis. When affective memories embedded in early object relationships become apparent in the patient's symptomatology, some reconstructions from the basic transference and from dreams may be made that have validity in analysis. In the ensuing case material, I will attempt to indicate how this may come about.

The analyst's interpretive work is guided by theoretical orientation and the knowledge that every human being has to pass through certain pivotal developmental points, or organizers (Spitz, 1965). My own work is guided by the belief that optimal consequences of development include internalizing a maternal image in which the balance favors libidinal over hostile cathexis; daring to say No (Spitz, 1957) without fear of losing the object; establishing "anal autonomy" (Mahler, 1971) and a clear sense of gender identity (Stoller, 1968); the capacity to develop a sense of self geared toward independent achievement, which promotes the developing ego functions; the resolution of the rapprochement crisis; a capacity for signal function that will prevent the reenactment of traumatic interactions in the patient's current life; and, finally, object constancy and the establishment of the Oedipus complex as an enduring psychic structure.

It was this orientation that underlay my first analysis of Maureen, beginning when she was 22, and that led me to formulate a relationship between her narcissistic pathology (as well as developmental fixations in the practicing and rapprochement subphases) and the emergence of both phobic character formation and phobia proper. These early developmental way stations were central to the patient's pathology. From both the preoedipal material of the basic transference and oedipal reconstructions, the relationship between pathological narcissism (arising from phase-specific maladaptations) and the emergence of phobic reactions became evident.

I was able to make reconstructions from the patient's memories dating back to the second and third years of life that enabled the patient and me to understand how her grandiosity was a substitute for phase-specific separation–individuation processes that postponed separation. These processes were set in motion because a psychic representation of a realistic, autonomous development of the patient's sense of self was fostered by neither parent. This situation later prevented adequate resolution of the rapprochement subphase and, still later, the development of a reliably functioning oedipal structure. In Maureen normal developmental sequence had been replaced by a cluster of phobic reactions and specific phobias.

CASE HISTORY

When I first saw Maureen, her appearance conveyed beauty and intelligence, but she sat erect and frozen, more like a puppet than a person. Throughout the session, her speech was controlled and lacked affect. Her appearance was overly neat. Unmarried and a virgin, she said that her love life was unsatisfactory and that her capacity to express her feelings was limited. She spoke of feeling detached, particularly with men, including her new boyfriend. She wanted to enter analysis because of what she called "a crisis in her love life." She had just broken off an engagement in order to begin seeing a man of whom her parents disapproved. The ensuing conflict between her addictive attachment to this new boyfriend and her wish to submit to her parents' wishes was what led her to seek analysis.

Maureen was a sheltered and indulged only child who had received a better education than either of her parents and who had successfully embarked on a professional career. She felt closer to her father, who she said worshipped the ground she walked on, than to her mother, who was a self-assertive but essentially dependent, anxious, and infantile woman. Her passive father's habitual way of maintaining family peace was to offer his wife and daughter money, which they spent exclusively on self-adornment. Any sign of anger was dealt with by these gifts of money.

Maureen often felt as if she were "in a fog" and avoided situations that were unfamiliar, preferring the security and shelter provided by her parents. With a complacency verging on arrogance, she reported that she saw herself, as her father did, as rather "special" and "perfect."[2] She conceded, however, that it was this feeling of perfection that inhibited her artistic proclivities, though she denied that it interfered with her social life or professional career.

During the first session she reported no phobic symptoms. During this first phase of treatment, Maureen maintained the aura of her specialness and perfection, which kept her distant and masked, and which I took as a characterological defense against hostility, as in Winnicott's "false self" (1960). She quickly became dependent, however, on her sessions, as the analysis itself became idealized and "special." She demanded that I help her maintain the illusion that she was perfect. The fact that early on she formed an idealizing transference suggested that her disorder was primarily a narcissistic one (Kohut, 1971), despite the fact that developmental fixations based on a traumatic core later emerged (Kernberg, 1967, 1975). In the beginning she made many demands, requesting personal information about me, attempting frequently to rearrange her

---

[2] "The inclusion of the child in the narcissistic world of the mother [or father] during certain periods of his early development creates the predisposition for the specialness of the child, around which the fantasies of the grandiose self become crystallized" (Kernberg, 1975, p. 276).

hours, and asking that I meet her new boyfriend. When these demands were not met, she retreated into coldness. I interpreted her demands as concealing an underlying wish for love that would conquer her hostile feelings and disappointments. I stressed that I could not indulge her in these constant demands, which were more prominent when she was angry, and which were echoes of her demands on her parents. I did, however, give her the encouragement she needed to express her anger and disappointment when demands were not met. I showed her that her parents had used gifts and indulgences as substitutes for love and as bribes against her expression of hostility, and that this set up, unconsciously, a familial compliance that prevented separation.

Step by step, the patient acquired a more realistic image of herself, accompanied by a corresponding decrease in feelings of detachment, an improved reality orientation, and a lessening of hostility toward me. In the second year of her first analysis, a greater capacity for delayed gratification allowed a lessening of her omnipotent fantasies, and, with it, a decreased need for indulgence. Maureen now experienced feelings of pride in her capacity to "take" it—to take life as it comes, without the need to be indulged as compensation for self-denial. As a result of her ability to verbalize her anger instead of demanding concrete evidence of being lovable, she began to feel self-reliant for the first time in her life. A quest for independence from her parents followed, and she started to talk about the issue of separating from them.

Now Maureen no longer idealized her parents; instead, the idealization was transferred to me, the analyst as magic protector. This idealization alternated with a view of me as someone who, unable to prevent the patient's sufferings, cared more for myself than for her. Maureen learned to work with this projection and with her ambivalence toward me, and to relate the latter to specific hostile fantasies or sexual wishes.

During this period, Maureen attempted to test what she experienced as her "new independence." She had sexual intercourse for the first time, but was disappointed at finding herself frigid. She retreated, reestablishing her ties with her parents. Her failures with men and her realization that she was still too dependent on her parents led to her becoming motivated to examine the events of her childhood.

She recalled scenes from when she was 2 or 3. She remembered clinging to her mother at the beach, and being terrified of the ocean waves. She discussed memories of her mother's phobic anxieties, her fear of water and of strangers, which were intensified when her father was not present. As a child, Maureen was encouraged by her mother to avoid playmates and was forbidden to use swings or slides unless closely watched. Yet she also remembered her mother leaving her entirely alone on a number of occasions, when she might have been even younger than 3.

At this point I offered my first reconstruction, telling Maureen that she seemed to have developed a conflict between feeling that she needed her mother's protection and wanting to explore the world by herself, but that the tie to her anxious mother had won out over her needs for independence.

Maureen now became interested in her very early years. Her parents cooperated by furnishing her with data. During the third year of analysis, her dreams, fantasies, and memories helped to lift a massive infantile amnesia and provided new material about the mother–child interaction and the father's role subsequent to the failure of that dyad.

When Maureen was a baby, eating problems became manifest when solids were introduced. She often responded by vomiting, which led to frantic scenes that were relieved only when her father took over. Maureen came to realize that her father had assumed maternal functions and that she had transferred many of her oral and symbiotic needs to him. Unlike her mother, her father encouraged exploration, often carried and rocked her, fed her when the mother was too anxious, and took her into the water. Unfortunately, he also overstimulated her.

Following her traumatic oral period, Maureen developed a defensive need to be empty. She "vomited out" to protect herself against her mother's feeding assaults. This stage manifested itself in the transference when the patient began responding to my interpretations with either nausea and a wish to vomit, or with constipation. I interpreted her vomiting as getting rid of anger against her "bad" mother or analyst. Feelings of "emptiness" were connected to emerging feelings of differentiation and represented a new feeling of separateness from her mother. The empty body belonged to her alone. In states of fullness from overeating or constipation, she felt as though she were part of her mother. She hated that feeling and at such times withdrew from social contact. Emptiness as a general somatic state defended her against facing hostile feelings toward her mother and later became the core affective state of her detachment, depersonalization, and phobic anxieties. Throughout development

Maureen dealt with her own fear and hostility to force-feeding by opposing various forms of indoctrination and by resisting the assimilation of new ideas.

Maureen now remembered having been coerced daily at the toilet. Her mother often sat on the edge of the bathtub, waiting for her to produce stools. When it took too long, her mother became angry and called her a "rotten kid." This was her first memory of not feeling "perfect." She was not allowed to be messy, dirty, hostile, or independent. Following the anal period, she tended toward chronic constipation. The onset of her doll-like and very proper behavior, similar to that which she presented in her first analytic hour, seems also to have begun during this period.

The connection between Maureen's oral traumata, anal restrictiveness, damaged self representations, and later frigidity unfolded during the third year of analysis. Her dreams and nightmares frequently contained frightening scenes of babies with injured bodies and heads, including tubes going into the mouth or head. She began to devalue her own genitals, to repress her feminine wishes, and became frigid. An increasingly frequent alienation from her body at this very early period in life became apparent in the analysis, following associations of intrusiveness experienced as a result of force-feeding and forced toilet training. The following dream was typical of this period: "I am in a bar with K. I love him, but our relationship is over. I am sitting in a chair. He leans over and says something affectionately. I say he has a big belly and no ass. I feel my head. It has a big dent in the middle. I felt very angry and constipated when I woke up. I wondered if I had hurt my head on my childhood high chair. I felt I had a head pain on awakening."

Associations led the patient to a typical kitchen scene (the "bar" is the kitchen counter), in which the child is in her high chair and the mother is holding the child's head and forcing the food into her mouth (the "dent in the middle"). Maureen remembered feeling overfed and constipated ("a big belly and no ass"). She further associated that K was her current boyfriend; his lovemaking seemed to her like force-feeding. In this context, the "dent in the middle" also represents the patient's injured and frigid sexual organ.

In addition to my earlier reconstruction, which was based on my understanding of a failure in separation-individuation during the rapprochement subphase, I now reconstructed what seemed to be a screen memory of a concrete event: Maureen was confined in her high chair, as though in a straitjacket, while her mother forced her mouth open. The feeding spoon represented a phallic extension of the mother, which had turned into an instrument of danger. This clarified her transference reaction to me as a force-feeder with "the spoon." The patient often felt that I withheld my real thoughts from her; she expressed the fantasy that my interpretations were force-feedings "for her own good." After an interpretation, she would come to the next hour feeling "full," "constipated," and angry.

As she began to test her new separateness from her parents, she felt anger, as well as a sadness and longing for once idealized childhood objects, feelings she called "sweet misery." With her ability to express her true feelings, instead of her doll-like constrictions, Maureen now began to feel that being "special" was a burden, and "being like everyone else," a relief. She had belatedly entered into the period of saying "No" (Spitz, 1957). She fantasized that I would retaliate for her wishing to separate, and would punish her for her newly acquired skills and negativistic attitudes. At the same time, she was terrified by her infantile wish to "injure" her mother by becoming independent. Nevertheless, she had learned to distinguish between archaic images of the "force-feeding and force-toileting mother" and more realistic ones. As a result, she became less afraid to lead an independent life.

Around this time, she found a new delight in physical experiences, although these did not as yet include the discovery of her feminine identity. As she relived the early, constrictive period of her life, she experienced a feeling of "undoing the past" as well as a thawing of her frozen affects. Maureen now began to enjoy food and to love her own body. She lost her self-consciousness about moving her bowels when someone was present in her apartment. She went through a period of being messy, of wallowing in not being perfect.

As the wall of perfectionism began to crumble, the patient was less afraid to verbalize her hostility. Her idealizing demands on me diminished. She learned to drive, to ride a bicycle, to ski, and to dance, delighting in it all. She began to think about what her real life goals were, and a process akin to the "second chance of adolescence" (Blos, 1967) took place.

These advances were impeded temporarily by a further lifting of infantile amnesia. She began to remember her infantile fears and, for the first time, the phobic reactions that followed them. She had had a fear of choking, allergies to animal hair, and occasional breathing difficulties. With her entrance into the phallic phase, these had congealed into true phobias—fears of animals, water, and new situations.

She now recalled her father's habit of spending long hours in a state of semiundress in which his genitals were at times exposed. The sight of his penis both stimulated and frightened her (Greenacre, 1953). The resultant conflict caused the patient's love for her maternal father to be repressed, which led to identification with the father's genitals during her own phallic–narcissistic phase and later prevented phase-specific oedipal strivings from being expressed. These disturbances set off by paternal overstimulation in the preoedipal and oedipal phases contributed to phobia formation. They led to a renewed need for protection from her mother—a regressive step and a retreat from positive oedipal feelings.

With the emergence of this trauma at the phallic level of phobia formation, Maureen remembered a "wild and unpredictable" puppy she was given at the age of 3. She lived in fear that he would bite her. Unpredictability also became associated with her father's absences when he left for work. Later, unpredictability stood unconsciously for her father's seminudity and the unpredictable state of his penis. Maureen's fear of the penis was displaced onto all that was moving—dogs, rats, mice, and especially cats, which she said were "uncontrollable, jump on you, and bite you," a fear that was related to the change in size and shape of the penis and that continued until the end of her analysis. As a child she had the fantasy that her mother did not want her to see her father's penis because it was dangerous. She projected her own oral sadism onto the paternal phallus and then displaced it onto animals. To defend against acknowledging the sight of the penis, she experienced the visual sensation of being "in a fog" and feelings of depersonalization such as she had described in her first hour of analysis. Her unconscious wish to possess the penis by biting it off and swallowing it represented her fantasy of narcissistic–phallic superiority over her mother whose breasts she envied. The fear of cats had its onset in this phase and continued until the end of the analysis.

Maureen remembered taking her only doll apart so that its straw stuffing leaked out. This attack was related to unconscious revenge fantasies aimed at her mother's body, from which she felt protected only when her father was present. Destruction of the doll's body also represented identification with the "attacking" father who exposed himself to her, and a warding off of anxieties related to her own body. Her anxieties set off these vivid associations: "My childhood must have been one big fear: a fear of water, a fear of seeing my father's penis. When I feel I am me, I feel my father's penis cannot hurt me. I used to think: Please, Daddy, cover yourself up! When I used to look at it, I didn't feel real. I used to feel I gave my father life, that I was not just his daughter. When I felt special, I was not afraid of being attacked."

When Maureen was experiencing her childhood animal phobia most vividly, our family cat darted into my office as I opened the door to admit the patient for a session. While the cat frolicked with a pipe cleaner, Maureen stood at the door motionless and rigid, reminiscent of her posture in the early stages of analysis, her eyes flashing with rage. I immediately picked up the cat and removed her from the room, apologizing for the incident when I returned. Maureen assumed her position on the couch, but spent the entire hour and the following three in total silence. I did not interfere with the silence, lest she take my talking as a reenactment of the mother's force-feeding. In the fourth hour, she said, "What I *really* minded was the loving way you picked up the cat and took her out."

After that, memories from the phallic phase, particularly about her father, intensified. She remembered that she began to experience separation anxiety from him around the age of 4, and was prone to screaming fits when he was about to leave for work. For months she had scratched her forearm intensively during analytic hours. She now recovered a memory involving the jeans that her father left hanging on the doorknob when he went to work. She was tall enough to reach the zippered fly area and would scratch at the trousers, which retained her father's odor. She claimed she did this to comfort herself over his unpredictable absences.

Maureen's sense of longing for her father was particularly intense when she was alone with her mother. What frightened her was that her mother seemed not only "impatient and rigid" but terrified underneath as well. Maureen had a nightmare that revealed a wish to get rid of her father, replace him, and have her mother to herself. Following intercourse, the patient dreamt about a big pouch that was full of semen. On awakening, she had feelings of uncertainty about her body image, and a sense of terror. These feelings reminded her of making a mailman's pouch in kindergarten. Her mother had bought multicolored felt and participated in the project. Associations brought to light that what disturbed her was her mother's *participation* in the making of a "male" man of her little girl, who, like the father, would make a baby with and for her. It was a recollection of her mother's *participation* that reawakened the shared fantasy which the patient—now in the phallic–narcissistic stage—took to mean that her mother had wished her to be a boy.

There were other incidents of collusion to exclude the father. At the beginning of her menses, her mother bought her her first bras, all of which were padded. Mother and daughter pretended Maureen was her mother's sister and that their breast size was the same, thus bringing them closer together.

As she grew up, Maureen continued to wear padded bras. She dealt with anxiety by using more pads, which soothed her. She called the bras an addiction because she felt unable to function or exist without them. In contrast to a male fetishist, who demands that the feminine object wear a fetish as a defense against his castration anxiety, Maureen seemed to use a padded bra as a magic phallus of her own (Greenacre, 1970). Maureen idealized her mother's breasts, while she felt she had only a large bra. She did not experience her growing breasts as belonging to her developing body. They became devalued and "fake"—thus, she needed the bra. The bra also appeared to unconsciously represent her father's penis, which she coveted. The penis–breast equation formed a particularly powerful theme.

When she wore a padded bra, she could have the fantasy that her breasts were as large as her mother's; therefore, she did not have to envy her. It was evident now that the false "breast-phallus," in addition to preventing separation from her mother, was also used to merge with the maternal father and to ward off sexual wishes toward the oedipal father. Whenever Maureen felt hostile or insecure, she added more layers to her padded bras. Struggling to give up her padded bras also produced fears about the inside of her body. She fantasied her vagina as a dark tunnel and dreamt it was a room in which her "nighttime" parents made love.

At this time in her analysis, Maureen remembered that during the "padded bra period" she heard her parents having intercourse in the next room. Primal scene episodes (in early childhood she had shared the parental bedroom)[3] were reconstructed from dreams such as the following: "We were on the ocean. The waves go up and down. I see moving shadows through slats or blinds, half open. It seems a child is crying. Perhaps someone drowned."

---

[3]Esman (1973) quotes Fenichel (1927) as tracing a hunger for screen experiences to having witnessed the primal scene and quotes Greenacre (1966) as attributing to primal scene exposure the overidealization of the analyst. Both my patient's hunger for screen experiences and her excessive idealization were prominent features in her character structure.

Maureen remembered that her crib had had vertical slats on the sides. When awakened in childhood by parental intercourse, she would pretend to be asleep while watching her parents through these bars. She would wet the bed ("someone drowned") and then cry. Over her mother's protests, her father would lift her into the parental bed. She recalled a fantasy of having divided her parents into "daytime parents, white, lovable, and rational," and "nighttime parents, black, wild, and dangerous, like animals." These recovered memories were followed by a phase of promiscuity with black lovers, in which Maureen, who is white, enacted the fantasy of being her father's "superwoman" or prostitute, thereby outdoing her mother. She dressed in slacks, boots, and padded bras under a sweater. She wore gaudy colors and used excessive amounts of perfume. She played at being very sexy, and would throw herself on the bed nude, wearing only high heels and theatrical makeup. She pretended to have orgasms. She admitted that "being wanted" was her "greatest need." Her lovers had to be black to fulfill the fantasy of finding her "nighttime" father and experiencing his penis in the sexual act, while displacing her mother. She was frequently angry with her white "daytime" father, who belonged to her mother. After intercourse with a black man, she fantasized that she had acquired his penis, her way of concretizing the fantasy of fusion with her father (Zavitzianos, 1982; Raphling, 1989). Maureen called this her "second addiction." Forbidden, intoxicating, it was her only way to feel sexual: "It transforms me away from being a woman. I become my father's penis—an animal, a cat: I don't feel like a woman, but I feel like an animal."

Maureen experienced heightened genital arousal with these lovers, but her still incomplete individuation and sexual inhibition produced feelings of insufficiency. These feelings appeared in the transference as a demand that I confirm her "conviction" that she lacked nothing and needed no one. Being needy meant admitting having a vagina, which aroused penis envy and orgasm envy. She demanded that I promptly cure her frigidity, declaring she would do better in other therapies, and claiming she could experience orgasm if hypnotized or drugged. She thought I was withholding knowledge of how she might achieve vaginal orgasm. She said, "Give me the orgasm!" This angry demand expressed her confusion about the difference between gratification from an external source and experiencing her own vagina as a pleasure-giving organ. "Give me the orgasm!" was also related to issues about her analytic fee: she felt cheated by having to give so much and getting back so little. I represented the force-feeding mother and not the "good mother of symbiosis." I interpreted that she had to remain frigid as long as the penis stood for the force-feeding mother of whom she was afraid.

At this time she also developed difficulty in wearing dresses and reported states of depersonalization when shopping for clothes—unless she was buying slacks. Her phallic competitiveness produced further narcissistic vulnerability, and she fantasized both becoming male and having large breasts like her mother. In such states the existence of her vagina was denied, and the patient felt narcissistically intact.

Interpretations of this denial uncovered the wish to experience being a woman who was not frigid. She admitted that during intercourse she felt stiff and corpselike—an identification with the father's penis—(Lewin, 1933)[4] and would weep involuntarily when her partner had an orgasm. This weeping was an affective reliving of her childhood enuresis and of her father picking her up when she cried. The stiffness expressed her fantasy of oral incorporation of her father's penis and was an attempt to prevent feeling overwhelmed.

Gradually we came to understand that Maureen's frigidity had phobic roots in its connection to early oral and anal training experiences, as well as in early somatic stress responses and a faulty body image supported by her mother. Later phallic–narcissistic conflicts reinforced this development, as did repeated exposure to the primal scene. The nature of her inhibitions related to her force-feeding mother, who had invaded her body, and to a sadomasochistic fixation on the father's penis as a destructive force. When her frigidity came up, the patient said: "The biggest lie was, I could not remember the bedroom. I was ignored there. The fear of the cat is like the fear of my father's penis and my mother with the spoon. I feel crazy when I feel I have the bedroom feeling. Lovemaking is a battle: will I win, will I come out alive? I'm going to be hurt."

The "bedroom feeling" was the name she gave to feelings of depersonalization. I interpreted these associations as indications of oral and phallic anxieties that developed into phobic character traits.

As the analysis of her frigidity progressed, she undertook a shift in her career, which ultimately recast the direction of her life. She

---

[1] I am indebted to Henry Edelheit (1976, personal communication) for pointing out that the doll-like stiffness of my patient was like the fantasies of robots and other man-made monsters representing a male pregnancy fantasy and the primal scene. During her "black promiscuity" period, my patient experienced herself as male, impersonating her "nighttime" father.

had always avoided using her talent because of her fear of exposure, an identification with her father's exposure. The idea of exhibiting herself was linked to uncontrollable impulses; an organized phobia against self-exposure had set in. She dreamt at this point: "I am being forced to participate in something I don't want; I am waiting my turn to go on stage. I'm forced to go, although I'm the wrong person. This dream turns into a nightmare because I will have to be impersonating on stage and bluff my way through. The feeling is that I have to do something alien to me, and this is the story of my life."

The "stage" of this dream is the parental bedroom. The patient's fear of public performance and her feeling of being forced to participate "in something I don't want" was rooted in her feelings about having been force-fed and the accompanying somatic stress responses. It was also a superego injunction related to the wish to masturbate when her parents were having intercourse. The patient associated:

> My feeling in the bedroom was: What is it all about? Why am I here? In masturbation I had the fantasy that I was part of my parents making love. I was in the middle. After it was over I felt abandoned; I got scared and made believe I was dead. I don't know whether this is true or not. I don't want to lie to you. I feel stupid. I was so afraid in this dream; I'm not sure I have a voice, as I'm not sure I have a vagina. I feel anger and nausea when lovemaking. Sex and food are coming together. I just want to pull out what is moving inside me.

In her masturbation fantasies she created a fused bisexual and omnipotent narcissistic image, which denied her exclusion. The understanding of these fantasies eventually permitted her to be in touch with her body and begin to experience her own sexuality.

In further interpreting the "stage" dream, I told her: "Unconsciously, you sometimes feel like a man impersonating a woman. At such times, you really feel you *are* a man, and then you cover it up with an unreal femininity." Later, I added: "This way, you conceal from yourself that you feel helpless and angry about being a girl." I also interpreted that her fear of appearing in public without the padded bras meant that she actually thought of herself as a female impersonator. For the patient, the fantasy of being a man impersonating a woman encapsulated the entire range of her narcissistic, phobic, and counterphobic symptomatology (Arlow, 1963).

Following this interpretation, the patient came to the next session and reported an outbreak of rage against me. At a party she had smoked marijuana and, when she looked in the mirror, saw her face cut in half. One half was clearly her own; the other half was her father's and had a mustache. Contemplating her mirror image infuriated and frightened her, but she understood the meaning of her visual image fantasy as a confirmation of her bisexual and omnipotent narcissistic wishes. Her associations to my interpretation of her bisexuality in her previous session became more specific:

> The padded bra makes me an ungirl. An ungirl is very sexy, maybe a prostitute. This is where the whole thing with my father comes in. He protected me from being forced so much. It feels good to cry. It feels good to feel. The invasion of privacy was like my mother's spoon. I used to wish I would be somebody else. Everything was foreign, like a big dangerous cat. I also wished that in the bedroom. I felt in a fog. I am so angry when I think of pretending. There's a sex confusion. I think: "Take me as I am." This is the feeling at an audition. I'm not going to wear my false breasts. I have a masculine feeling with a bra. I feel angry now. I'm thinking about having a pizza. Sometimes I feel omnipotent.

It was not until the patient was able to experience herself as female rather than bisexual that lesbian fantasies entered consciousness. The wish to experience her femaleness finally prompted attempts to relinquish the padded bra "addiction." During this struggle, she remembered the following: "My father encouraged fakery. He told friends I made 95 in school when I had made 85. I was not allowed to be average. It was like the bra. I became elevated [she laughed at her own pun] and felt like a fake. It's amazing how much I put into the bra."

I said, "A small piece of cloth that made you stick out more."

"I never thought of it as a small piece of cloth," she responded. "I thought of it as something dirty. Like sleeping with dangerous or forbidden black men, like slums, like being a prostitute, like not allowing myself to have things. I am not entitled because of that piece of cloth."

Once she succeeded in relinquishing the padded bras, wishes for union with her mother—first as a man, then as a baby—emerged. She then was able to establish a better relationship with her mother. She was unable, however, to reach her symbiotic needs for her mother in her first analysis and therefore could not fully relinquish her need for protection from her maternal father. Although the patient experienced oedipal wishes with strong affect, she was unable to synthesize fully in analysis her oedipal feelings (toward either parent) into a developed, mature, and enduring psychic structure.

DISCUSSION

In normal internalization, the developing personality draws on positive, real experiences with the mother and adds fantasy images to the representation of the "good" mother. Maureen built up a fantasy image of a "good" mother as a defense against interactions with the "not good enough" mother (Winnicott, 1953). Because the "good" mother remained largely a fantasy, in opposition to the forcing, menacing mother, the patient proceeded to cling to the concrete and *real* mother as a protection against the introjected "bad" mother. Inability to internalize an image of a "good enough" mother, compounded by identification with the phobic mother, prevented establishment of the psychic structure that could have supported strivings toward independence. In view of Maureen's lack of permission for independent self-expression, it was necessary for her to use the external mother as an affect regulator (McDevitt, 1971).

The patient's use of the *real* mother in place of her object representations could be described in the context of the subphases described by Mahler (1968, 1975b; Mahler, Pine, and Bergman, 1975): the grandiose fantasies of the practicing subphase persisted so that the patient was unable to explore, enjoy, and master the environment on her own under the approving protection of her mother.[5] Instead, her injured self-structure remained insufficiently differentiated from the real mother.

---

[5] I am indebted to Margaret Mahler for the following comments in connection with this case: "Through 'good enough mothering,' which implies a preponderance of libidinal nutriments and protection from trauma, primitive structure formation is facilitated. Concomitantly the body ego can engage in differentiation, especially boundary formation, without undue protection of rage violence and undue fear of loss of the still symbiotic half of the self. If, through intrinsic reasons of pathological mothering, the mother is not good enough—the predominance of aggression hinders adequate structure formation, i.e., reconciliation and integration of the good vs. bad (self &) object representations. That means that, as early as in the early practicing subphase, the active defensive splitting mechanism has to be resorted to— because the good image has to be protected against the unneutralized aggression and rage that the bad introjected mother-representation generates. Splitting as an active measure is then used for gaining time, so to say, for the ego to catch up" (personal communication, July 29, 1977).

I have characterized this mutually idealizing relationship between child and parents as a "narcissistic alliance." I use the term *alliance* in order to emphasize the *real* mother's role in the initial injury of the child's emerging self during the separation–individuation process, as well as her role in maintaining this injury. The narcissistic alliance has an interpersonal as well as an intrapsychic meaning. Dynamically, it has the function of preventing the expression of hostility between parent and child (Loewald, 1960). In the case of my patient, the alliance had the additional function of furnishing each participant the necessary missing elements of narcissism (Freud, 1914a). The investment in sustaining this alliance came about because neither mother nor child could tolerate the child's separation attempts. When pressures for separation finally reached an inner urgency during the rapprochement subphase, Maureen seems to have produced her first somatic and phobic symptoms, and clinging to the real mother increased. After this alliance was analyzed, hostility emerged in analysis. Only then did phobic symptoms begin to appear.

According to Schur (1955), somatic stress responses indicate the preponderance of hostile over libidinal components while the child is developing a representation of the mother. In my patient, breathing difficulties, choking, and allergic tendencies during the second and possibly the first year of life were the precursors of later phobia formation (Wangh, 1959; Schur, 1963, 1966).

I observed a specific developmental line of "phobia proneness" on a characterological continuum, beginning most likely with a premature separation before completion of the symbiotic phase and followed by an unconscious search for "the good mother of symbiosis" and by somatic stress responses, a failure to develop signal anxiety, and a faulty self representation. During the rapprochement subphase, she could not leave her mother because of the latter's phobic anxieties, with which the daughter identified. Maureen's identification with her phobic mother prevented the normal hostility of the rapprochement subphase to emerge and paved the way toward later phobia formation (Mahler, Pine, and Bergman, 1975). A true phobia is a highly organized and complete system, but precursors of phobia may already appear at the beginning of structure formation (A. Freud, 1965; Schur, 1953).

The child who is perfect in the eyes of both parents and herself, devoid of hostility and of individuality, represents a wished-for self-image (Jacobson, 1964; Milrod, 1977) that replaces the beginning of the development of a genuine ego ideal. In my patient, very premature separateness during the symbiotic phase was counteracted by the mother during the rapprochement subphase, preventing phase-specific separation. Because the mother herself was phobic, it is likely that she discouraged autonomous ego functions during the rapprochement subphase that could have promoted the child's distancing. During this phase, Maureen felt threatened whenever she attempted to master tasks independently, and it was at this point that she internalized many of her mother's restrictive, phobic character traits.

While such predispositions may not always be sufficient to predict specific symptoms, in Maureen they seemed to have constituted the necessary conditions for later phobic symptomatology. Treatment revealed that what was critical to the patient's phobia-proneness was rooted in confusion about real and imaginary dangers. The child was unable to learn from her phobic mother to distinguish the "dangers" of separation from the real dangers of the environment (Freud, 1926).

The active early participation of a maternal father as a protector against the mother's intrusion and domination over the child's bodily functions further complicated the clinical picture. Crucial differences in the caretaking functions between mother and father led to a heightened, tactile sense of overstimulation that frightened the patient, and to a sense of narcissistic bliss in the presence of the maternal father.[6] Simultaneously, earlier wishes for a symbiotic merger with the mother were still present, recast now in the form of a negative oedipal conflict. Rudiments of the normal Oedipus complex appeared as well, but the oral wishes left the patient open to the dangers emanating from the father's exposed penis and the fear of losing her mother's protection. Her multifaceted phobias were displacements of all these conflicting wishes and fears. I believe that the maternal activities of the father made him less available as the main carrier of the patient's libidinal wishes during Maureen's phallic and oedipal phases. The patient therefore exhibited features of oedipalization (Kernberg, 1975), rather than a full expression of the Oedipus complex as a new psychic structure (Shapiro, 1977).

Although oedipal themes increased during the course of analysis, Maureen's relationships to men remained strongly narcissistic, and her maternal wishes were sporadic. I was initially puzzled as to why her

---

[6]A situation reminiscent of Little Hans (Freud, 1909) whose father fulfilled protective paternal as well as maternal functions.

frigidity and phobias disappeared without there having been more oedipal material in the transference and without her relationships to men having reached greater depth. Paradoxically, reaching orgasm enhanced feelings of bisexuality and unconsciously served as a substitute for the padded bra of her puberty and adolescence. The padded bra, which the patient clung to until the last phase of treatment, represented her bisexuality and thus a protection from bodily harm.

Clinically, the patient presented a paradoxical picture: she functioned well in her social contacts, yet she was extremely inhibited, to the point of phobic character pathology. Initially she established an idealizing narcissistic transference not unlike the mutually idealizing relationship she had had with each parent. In analysis this transference had had the function of binding hostility.

This complex diagnostic picture may throw light on obscure developmental issues in cases in which the diagnosis remains less clear-cut. In Maureen, her narcissistic structure substituted for phase-specific separation processes and needed to be the first concern of the treatment. Individuation from her two hovering parents needed to get under way before intrapsychic conflicts could be reached.

Initially, the idealizing transference as postulated by Kohut (1971, 1972) was the reason for the patient's rapid progress and was based on a fantasy exchange of the analyst for the mother as a better maternal model. Hostility, stressed by Kernberg as crucial in narcissistic pathology, could clearly be observed as emerging from below the narcissistic alliance.

I believe that what permitted the working through of the phobic symptomatology was the fact that in the first two years of analysis, treatment focused on the narcissistic rather than the oedipal elements of the patient's character structure. It was the combination of the patient's aloofness, anger, and the need for love and idealization that led me to focus first on the origins and development of the narcissistic alliance.

A great deal of analytic time had to be devoted to the patient's dependency on her parents, and to the emergence of long-postponed anger directed toward them, which was manifested in an ongoing idealizing transference alternating with narcissistic rage. Analytic hours during which the patient struggled to unify the split of her good and bad parental images were particularly stressful. When she attempted to integrate her internal objects, she suddenly developed phobic reactions to separation in the transference and feared that her expressions of hostility might lead to object loss (McDevitt, 1971). In heightened anxiety states, there was a temporary regression away from self- and object constancy. There was also a reliving of narcissistic injuries and the phobic reactions that accompanied them.

The continued analysis of, and separation from, these aspects of her relationship with her parents made more realistic self- and object internalizations possible, devoid of narcissistic grandiosity, and without primitive rage. This capacity, which the patient reached in the analysis of the oedipal phase, represented a new integration. The final emergence of the beginnings of oedipal conflicts appeared once the patient relinquished her fantasy search for symbiotic connections to her mother and particularly to her maternal father—a relinquishing, however, that was only partially accomplished. At the very end of the first analysis, symbiotic needs were amalgamated into genital experiences. The patient discovered new pleasures in being rocked by a penis, in preference to a phallic thrust, which helped her to cathect her vaginal feelings in a new way. The thrusting penis represented the force-feeding mother, while the rocking penis represented the good symbiotic mother. Not until the last year of this first period of analysis could oedipal conflicts be worked through to some degree without being blurred by problems of separation anxiety and phobias.

SUMMARY

In the case of Maureen, early maternal failures reconstructed from separation–individuation subphase developments revealed a narcissistic alliance between the child and her parents. This alliance stood in the way of separation–individuation processes and blocked the expression of hostility. Identifications with the phobic mother prevented the ego from developing a signal function for anxiety as an anticipatory capacity against internal dangers minimizing phobia formation.

A maternal father, who in many ways counteracted the deficiencies of the mother, could only partially become the principal love object during the phallic and oedipal phases. A strong bisexual orientation prevented the full emergence of a feminine gender identity. Only after the narcissistic alliance emerged in transference and was given no gratification did phobic symptoms appear. The transference recapitulated a segment of the childhood neurosis in which phobia-proneness was held in check by the "narcissistic alliance" between mother and daughter.

6.

A Pathological Oedipal Constellation in a Female Patient: The Second Analysis of Maureen

Generally, patients whose psychic development is dominated by perversion have been regarded as fixated at a preoedipal level. As a counterinstance, I will present the case of a patient with perverse psychic structure who reached the oedipal level of development, even if aided by characteristics of perverse fantasy formation.

When Maureen, the patient described in the previous chapter, first came to analysis, her perversion remained repressed; upon returning for a second analysis, however, an unconscious perverse fantasy emerged that was oedipal in nature.

In Maureen's first analysis, we explored her infantile neurosis, which was characterized by symbiotic-like clinging, phobias, eating and elimination disorders, and primal scene traumata. She was frigid during intercourse, and her relationships were dominated by narcissistic pathology. Maureen needed to be admired by men rather than to love and be loved. In her first analysis, we worked on her narcissistic problems, her phobias, and her incapacity to free herself from her closely knit family ties.

Upon experiencing feelings of internal liberation and a new sense of selfhood, Maureen wished to terminate her first analysis. Although work on the patient's oedipal conflicts had aided maturation, conflicts related to narcissistic pathology remained and interfered with the analysis of oedipal conflicts. Nonetheless, Maureen had developed a more integrated sense of self. She had achieved considerable separation from her parents, changed professions, and became a performing artist. I did not believe she could go further in analysis at that time, especially since she had never lived in the "real world" as an independent individual. I did not oppose termination, and Maureen left analysis cheerful and content.

A few years after her first analysis, Maureen returned briefly for psychotherapy because she had developed bleeding ulcers, her father's lifelong psychosomatic illness. Her father had died, and she was in an intensely erotic relationship with a man who substantially resembled him. Her lover was married and uneducated, like her father. Submissive to her whims, he showered her with gifts. During intercourse she fantasized that she had resurrected and possessed her father. She was his "superwoman" and "prostitute," receiving the narcissistic gratification and sexual satisfaction she craved via the fantasy of regaining her father's penis.

Maureen's fixation on her father made it difficult for her to free herself from the fantasy that her lover was her father. At times the power of psychic reality—the feeling of being in bed with her father—was overwhelming. Although Maureen claimed not to know "what was so wrong with incest," unconsciously she felt she was the injured father with whom she identified.[1] During her sexual relationship with that lover, she fantasized that she could protect her father and bring him back to life. Having ulcers represented a fusion with her father, whereby she magically created the feeding father who is both father and mother and who is not differentiated from her. While this symptom was active, Maureen was unconsciously casting her father in the nursing role and excluding her nonfeeding, nonnurturing mother. Her father could eat only milk products because of his lifelong ulceractive condition. When Maureen had bleeding ulcers, she was forced to follow an all-dairy diet similar to the diet her father followed. She lived out a condensation of her oedipal wishes on the oral level, in which her

---

[1]Chasseguet-Smirgel suggests that perverts do not experience the "horror of incest," because oedipal prohibitions are "less absolute" (1986, p. 90).

father gave her only milk products to eat. Maureen struggled to leave her lover because of her incestuous conflict, but whenever she returned to him intermittently, her ulcers began to bleed again, despite her medication.

Our work together enabled Maureen to understand that her sexual relationship with this lover had prevented her from mourning her father. After a few weeks of working with me, she was able to leave both her lover and the treatment. Subsequently, mourning her father generated the wish to find a new type of love relationship.

Two years later, and nine years after terminating her first analysis, Maureen returned for a second analysis because she was in love and planned to marry, but felt insecure about being a wife. She had difficulty coping with the social, economic, and cultural pressures imposed by the new relationship.

During this second analysis we were able to work on a more profound level and uncover Maureen's perverse character pathology, fetishistic fantasies, and psychopathic traits (Arlow, 1991; Grossman, 1992; Kernberg, 1992). I found that infantile traumata specifically related to the primal scene had been overlaid by characterologically embedded narcissistic traits that had formed a defensive structure. A fantasied self-image of a narcissistic nature aided Maureen in denying myriad narcissistic injuries of early childhood. In this self-image, she was special, beautiful, very talented, and able to control the people who surrounded her or who helped her. This self-image formed an intermediary defense between her overtly apparent neurotic structure and her more severe underlying pathology. During the second analysis, a network of perverse oedipal fantasies emerged, some of which she had been able to sublimate as a performer.

In this analysis, Maureen's body image confusion, which now could be addressed more meaningfully than in her first analysis, was brought to light. Maureen became increasingly aware that she experienced a lack of contact with her own womanly body and female appearance. Her early feeding and elimination disorders, enforced by her mother's phobic reactions, constricted Maureen's body feelings from early childhood on, and her father's overstimulating, seductive behavior had led to a denial of, and subsequent alienation from, her physical self.

Whenever Maureen shopped in a department store, for instance, she had an anxiety attack, which frequently led to feelings of depersonalization. She felt that such stores were for "real women" who had "real women's bodies." She expressed the wish to be like me, to feel and look feminine, to be serene and not hostile. She envied women patients she saw in the waiting room, whose feminine appearance made her think they had a secret she did not possess. Maureen liked to buy clothes in a thrift shop, which she found sexually exciting because it "was so cheap it felt like stealing." Thrift shop clothing enabled her to "impersonate" a woman, since another woman had already worn the garments she bought. She said it was like wearing her mother's skin. When she married, soon after beginning her second analysis, she had a padded bra sewn into her wedding gown to relieve her anxiety about not being a "complete woman," which led back to her idealization of her mother's breasts, and her addictive and fetishistic need to create false, larger breasts of her own.

A complicated fantasy system emerged, which helped us discover a variant on the Oedipus complex that revealed the patient's core pathology: Maureen fantasized stealing the sexual organs of one parent and using them in intercourse with the other. While these fantasies remained active, Maureen's gender identity fluctuated between a fantasied masculine and a fantasied female identity, but whichever identity she impersonated, her sexual organs were "stolen." Unconsciously, Maureen gratified her father with breasts and orgasms stolen from her mother, while simultaneously gratifying her mother with her father's penis, stolen from him during intercourse. This double theft enabled her to reach her own perverse fantasy version of the Oedipus complex.

Whenever Maureen pretended that she possessed the genitals of her father, she exhibited distorted reality testing in other areas of her life as well (Bak, 1968, 1974; Raphling, 1989). In the second analysis she came to understand that the theft fantasy had enabled her to attribute magical powers to herself and had prevented her from realizing either her positive or her negative oedipal wishes "on her own." The theft fantasy was also a means of healing the narcissistic injuries inflicted in her parents' bedroom. If she had the special attributes of each parent, she could simultaneously possess each of them but also separate them from one another.

Maureen became consciously aware of the conflict between wanting femininity and sexual gratification with a man and holding on to her fantasies and enactments of the superwoman who is "a fake in bed." These conflictual wishes about her femininity were expressed in a contradictory transference fantasy: she hoped to reach femininity through a magic union, via intercourse with me, which represented a wish for the missed early closeness with her mother. This wish also came to be understood as a transference experience of Maureen's negative oedipal phase. This emergence of erotic feelings toward me, which expressed a wish for an archaic fantasy of fusion, was Maureen's first expression of wishes for the erotic closeness with her mother that she had missed as a little girl because of the frightening conflicts over feeding and toileting. Maureen had the fantasy that through intercourse with me she could get close to a woman, and by finding out how a woman experiences an orgasm she would be able to feel like a woman herself. In this transference-fusion fantasy she was the man, and through her wish to experience my body sexually a magical fusion state would be created. She could become loving because I would become the mother she never possessed, a mother she could idealize, who was feminine and not phobic.

Maureen's earliest traumatic experience of childhood had related to her eating and elimination disorders, which were woven through with her mother's own phobias, which included the fear that her mother would die or that she herself would die by choking from eating or by swallowing water while swimming. Mother and daughter shared the fantasy that eating was dangerous but that not eating would lead to death. When Maureen would vomit after being force-fed, her mother would become frantic about her not having received enough food and feared she would become ill or even die. These childhood events prevented Maureen's separation from her mother and her development of autonomy from early childhood on. She became a phobic, clinging child, with the feeling that the "outside world" was unreliable: the water does not hold you up when you swim, for instance, but if it does you could swallow some, choke, and die.

Maureen experienced me as someone she could love and be close to without becoming frightened, and in that sense I was a desexualized maternal image. She also saw me, however, as someone with whom she wanted to merge sexually. In that sense, I became the maternal figure toward whom she could have erotic wishes and whom she could idealize, unlike her own mother, whose possessive, clinging, and phobic behavior during Maureen's negative oedipal phase had induced in the young girl feelings of revenge and anger.

Maureen had been unable to internalize my interpretations as long as her grandiose fantasies of being a "superwoman" defended her against the full affective experience of having been overstimulated when her father exposed himself and having been ignored in her parents' bedroom during their lovemaking. Interpretations relating to Maureen's infantile traumata and narcissistic injuries, particularly her rage when she felt ignored, had been ineffective. At times, feeling force-fed, she was unwilling to accept an interpretation and changed the subject. There were also periods when she acted "constipated," refusing to talk and withholding information.

In her first analysis I had interpreted: "Unconsciously you sometimes feel like a man impersonating a woman. At such times, you really feel you *are* a man, and then you cover this up with an unreal femininity . . . . This way, you conceal from yourself that you feel helpless and angry about being a girl." That interpretation had produced an outburst of rage against me. I now realized that Maureen was unable to accept this interpretation while she still needed to defend herself against the overwhelming anxiety of feeling she could cease to exist without her mother's illusory breasts and her father's illusory penis, without her fetishistic fantasies, which gave her a "borrowed," bisexual fantasy self and a "borrowed" narcissistic sense of well-being.

As the enactments of being a "superwoman" and being an "exception" based on her incestuous feelings toward her father became better understood, Maureen developed a genuine wish to feel like a woman and give up her fantasies of possessing her father's penis. Her frigidity became clearer now. We understood that she felt injured by her mother's force-feeding and harsh toilet training in childhood. She felt she had an injured mouth, anus, and vagina, which led to feelings of body inadequacy and self-devaluation. Thus, she disavowed her body and created a self-image of a body with large artificial breasts and a secretly stolen penis. Until this fantasy could be analyzed, the only strength Maureen knew was "borrowed" or "stolen."

Analytic work was needed to help Maureen accept ordinary fluctuations in her husband's attentions. She went through a phase in which she was convinced I took her husband's side whenever she reported feeling ignored. She relived the extraordinary contrast between being the center of her father's attention in the daytime, and being both overstimulated and ignored in the bedroom at night. Maureen's experience "in the bedroom" had led to her feeling abandoned and had impeded her capacity to feel empathy for others. Whenever the analysis became "the bedroom," she ignored me, not responding to questions or interpretations, and treated me as though I were not present.

As we were analyzing the conflicts that arose from her repeated exposure to parental lovemaking, Maureen told me that from the age of 10 she frequently read pornography and masturbated in the bathroom before a large mirror. She set up a "stage" with lights in order to see herself better.[2] My impression was that keeping this a secret from me until this moment had enabled Maureen to differentiate herself from me. She said:

> I put time and energy into rearranging the furniture into a particular position. It was my gift to myself, my entertainment, particularly after a performance as an adult. It was my secret. Sometimes I had the fantasy that it's not my hands I see in the mirror. When I felt Father was doing it to Mother, I felt disembodied. I also fantasized that Father's hand was on me. I was recreating something: being half mother and half father. I experimented with my fingers in the vagina; I fantasized it's my father inside, that I have his penis and . . . that's why I didn't need a man. I obviously prevented myself from knowing what I was missing. I had to be in control—I couldn't just experience, I didn't believe you.

During her masturbation enactments, Maureen read only pornography describing three people making love. This illuminated her unconscious attempts to control the primal scene by being included in it.

Maureen had one masturbation fantasy in which she was her father stimulating her mother clitorally. Another fantasy condensed her early bedroom experiences: she was in a prison with bars, where the men came one by one for cunnilingus, saying she was "the greatest piece of ass" they had ever seen. She recreated this fantasy with each of her black lovers. Maureen then associated that the bars might stand for the bars of her crib in the bedroom: she was lying with her legs stretched through them, and her father may have touched her clitoris or made her suck his penis. In discussing this association, I said: "In this fantasy you are 'the greatest piece of ass' ever, and your father is with you and not with your mother."

"And what if it really happened?" she answered. "You sound as if you don't believe me." I was silent. "I'm not sure I believe it myself," she went on. "Whether or not it happened, I have to get out

---

[2]William Grossman suggested my patient deliberately withheld the information about her masturbation during her first analysis. He has noted similar behavior in several patients in his own clinical experience (personal communication).

of the bedroom and stop feeling ignored and angry at my husband. He appreciates my body; why don't I believe it?"

"You need to find out why you devalue your own body," I said, "because as long as you do, you can't enjoy his loving it."

Maureen was unable to remember whether an actual seduction had occurred during her childhood, other than her father's exposures, his touching her breasts in puberty and adolescence when he embraced her, and his taking her into the marital bed (probably unclothed) after she wet her bed (a nightly occurrence until the age of 8 or so).

One of her "sexual secrets" was having masturbated a little girl for whom she baby-sat. Maureen was 10 or 11 and the child less than 2. The child "couldn't talk and tell anyone," recreating Maureen's own silence in her parents' bedroom and the theme of having been touched by her father. As is typical of patients with perverse fantasy needs, Maureen also periodically longed to reacquire the addictive fantasy state in which she possessed her father and became part of his masculinity. In this feeling state she displaced her rage against her father onto her husband and produced dreams and fantasies of having been seduced by him.

During her second analysis, Maureen went through a period during which she feared she would choke while coughing. She had a dream about little white bodies swimming in mucus in the water, possibly the ocean. Maureen had always swum only in shallow water because of her fear of choking. During one of our sessions, Maureen had an anxiety attack and said she wanted to go to the bathroom for water. I said she could do as she wished, but as there was manifestly nothing wrong except acute anxiety, it would further our understanding if she could put her anxiety into words. She became pale and suddenly looked like an old woman. She said: "Maybe my father really did do something to me. Maybe he did put his penis into my mouth and I felt like choking. I couldn't breathe." Her only memory was this physical one. Then her color became normal again, and she began to look her true age. When she got up to leave, her entire body trembled. She held on to a chair as if she were afraid she would lose her balance. I pointed that out to her, and she asked to sit in the waiting room until she felt strong enough to go home.

After this episode Maureen dreamt that her husband and a friend she admired for her femininity swam nude together in deep water. Maureen awakened from this dream in a fit of rage and envy. She said it was clear that this dream was about her parents having intercourse. "I was a caricature," she said: "with all these men I was like a man, not like a woman. I could not receive, but I put myself into the role of a receiver. I was aggressive and a performer."

Maureen blamed me for her failure to have a confirming memory about her father's seduction. Her reproach became a transference issue: a memory of her father's seduction would equal a gift from me, and giving her the memory would equal giving her father to her (and taking him away from her mother). She demanded that she stay in treatment until such a memory emerged. She could then continue to enact turning her husband into her father, and in the transference reenact being both mother and father in the bedroom, thereby taking revenge for being ignored and excluded there. This fantasy would have cast me in the role of observer in the bedroom and displaced her fantasies of revenge onto me in a fully experienced negative therapeutic reaction.

I was uncertain, but decided to treat the idea of paternal seduction as fantasy unless proven otherwise. I felt that if I treated these fantasies as memories, as Maureen wanted, they might only enhance her fixation. I might thereby unwittingly assist her in distorting her psychic reality and reality perceptions. In Maureen's unconscious, fantasy and possible memory were treated equally as reality, which was confirmed by her dreams. The current debate about real childhood seduction vs. seduction in fantasy of course continues to rage. By maintaining analytic neutrality here, I hoped to prevent the issue from becoming channeled in either direction in the transference.

Maureen's internal struggles and fantasies made it clear that she was a "survivor of the parental bedroom." Gradually, she developed a need to "get out of the bedroom" and a hunger for identification with me. She decided to stop masturbating and threw away her pornographic literature, which she had hidden from her husband. Ultimately, the question of memory or fantasy lost its centrality. "Whether it happened or not," Maureen said, "whether I remember it or not, before I can terminate, as long as I cling to it, I am Father's other woman. I am not myself. I need Father's penis rather than my husband's and I hang on to not finishing my analysis."

As I continued to interpret Maureen's projections of her "bedroom situation" onto her present life, her capacity for internalization increased. When she could struggle successfully and find her own answers, she stopped feeling ignored and began to feel friendly toward the world; she began to grow up.

When she then began associating to her fantasies with a less perverse and better organized internal structure, as a neurotic patient does, she began to direct her rage and anger toward me. She was reluctant to give me anything, including my fee. She envied me and therefore had difficulty identifying with me. She was enormously curious about my life—particularly my sexual life—my way of doing things, and my thoughts. She fantasized she would have to get "inside me" to obtain what I had. At the same time, her narcissistic fantasies of grandiosity and bisexuality (a split body image experience—"I am a woman from the waist up and a man from the waist down") defended her from envy and convinced her she had it all and needed no one. Eventually, Maureen was able to accept that her rage against women who were sexually gratified by men stemmed from envy of her mother, as well as envy of her father's erect penis and her mother's gratification by it.

She then went through a period in her treatment during which she wanted to be the little girl she could not be as a child. She wanted an asexual but tender relationship with her husband in which he represented the nonseductive father and the feeding and gratifying mother. When I interpreted these wishes, she experienced vaginal feelings during the hour and reported feeling more feminine than she had for a long time. She understood better her need to fantasize being a man, as well as why she had needed to wear falsies and plunging necklines to prove to herself she was female, and why she had needed the bathroom mirrors when she masturbated to prove she had a female body. Once she began to feel truly feminine, she expressed great sadness about not having been able to have a child.

Ultimately, Maureen was ready to bring her "tender currents" (Freud, 1910)—love feelings and sexual needs—together. After she reached full vaginal orgasm for the first time, she said, "I must have been a normal little girl with normal sexual feelings like other little girls. I wonder what happened to me and how I lost them? I must have lost them in the bedroom. I pretended I could be my mother with my father or my father with my mother. Therefore I never felt like a child. As I wanted to steal my mother's body and be my mother rather than myself, I couldn't have sexual feelings because I wasn't myself. Therefore I didn't know what it was like to be a woman."

At that point it seemed that Maureen was ready to terminate her second analysis. She was jubilant and felt she had "joined the human race." She set a termination date to which I agreed, but as

the time drew nearer Maureen became increasingly more uncom-
fortable and finally confessed that she had lost her capacity for
orgasm, that she was afraid of dying, and that she couldn't leave me.
She had embarked on a full-scale regression, experiencing total
vaginal anesthesia; she felt like a corpse, and suffered severe anxiety
attacks. She oscillated between feelings of rage against her husband
and against me. She began to bring bottles of water to her analytic
sessions, because she was afraid of choking. She felt betrayed and
became increasingly disengaged from the analytic process.

It was clear I needed to help Maureen recapture certain fragments of her sense of self before we could resume work on her
internal conflicts. I pointed out that she had surrendered her adult
self to the frightened little girl who clung to her mother. It became
clear to us both that her fear of death, now more prominent in analysis than ever, was a traumatic reliving of certain aspects of her earliest relationship with her mother.

I interpreted that when she and mother felt sick together, she
felt loved. As she regressed in analysis, she became like her mother,
overconcerned with her body and potential illness. To that very day,
each of them carried a whole pharmacy in a bag when they visited
each other, "just in case." Their exchanges of cautionary warnings
not to choke, to eat slowly, or to be careful in the street in rain or
snow all were "signs of love." I interpreted that as long as she felt sick
she had to stay in treatment so she could feel I was concerned about
her: it was a reliving of being sick with her mother and thereby
feeling loved. This feeling state also excluded her "father-husband,"
a sexual person she had temporarily lost in her feeling state of infantile rage. Death anxiety emanated from the deepest level of separation anxiety, and in her transference behavior Maureen reverted to
being an angry, clinging child who could not leave analysis.

Maureen was extremely reluctant to describe her recent sexual
feelings when with her husband. Finally, with a great deal of difficulty and hesitation, she admitted that when she and her husband
made love, she fantasized that it was her father stimulating her,
which she felt was "the only way" she could "feel something." At the
same time she was reenacting a revenge fantasy against her mother
for her sexual relationship with her father and for allowing her to
witness their sexual relationship in the bedroom as a child. She felt
that she was betraying her husband by having fantasies about her
father and enjoying the feeling of being a little girl. In fantasy she
was also "impersonating" being a wife (her mother), who "felt

nothing" in her sexual relationship with her father. She now enacted being a wife who "felt nothing" with her own husband, but longed to experience herself as a little daughter who adored her father and had sexual feelings toward him. Meanwhile, she had made a non-sexualized father out of her husband. During brief moments of active sexual arousal with him, she fantasized being a little girl with her father as he stimulated her clitorally. Whether experiencing arousal with her husband or not, she would invariably resort to the fantasy of being stimulated by her father. Feelings of guilt then ensued, causing her to stop feeling aroused, which in turn filled her with rage. Her rage then brought forth the old fantasy that a wife (her mother) felt nothing in bed.

Maureen had two dreams that took the analysis further. In the first dream, she has murdered her father. She is lying in bed and there is a can of 7-Up next to his bedside. Her fingerprints are on it, and she is trying to "do away" with the evidence before the police come. She is very frightened. Her mother is also there. In the second dream, she stuffs her father into the freezer, but after the police leave he comes out of the freezer, is alive again, and she feels very relieved.

These two dreams led to associations of believing she may have touched her father's genitals with her fingers, perhaps even having stimulated him to ejaculation. She thought the can of 7-Up represented an erection. There had been repetitive dreams of wiping off white mucus or scraping it off her thighs, which she thought might have represented her father's ejaculation onto her body. Her sexual arousal was fixated on these images. She had felt a strong sense of loyalty toward her father and a need to keep "her secret." At the same time, she had also experienced tremendous guilt for feelings of revenge toward her mother, for the wish to kill her father for what he had done, and for her fantasies in bed, through which she betrayed her husband and caused the return of her frigidity. We could now understand together why her sexual anesthesia had returned, and why she felt that her husband and I had betrayed her. It was a projection of her feeling that she had betrayed her husband in bed by having a fantasy of being with her father, and that she had betrayed me in analysis by withholding this fantasy, but wishing at the same time that I would "do something" so she would not feel frigid anymore.

I told Maureen that I could understand how as a little girl she had wanted her father not to excite her sexually by exposing himself, and that this might have prompted her unconsciously to make her husband a desexualized father figure. I also pointed out that she was sometimes duplicitous toward her husband and toward me (McDougall, 1985, p. 279). She expressed this duplicity through her unrelenting and rejecting asexual behavior toward her husband and her dramatization of her "hopelessness as a patient," her unwillingness to be cured, and her secret wish to remain "father's little girl" in bed. I said that by living out these fantasies she had created "two saintly parents," her husband and myself, whom she kept apart and whom she tried to control through this behavior. The excessive overstimulation in childhood and possible seductive experiences with her father had prompted her to hide her excitement, to play-act, lie, and take on a stance of duplicitous behavior toward each of her parents; she now relived this with her husband and with me. Maureen's behavior represented an attempt to hold on to her fantasies of infantile gratification from her father, which presumably she had actually experienced in childhood.

Maureen's manipulations of her environment grew out of a lack of a cohesive self. Maureen's perversion appeared to be a psychoticlike symptom confined to the sexual area. In her second analysis, she developed a capacity for giving up some of her narcissistic fantasies about controlling her environment and getting special treatment. She began to be able to genuinely love her husband and to function extremely well in all areas of life, except sexually. In that area her duplicity, her secrecy, and her active fantasy life continued intermittently, increasingly interspersed by normal sexuality to the point that, when her sexual life had become very good, we had thought we could end her analysis. But as soon as separation from me had become a reality, a pervasive regression had taken place.

By that time, however, Maureen's perversion had become ego dystonic. The problem was how to get the healthy part of her sense of self to function in the service of analysis in the face of very strong opposition to cure, which Maureen herself came to call "my craziness about my sexuality." The perverse structure consisted of a fusion with her father and revenge against her mother, and was lived out in a fantasy of total exclusion of her husband in favor of her fantasies about her father during the sexual act: "I don't know who I am in bed" also meant "with whom." This alienation from the genuine part of her personality and her depersonalization during the sexual act was her way of preserving an organizing fantasy in which she and her father became a loving couple, but in which she could also remain his "very special little girl" and exclude and replace her mother. Prominent envious and jealous fantasies about me in the transference were derivatives of her feelings toward her mother. This problem had constituted the core of her perverse oedipal fantasies.

As Maureen's perversion receded, murderous rage surfaced toward her mother, her husband, her father, and toward me. While in the past her perverse fantasies and actions had permitted her to disavow her rage toward everyone, giving her the feeling that she could control all situations and that she would live forever, she now became increasingly aware of her fear of death. Her opposition to cure brought to light the full extent of her rage, revenge fantasies, and jealousy toward her mother, as well as toward me in the transference for having destroyed so many of her illusions. She felt I had robbed her, "stolen" her fantasy life. At the same time, she respected me for having been able to help her become honest, rather than duplicitous, by being able to see through her deceptions without condemning her. It was through these insights that her split values became unified, thereby decreasing her guilt feelings toward her parents.

Maureen could now understand the various strands of her perversion. The men with whom she had had promiscuous sexual relations had allowed her to merge with her father in unconscious fantasy. She could fantasize that she had his penis inside, which in turn had led to a total alienation from her female body. Her frigid genitalia were the "freezer" in which she had kept her father alive. Maureen had a childhood memory that her mother locked the bedroom door to keep her out when her father was asleep in the daytime, so that she would not disturb him, something she always wanted to do. She now was sure that her father had allowed her to touch him and maybe even stimulate his genitals when he was resting. I had the impression that if this indeed was a genuine memory there must have been an unconscious collusion on the part of her mother. In the dream in which she murders her father, her mother is present.

In recounting that dream, Maureen associated that separating from her father would be killing him; that she was needed to give him life. Putting him into the freezer was a way of preserving him. Cleansing herself of the semen, or "getting rid of the evidence" represented not knowing what to do after her father had ejaculated. She now told me, for the first time, that as an adult she had gone through a cleansing ritual after each sexual experience with a lover and now felt compelled to do this with her husband. In all these ways, the fantasy of keeping her father inside and taking revenge on her mother had been her basic resistance to the analytic process. As long as she had the fantasy that she needed to keep her father alive inside of her and needed to replace her husband with him, she could not hold on to her sexual gains in analysis and terminate treatment.

This work brought about a wish that she could find within herself "the sexual little girl I was in childhood before I lost all sexual feeling, before I became a 'corpse.' " I replied that to find the "sexual little girl" was not as difficult as she thought, because this is what she felt in bed with her husband when she fantasized that she was in bed with her father. Maureen then emphasized very strongly that with the help of analysis she had really loved someone deeply for the first time, namely her husband, except for the fact that she had hated him in bed. I repeated that she had made a desexualized, loving father of her husband, a father she had never had in childhood—a father with whom she could be a playful little girl without feeling overstimulated and frightened by her own excessive sexual arousal.

Preceding her termination phase, Maureen's hatred of her mother moved to the center of our work and accounted for her current fear of death. She had shared her mother's phobias and fantasies of bodily harm, which had inhibited her mobility as a young child. At the same time, Maureen resented her mother's lack of protection from the exposure to parental lovemaking and her father's sexual exhibitionism. Maureen had to work through these conflicts to lose her fear of death, to rediscover her love for her mother, to forgive her, and to reach the capacity for identification with her as a woman.

Maureen now became increasingly able to let these fantasies go and to relinquish her sexual perversion. She could then commit herself to her husband without being afraid that if she separated from me, one of us would die. This made it possible for her to terminate her analysis.

DISCUSSION

The analytic literature has described women with fetishistic tendencies, particularly where primal scene traumata play an important role, as needing the fantasy of using their sexual partner's penis as their own illusory phallus, which gratifies both sexual and hostile fantasies. Raphling (1989), Zavitzianos (1982), and Chasseguet-Smirgel (1984) all note cases of perversion in which, in Chasseguet-Smirgel's words, "the wish to steal the longed-for penis of the father . . . and to keep the love object, the father or his penis, inside herself, are prominent" (p. 170).

In normal oedipal development the sexual organs are sufficient to establish sexual union. In the perverse oedipal act, fantasies of aggression or castration precede the act of sexual gratification (McDougall, 1972). In the ordinary oedipal complex gender difference and incestuous fantasy have been established. In Maureen's case, the fantasy is bisexual and belongs to the phase of predifferentiation from mother and father. In her oedipal fantasies Maureen supplies the missing sexual part to each parent by "borrowing" it from the other. In the usual oedipal fantasy, more libidinal cathexis goes to the parent of the opposite sex and more ambivalence or hostility to the same-gender parent. In Maureen's case the oedipal fantasy contained an alternative solution related to each of her parents: she wants to receive from one and give to the other. Her sense of self was not expressed except in making these alternate exchanges. Her hostility was expressed in the manner in which in her fantasy the sexual organs are obtained.

The configuration of the father's seductive relationship with Maureen and her mother's "game" of buying padded bras led to gender identity confusion and promoted fixation on part objects that replaced fully internalized parental images. The padded bra originally introduced by Maureen's mother became a fetish. The ongoing overstimulation of being one of her father's "two girls" in the bedroom impeded Maureen's ability to differentiate herself from her mother and may have stunted the development of her ability to distinguish fact from fantasy—e.g., to distinguish observing the primal scene from being seduced herself. Thus, when Maureen reached the oedipal stage, an incomplete separation from her mother and a fixation on her sexualizing father facilitated the formation of the theft fantasy. Maureen's fantasies resembled more closely those of a perverse patient than those of a neurotic patient struggling with oedipal jealousies. Maureen's case highlights the fact that people who suffer from perversions also develop an oedipal constellation. In Maureen's case, the Oedipus complex became embedded in specific perverse fantasies that gave rise to her perversion and were traceable to the circumstances of her history.

The fantasy of genital theft—satisfying her mother with the penis stolen from her father, and her father with breasts stolen from her mother—defended Maureen against feeling helpless and overwhelmed in the bedroom and organized her deepest conflicts in adult life. She remained an incestuous bisexual fantasy participant in the primal scene and thereby gratified both positive and negative oedipal wishes, but in a perverse fantasy mode (McDougall, 1995, p. 177).

Loewald (1979) stated that incest destroys the oneness of mother–infant unity and the narcissistic bond within the family unit. Incest contains the exclusion and destruction of the third person in the triangle; a "hateful vengeance" (p. 396) is perpetrated on the incestuous object that is wanted or has responded to the rival. I believe that Maureen's theft fantasy exemplifies this hateful vengeance.

Initially, direct transference material was sparse. In that way, Maureen typified patients who suffer from a perverse character structure and psychopathic traits and who relive early traumata through perverse fantasies and enactments in the transference rather than through associations. One has to "read" the meaning of these enactments and wait to obtain verbal confirmation from the patient. Boesky (1982) has pointed out that action in analysis can be important as a form of communication (p. 46) and that "ontogenetically, action tends to precede thought" (p. 49). It was characteristic of Maureen's transference, in both her first and second analyses and the intervening psychotherapy, that enactments derived from the original traumata preceded discussion of fantasies or feelings related to the analyst. Following these perverse enactments or fantasies, a patient initially cannot integrate and internalize interpretations— such as in the case of Maureen's fantasy of being a transvestite male posing as a woman (Sandler and Sandler, 1978; see also chapter 7).

Analysis demonstrated to Maureen the degree to which her "bedroom behavior" had impinged on her reality testing and had led to self-destructive behavior, even in her marriage. When she had read pornographic literature or masturbated in front of the mirror, she had been attempting to recreate "the bedroom" both as an actor and as an observer. In analysis she began to experience "my way" as an advantage. (Originally this was "opportunistic"; only later was it internalized.) Gradually, internalization of the analytic experience made feminine identifications possible and led to psychic change. She realized she had needed her theft fantasies when she felt oedipal hatred, when she lacked the ability to feel and internalize love.

Before the analysis of her theft fantasy, she could not experience herself as a little girl who loved her father and may have wanted his baby. When she reached the stage in her second analysis when she could experience that, newly discovered vaginal experiences together with feelings of bodily interiority led to an increased capacity for internalization, which made Maureen more capable of loving.

In Maureen's first analysis, I had followed the neurotic model of treatment and dealt primarily with helping her develop better ego functions and become more reality oriented and more capable of functioning in the outside world. This work led to the establishment of the patient's autonomy and individuation and to her wish to function on her own. Today, the mechanisms of Maureen's perversion would have been much clearer to me much sooner. As it was, these mechanisms became clear only in the second analysis. The perverse and transvestite fantasies underlying Maureen's promiscuity were not sufficiently understood in her first analysis. In her second analysis, when her perversion became more evident, it became clear that my earlier, classical model of analysis required some modification.

As Stoller (1975) emphasized, perversion consists of the pursuit of gratification through hostility and vengeance designed to deny and defend against frightening sexual curiosity, mystery, and danger that surround the traumatic attachment to the mother (p. 429)—and, we may add, in this case also the father.

Chasseguet-Smirgel's emphasis (1986, p. 141) on the magical attempt to deny infantile traumata by creating omnipotent fantasies to ward off the fear of the menacing and archaic maternal image was certainly true for Maureen. The majority of psychoanalytic writings on perversions emphasize the enormous threat the maternal figure poses for the child who later develops a perversion. Submitting to her through helpless passivity or through feeling dead in order not to feel pain creates these fantasies in order to help deny that the mother has hurt or can hurt the child. The child says, as Cooper (1991) points out, "(1) She doesn't exist, (2) I don't exist, and (3) I force her (to give me pleasure)" (p. 24). As Cooper further notes:

> The perverse exhibiting woman uses her capacity to excite a male by the sight of her breast or body to overcome her own sense of small-ness and unfemininity compared to her mother, as well as to demon-strate the greater power of her breast or whole body compared to the male penis. The sexual excitement she experiences in this triumph

involves the dehumanization of her own body and that of the male's as well as the symbolic murder of the mother. The fetishistic object is not a phallus but a breast. In fact, one can raise the question whether fantasies of the huge breast do not underlie the fantasies of the ← phallus in fetishism [pp. 30–31].

In Maureen's case both the breasts and the phallus were fetishistic objects that permitted her to feel sexual.

Bach (1994) has stated eloquently how the profound libidinal deadness in this type of pathology is traceable to a defective libidinization in the early mother–child relationship. He also suggested that when this is brought into the transference and analyzed, there is a danger that the therapeutic alliance may break off. This tendency was certainly apparent in Maureen's oscillations between cooperation and resistance.

Classical psychoanalysis held that perverts cannot love because they do not reach genitality. Martin Bergmann (1987) has shown that love and sexuality have different lines of development. People fixated at pregenital developmental levels may be capable of loving, but the nature of their love is different from that of individuals who have reached genitality. The capacity to love is based on a long development of internalized object relations and their stable representations. Perverts can also love, but only with the grown-up part of themselves.

Maureen's analysis eventually led to the emergence of a significant difference in her capacity to love. In her second analysis, a gradual desexualization of her relationship with her father (which had become understandable through her dreams), a greater capacity for symbolization, and a newly found quality and depth of love for her husband led her to abandon her former sexual preoccupations.

Because of Maureen's need to dissociate periodically from a part of herself, particularly in sexual situations, but also in analytic treatment, she remained for a long time unable to mourn the losses she had experienced throughout her life, particularly her previous psychological inability to have children. As long as she needed to disclaim those aspects of herself that had become attached to a defense against infantile traumata, she was unable to go through the process of mourning in analysis. When this process finally took place, it was extremely painful for her but ultimately culminated in a sense of triumph and pride in all she had been able to master. She said repeatedly that by relinquishing her perversion she had "joined the human race."

Part III

Trauma and Retraumatization in Clinical Work

7.

Thoughts on Superego Pathology in Survivors and Their Children

The Holocaust experience of patients has been found to constitute a powerful paradigm for the study of universal phenomena related to trauma. In the vast literature on trauma, insufficient attention has been given to the superego structure of the traumatized victim, to superego functioning after the external traumatic agent has ceased to exist, and to the transmission of parental superego pathology to the second generation.

This chapter will address some of these issues, focusing on my own work on superego pathology transmitted by traumatized Holocaust parents to their children in their reconstituted families after the war. Not all survivors reacted to their camp experiences and other traumata in the manner I will describe here, nor did all their children. Nor is the need to externalize events from a painful past and relive them repeatedly specific to these cases. Many case reports have demonstrated, however, that as soon as survivors of the Holocaust had created a new family, a "holding environment" in Winnicott's sense (1965), they internally confronted their traumatic losses once again.

After the war, a new environment provided survivors with a non-punitive affective milieu for the reliving of traumata. It furnished a less threatening atmosphere, in which survivors could test and internalize new experiences, newfound capacities for mirroring, and selective identifications with objects. Under these conditions, perceptions and affective experiences could be validated afresh. When traumatic events related to the Holocaust past resurfaced (sometimes after years of suppression) and were subjected to reality testing in a saner and more stable environment, a thread to the pre-Holocaust past could be restored.

In an attempt at "self-healing," traumatized people generally use their families as a means of psychic recovery, to a far greater extent than less traumatized individuals do. In most Holocaust cases studied, two major fantasies were transmitted from parent to child. In the first, the child is a replacement for a beloved lost family member—a child, a parent, an idealized relative. In the second fantasy, the child has a special mission: his or her life is to be devoted to restoring family pride by personal achievement, thereby healing past injuries.

Parents subjected to Holocaust experiences frequently relived their experiences, or their memories of events from the past, which now were overshadowed by fantasies and colored by illusions. These fantasies were threaded into current reality and affected the parents' interactions with their children, whom they frequently cast in roles belonging to a reality, now long past, that they unconsciously wished to restore. Children were unconsciously expected to undo affectively charged traumata that had damaged a parent's psychic structure and destroyed superego guidelines and functions. Themes of disillusionment related to a formerly cohesive ego ideal were prominent.

A fantasy role of a narcissistic nature is cast upon survivors' children: by being special, they have to make up for the traumatic losses, disappointments, shame, and defeat that had led the parents to narcissistic self-devaluation. The children's success thus plays a decisive role in establishing a new, coherent value system, with new ideals for the parents: the children are expected to develop identical values.

The psychic picture described here is found not just in Holocaust survivors but in traumatic parent–child relationships affected by other religious or ethnic persecutions that have led to genocide. Both persons traumatized by genocidal events and their children will create personal myths or fantasies different from those of people who have experienced other forms of traumatization. This mythmaking serves to contain memories from the past and may have the function of preserving a traumatic screen (Kris, 1956) hiding massive amounts of anxiety, personal symptomatology, or hostility unleashed by brutalization. Hillel Klein (1981) has stated that every survivor can be expected to create a personal myth about his or her traumatization.

When people are engaged in mythmaking and magical ↤ thinking, only a certain portion of their ego capacities and cognitive processes are turned toward present-day reality. Mythmaking distorts current reality and influences survivor-parents in their displacement of affect, which is then transmitted to their children. The relation of the self to reality has been altered and frequently expresses itself in nonverbal behavior and in concrete acts symbolizing internal conflicts. Mythmaking is related to coping mechanisms deployed both during and after traumatization. Myths may not be the same for survivors and their children, but both have great difficulty comprehending the Holocaust trauma as actually experienced.

I propose the hypothesis that the unconscious need of the survivor-parent to put a child into the role of replacing a lost loved one, and consequently to respond with merciless threats toward the child who seems to fail this mission, rests on *values that have become externalized so as not to be lost.* Reenacted in the new family milieu, these values, in order to be preserved (a variation on repetition in the service of mastering trauma), are displaced onto the child *and thereby retained.* Externalization and concretization of thinking and action in favor of fantasy help to preserve an established value system and to protect it from being lost as a result of trauma.

As survivors' children are drawn into the parents' psychic reality, superego and ego ideal elements constitute a central organizing principle of their involvement in parental readaptation. This involvement interferes with development of the child's self representation and the autonomy of the child's developing superego and ego ideal. Boundaries between the generations are thereby lost.

Parent–child interaction cannot be explained as having had the *purpose* of self-healing. However, traumatized parents under the sway of the repetition compulsion who were in treatment were observed as having been unconsciously motivated to use their new objects— primarily their children—to confront traumatic themes from the past and to recathect a new world through interaction with their children, so that new coping mechanisms related to internal structure and external phenomena could develop.

Pre- and post-Holocaust themes merge in survivors that lead them to misread the motivations of others and to become confused in interpreting reality. Thus, a reality-testing burden is placed on their children, who are slated to rectify the horrors the parents have brought to light. Not only parental needs but also confusions are transmitted to the children, particularly where "the pact of silence" prevents verbalization and explanation of past experiences. Thus, the children's uncertainty increases, and the ground is prepared for the emergence of flourishing fantasies.

In many children of survivors, a sense of pressure to return to the survivor-parent what he or she has lost is transmitted and creates overwhelming feelings shared by the children. Tasks are imposed on the survivor's child at the expense of the development of an independent self. Because of this ongoing conflict, the parent–child bond frequently turns into a hostile obligation, creating a lasting hostile bond in which the child's superego structure motivates the child to fulfill parental needs. Only an intrapsychic act of separation from an imposed fate can free the child; a new freedom from a shared bond of survivor's guilt can strengthen the child's separate identity, feelings of healthy narcissism, and consolidate a sense of autonomy.

SUPEREGO FUNCTIONS UNDER THE IMPACT OF TRAUMATIZATION

We have learned from Freud that under favorable conditions the superego has an organizing function, promoting ego development and reality testing (Freud, 1923, 1926; Jacobson, 1964; Stein, 1966) and prohibiting certain unconscious impulses from reaching consciousness.

Despite the great variety of social, cultural, and pathological problems found to characterize the human condition throughout the world, unconscious drive-related id wishes are predictably few: they are incestuous, cannibalistic, and murderous. They encompass the sexual wishes of the Oedipus complex and those of earlier regressive needs, bisexual wishes, and perversions. The superego does not permit possession of the oedipal love object or removal of the rival. The superego also suppresses revenge fantasies and narcissistic triumphs; the latter are often based on omnipotent or megalomaniacal fantasies, with themes of frustrating experiences between the self and early objects.

Whether expressed in developmental, phase-specific terms, in terms of object relations that may have led to developmental fixations, or as intrapsychic conflicts or symptoms, these themes are predictably few. Although specificity of meaning needs to be clarified in the therapeutic work with each patient, love–hate wishes, splits, or unconscious fantasies defensively isolated from each other remain guarded by the superego and do not become conscious with their full implications, except possibly in some psychotic conditions. In the analysis of neurotic patients, unconscious fantasies appear as derivatives of id impulses, and conflicts reach consciousness only as a result of arduous therapeutic work.

Unconscious sadistic wishes normally forbidden by the superego emerge in the treatment of children of Holocaust survivors with a great deal of pain and under the aegis of the therapeutic alliance. Usually, however, these sadistic fantasies, even when the children are identifying with their parents' persecutors, seem never to have included specific detail of the Nazis' most unspeakable excesses, such as the making of soap from human beings or lampshades from their skin, or the use of gas ovens for mass murder. It is not clear whether most people successfully repress their most archaic or paranoid fantasies or whether their unconscious wishes simply do not contain such elements in the first place.

EFFECTS OF MASSIVE TRAUMATIZATION ON THE PSYCHIC STRUCTURE OF HOLOCAUST SURVIVORS

Observers of massive traumatization and its effects on the survivors' psychic structure reported muted affects, sometimes to the extent of depressive reactions, sexual dysfunction, psychosomatic symptoms, phobic states, or paralysis resembling a catatonic state. There was a generally diminished capacity to use ego functions, to anticipate and register anxiety-producing situations, and to judge perceptions related to reality. There was affect withdrawal to the point of depersonalization and destruction of feelings of individual identity; cognitive regression; and a marked loss of a sense of time and causality (Krystal, 1968; Krystal and Niederland, 1971; Grubrich-Simitis, 1979). Without the reliable use of the anxiety signal for the registration of potential danger, the camp survivor gradually moved from a hyperalert state forever ready to register a danger of death, to a state of inhibition and blocked emotions (Sandler, 1967; Krystal and Niederland, 1971).

A constant state of terror (Stern, 1959) overwhelmed the intactness of ego functions and threatened their extinction (Keiser, 1967). Impaired verbalization of emotions lowered or abolished entirely the capacity for symbolization, and fantasy formation became impaired or came to a halt. Krystal (1978) has pointed out how the settling in of the chronic traumatic state, with its numbing and closing off of affects, affords a certain relief from constant pain and anxiety to the persecuted individual.

The survivor's way of life centers on the here and now rather than on the future. While the survivor's own aggression is minimized experientially because experiencing it has become too dangerous to deal with, there is simultaneously an ever-present focus on escaping from death. Sometimes the belief in an existence after death modifies anxiety. Often a narcissistic gain is taken in having survived one more day (DeWind, 1968).

Under the aegis of death anxiety, functions become automatized, and an inability to relate to others becomes manifest. A marked loss of empathy (Grubrich-Simitis, 1979), and with it a blockage of the mourning process, follows loss of the capacity to relate to other individuals.

With loss of basic trust and healthy narcissism toward one's own self, hostility is readily turned against the self. The first signs of fragmentation and regression in the capacity to symbolize brings with it a loss of necessary self-protection and alertness for survival. Sometimes this regressive process leads to developing a "psychomotoric" organism, whose automatized functions are the first signs of impending death. There were, however, concentration camp inmates who, after a period of deepest regression, experienced a reorganization that permitted a part of the personality to be reawakened libidinally and become directed toward survival once more (DeWind, 1968).

In the concentration camp, massive assaults of hostility from an external source created an affective disturbance of overstimulation that constituted a central ongoing strain trauma: whatever sadistic fantasies or retaliatory wishes may have broken through from within the individual psyche needed to be suppressed. In addition, the signal function to respond adequately to imminent danger or violence from environmental dangers had lost its reliable anticipatory function to protect the individual. Thus, the individual psyche found itself helpless and unprepared, and the superego's normal function of protective guardianship became ineffective. Familiar moral guidelines proved useless. A constant fear of death became the basis for registration of affects and external perceptions. A curtailed capacity for verbal communication and symbolic function robbed the self and object representations of their uniqueness. As a result, self-protective narcissistic self-love and a useful sense of identity gave way to identification with the rules of the aggressor, which created a new system of anticipation geared toward survival.

This extraordinary capacity for adaptation among those who survived may be explained in part by the creation of what I have termed an "emergency morality." Self-renunciation, which had the advantage of creating distance between victimizer and victim, so that disaster could sometimes be anticipated and avoided (at least in the short run), was a means to a new type of self-protection. When successful, this emergency "moral code" apparently was learned without feelings of disillusionment or hostility toward the person's own internal parental representations. In the case histories studied, this disillusionment and resentment surfaced only decades later, after the survivor had established a new family. The traumatic reactions, silenced for years by the survivors' "emergency morality," were then revived and projected onto members of the new, reconstituted family, particularly the children.

Three brief vignettes, retold by two colleagues from personal experience, highlight the gradual unfolding of this "emergency morality." They demonstrate how within the concentration camp one needed to suppress empathy toward others in order to become less vulnerable, and how only through secret assistance, mostly from the outside, as well as by mutual aid among concentration camp inmates, a certain amount of narcissistic self-love could be maintained and aid in one's survival.

One colleague recounted the following: "When I was first taken to the concentration camp I wore a suit with a warm jacket, and another woman had on a summer dress. She was very cold and asked to borrow my jacket, which I gave her. When she felt warm, she returned it. Two months later I thought, 'Now she would not have asked for the jacket anymore, and I would not have lent it to her.' " This colleague also remembered a woman "ladling out food which passed for soup. On the bottom there were a few pieces of meat. I thought: 'On this meat one could avoid starvation.' The woman skillfully kept the pieces of meat until the end and ate them herself. I was infuriated. Then I thought: 'Why shouldn't *she* survive instead of someone else?' "

Another colleague reported, at the IPA Congress in Jerusalem in 1977, that there was a great premium on having books smuggled into camp. They aided in preserving a person's intellectual identity as a counterforce against Nazi barbarism. He said: "I often thought as long as I can read Goethe I know I am not crazy."

It is likely that this emergency morality gradually converted into a "moral absolutism" (Piaget, 1932) based on a regression to superego precursors and a fear of external authority. Primitive, magical, and unrealistic identifications, experienced within an ever narrowing frame, were used to protect one's psychic core from injury and death. It would seem that the pressure of this atmosphere of danger and torture, brought about by the constant use of violent force, led the victims toward reexternalization of formerly internalized superego representations. After liberation, the superego of the survivor was often left in a precarious state, in danger of further regression and lack of differentiation from others. Against this danger the victims undertook a series of defensive maneuvers in the environment.

SUPEREGO PATHOLOGY IN THE POSTWAR FAMILY OF THE SURVIVOR

Before evaluating case material, we must ask how superego functions and pathology can be assessed. The ego is known by its functions and is closer to consciousness than is the superego. The id is known by drive derivatives, affects, impulses, and fantasies. In order to assess the level and quality of superego functioning vis-à-vis other objects, the following questions helped to assess superego pathology:

Are there superego lacunae?

Is there a capacity to experience guilt when causing injury?

Does one differentiate between acts and wishes, and is self-punishment as severe for the former as for the latter?

Does the person wish to evoke guilt?

Does the superego give a warning signal before one commits prohibited acts, or does one realize consequences and dangers of such acts only in retrospect?

Does one experience feelings of love from one's superego, or is the superego only a criticizing agency?

In many Holocaust patients, superego functions appeared to be more disturbed than ego functions: many survivors could function adequately in the external world, but other people's motivations or value judgments, or an encounter with an unfamiliar environmental phenomenon left many of them in a confused state.

The superego structure of the survivor-parent was frequently found to have undergone severe destruction by exposure to Nazi ideology. In many case histories, splitting of self and objects within superego representations became manifest: at times the survivor-parent identified with Nazi morality but also condemned it. Because of such splitting, parental messages toward children were often confused.

Ego ideal pathology also had to be considered and the following questions asked: To what extent does the survivor project his or her disillusionment onto the children? How is the Holocaust theme transmitted by parental demands to restore the narcissistically injured self-image of the parent? Does the survivor's child feel that he or she cannot aspire to fulfill the ideals set by the parents?

Independence and autonomy from both the parental authority and the social group depend, as a rule, on the extent to which the superego has been internalized. In survivors' children, the strain trauma of upbringing by survivor-parents disturbed internalization processes and led to external behavior that was destructive or self-destructive.

Externalization of aspects of the superego and ego ideal put many of the values and goals of survivors' children into a utopian realm, leaving the children dependent on parents and external authority figures for approval.

In reconstituting their families with a new generation of children, many Holocaust victims experienced yet another shift of values, as new norms of behavior were created. In the traumatic past of the concentration camp, signal affect and wordless behavior substituted for language and resulted in the loss of symbolic functions: in the new family, typically, parents were outspoken in making demands on the children, who often were identified with exterminated family members; in a resurrection fantasy, a child might have been required to live up to expectations the parents had had for a lost child. The new child tended to acquiesce, feeling that he or she owed a debt simply for being alive.

THE SURVIVOR'S CHILD

The survivor's child has come into a family of parents who, before their persecution and since, lived in a world before the child was born, a world described as having provided a sense of belonging, a chance for personal achievement, and "ideal children." This world (which in memory seemed like an idealized dream) was suddenly lost and replaced by cruelty, loss of loved ones, and a constant fear of death.

The miracle of the parent's survival led to the miracle of the survivor's child's birth. As a rule, the fact that parents and children are alive is taken for granted by both. But survivor-parents frequently remained incredulous that they were alive, an idea they transmitted to their children. A child in such a family did not take existence for granted and felt "special"—an exception (Jacobson, 1959).

Such a child felt that one has to "pay" for having been born and surviving when so many others had been killed. A fantasy that puts a child into the role of a lost child eventually becomes concretized in certain life goals or practices. As a result, survivors' children identified with dead or lost children (as transmitted in parental narratives), who then also became part of the new child's self representation in superego and ego ideal.

In spite of the fact that survivors' children were Jews, we noted in our studies a strikingly frequent identification with Christ. One may venture a guess that the recurring fantasy in which a survivor's child identified with the suffering Christ suggested an identification not only with an innocent victim who suffered and died for the crimes of others, but with a child miraculously born, who in later life would fulfill a destiny of saving others. Christ's miracles reduced suffering and redeemed the worthy. He took over the fate of the victims, setting them free. Identification with Christ also offered a successful momentary silencing of hostile parent–child interactions, comparable with Freud's description (1921) of the beloved and idealized leader to whom the group submits uncritically. Its members are allowed a temporary relief from sin, as he takes responsibility for all their actions.

A survivor's child who has taken a deceased child or other lost family member into the self representation is unconsciously attempting to establish a bridge to the traumatized parents' inner life. In a shared unconscious fantasy the child takes on the parents' conviction that deceased family members are superior to the living. To establish an enduring emotional tie to the parents, the child has to submerge his or her narcissistic strivings and individual wishes and instead share parental fantasies, often of an idealized dead child, that are kept alive within the family. This process transforms the new child's ego ideal. That the survivor's child has come to share the parental fantasy is manifested by attempts to resemble the dead child or other lost person, at times even in physical ways. In both parent and child, a fantasy becomes entrenched in which the lost child is seen as having been more lovable. The new child maintains a sense of self as lovable or narcissistically valued only by trying to fulfill the destiny of the lost child. Yet it is impossible to compete with an idealized rival whose sins have all been paid for by death. Thus, the dead child becomes a hated "sibling" who destroys the autonomy of the new child's ego ideal. A genuine ego ideal can develop only after resolving survivor's guilt, shared with the parents, and after a severing of the legacy of commitment to the dead. Shared fantasies that sacrificed the child's autonomy to preserve the parents' value system were found to have led in some parents to narcissistic self-healing.

When shared fantasies become entrenched during the growth process, an unconscious narcissistic union with the parents makes survivors' children rescuers of dead brothers or sisters. In addition, parental goals set for the living child's future are expected to be carried out and are not looked upon as mere wishes. The child hopes to restore narcissistic defects (engendered by parental expectations and by survivors' guilt) through bringing new honor to the parents by trying to fulfill their expectations and replace what the parents have lost (a variant on Freud's categories in "On Narcissism" [1914a]). It is possible that the superior capacity for adaptability and achievement in many survivors' children has been motivated by unconscious adaptation to such parental goals and by the wish to obtain the love they thought had earlier been bestowed on a child now dead.

Identification with the parent's past through a shared fantasy concerning a dead person may provoke the child to become a victim and to develop masochistic fantasies. The survivor's child then may become self-destructive instead of destructive. Destructiveness toward the parent and straightforward hostility are often impossible for the survivor's child to express because of constant awareness of the parent's suffering. In addition, survivor-parents had difficulty helping the child learn impulse control because they had lost the scale of values related to expressions of hostility and deprivation. Thus, in severity of punishment, they fluctuated between undue pressure and excessive leniency. The severity of superego pressures sometimes led to psychopathic traits in the children, who frequently were found to believe that their parents had survived because they "got away with something."

As the parents placed the child in a restitutional role early in life, it could be assumed that magical expectations toward self and parents lived on in archaic fantasies and as part of the psychic reality of the growing child. Although survivors' children grew up under specially imposed superego pressures colored by rescue fantasies, they also rebelled against these pressures. Shared fantasies, while active, curbed hostile aggression, reduced the child's guilt toward the parents, and promoted object constancy, loyalty toward the dead, and an adaptation toward a life that became a substitute for mourning.

Through their fear of object loss and their use of the child to retain their values, the parents discouraged efforts to separate. Archaic superego identifications, shared with the parents, carried feelings of victimization and narcissistic injury, and heightened the intrapsychic conflict of the child by strengthening incestuous ties. Thus, having to be special in order to fulfill a parent's unrealized wishes, instead of one's own destiny, interferes with individuation during rapprochement and, later, in the preoedipal and oedipal stages, and with the formation of an oedipal and postoedipal superego. The oedipal fantasy becomes infused with themes of aggression and magical goals stemming from the myth of the parental past. Thus, triangulation is impeded by hostility and guilt "imported" from an earlier, fantasized reality.

In the survivor's child, therefore, empathy and identification with the parent as a persecuted victim, or as a Nazi aggressor, led to splitting of both ego and superego representations. Frequently the child could not idealize the parent who was victimized, particularly if the child had witnessed the latter in a subservient role vis-à-vis a government official or other authority.

Once parental authority is devalued, the superego cannot internalize the parent as a self-protective agent. A fantasy often found in survivors' children, that they ought to be given special privileges or dispensations, stems most likely from the feeling of having been unprotected by a reliable parent. In this way, a reciprocal conflict was established: a defeated parent required the child to restore honor and strength to the family; but if the child suffered from premature disillusionment in the parent as an idealized and protective force (Jacobson, 1937), the child felt disappointed and unable to act in meeting parental needs.

ON TRYING TO BE A DEAD, BELOVED CHILD

When Holocaust traumatization is transmitted by the parents, the child may reproject onto the environment superego components that initially were internalized. This seems to occur particularly when the child has identified with parental suffering and losses.

The child who is psychotic may develop messianic delusions. In a nonpsychotic survivor's child, the fantasy may be somatized, as in the case of "Rachel" (see Kestenberg, 1982), who felt that she had to carry the Jews of the world inside her stomach in order to protect them. Many survivors' children, whether primarily neurotic or afflicted by a more damaged psychic structure, give evidence of phobic states and anxieties stemming from an effort to either implement or reject the tormenting tasks imposed on them by their parents. Frequently hostility created by these pressures turns into passivity, a stance of victimization in identification with dead children, so that the parents' fantasies of restitution cannot be fulfilled. Alternatively, a conflict may ensue when the child "goes along" with the parents' wishes by striving for an exalted career, thus making the idealization of dead children a personal task. Because of its role-playing aspect, however, such a course may interfere with development of a sense of identity and so may result in a fragmented psychic reality.

A patient named Aaron reported he had felt overwhelmed by having to take the place of a dead relative. It appeared to his analyst that in identifying with his family, Aaron was genuinely mourning relatives he had never known. The patient described how an atmosphere of loss prevailed at home. One relative demonstrated a constant preoccupation with death and performed compulsive rituals to avoid any thought of it. In love-making, Aaron treated his lover as though he were holding a dead body. He sexualized death. He suffered from obsessive dreams that revealed his wish that the family members who had cast him in the role of dead relatives might die themselves. Aaron found it difficult to succeed in his career; an exalted profession had been chosen for him, but he was afraid to become successful, as he had the conviction (a conscious fantasy) that success puts a person on the side of the Nazis.

A variant on this theme has been observed in cases where a living parent behaves as if already dead—an attitude that undermines the child's capacity for communication with the parent and may create verbal and cognitive disturbances from early child-hood on. The child will feel guilty at any opportunity to enjoy life. When one parent behaves as if already dead, the child may develop difficulties in thinking and reality testing. Frequently an identification hunger (Greenson, 1958) with people who feel alive sets in.

Rachel said, "If none of my family is alive, how come I'm alive?" This patient alternated between bodily feelings that confirmed life and others that confirmed for her that she was already dead. She also fantasized that she represented a dead beloved relative, and that she had a life to lead in which she would rescue not only this relative but all the Jews who needed to be saved.

Another patient, Edna, a young woman who was attempting to help her father mourn his first wife and their dead children, whom he had lost in the Holocaust, tried to come closer to him emotionally by working in a morgue and washing the dead. At one point she joined a group of people who performed a chanting and dancing ritual in a cemetery. She was fascinated by the suffering of the tormented Christ and loved pictures in which he was portrayed as having been cruelly beaten and as bleeding and about to die. She admired painters of the suffering Christ, such as Matthias Grünewald—particularly his painting of the suffering Madonna. The patient expressed her oedipal relationship with her father by attempting in symbolic ways to be close to him and experience what he had lost. She expressed the feeling that in these ways and by certain sublimations—her studies—she could help her father carry his grief.

Leah's survivor-father had a habit of communicating with the dead on the Sabbath in a kind of gibberish, a language he had created himself that was not meant to be understood by his living family. It seemed to be a private communication with those he had once known. Leah felt very excluded. In a state of great longing for her father, she took medication and alcohol and had herself hospitalized in a confused state. In her therapist's judgment, she was not psychotic, though it was difficult to convince the hospital staff that this was true. The therapist sensed, and Leah later confessed, that out of a deep longing for closeness with her father she had tried to enter the world where her father communicated with the dead "in gibberish." By talking an incoherent language, as if in a trance, she hoped to reach him in the innermost aspects of his former but still present world.

Concrete action can lend an aura of reality to the fantasy that a dead person or idealized parent is part of oneself. Sometimes, however, it gives credibility to a fantasy that the opposite is true, that one can be a rebel and avoid becoming part of a dead person. Herzog (1982) has called some aspects of concretization via fantasy a "world beyond metaphor"—a particularly apt term for designating a temporary loss of symbolic capacity and its translation into external action. Such action often expressed, in however coded a fashion, is a central aspect of a major trauma.

"LITTLE HITLER"

Survivors of concentration camps have frequently called their children "little Hitler" when the child was hostile or misbehaved. Such parental behavior may stem not only from identification of the child with an internalized image of the aggressor, but from an attempt to externalize a disavowed aspect of the parental self representation, internalized under extreme stress, when identification with the aggressor was the only available means for adaptation and survival. It is now known that survivors of concentration camps usually identified with both the aggressor and fellow victims. This is documented clinically by transference fantasies and projections in which either patient or analyst came to be seen as the Nazi in conflictual situations involving hostility.

The feeling state (expressed by parents via projective identification) that gives rise to the image of "little Hitler" naturally varies in each family. In many cases, once the parents were in treatment they realized that their child was a "little Hitler" only in their own minds. While reliving the camp atmosphere may be an attempt to teach the child survival mechanisms, it translates a former experience into a concrete mode. Since hostility had to be suppressed in order to survive, aspects of the camp atmosphere that made normal interaction and object relationships impossible motivated this hostile reliving and the projection of hostility onto the children.

When the child identifies with and then externally acts out the role of internalized parental images, it appears as if he or she becomes the parent of his or her own parent (see chapters 1 and 2). This may happen when the survivor's child identifies, or is being identified, with the *victimizer* of the parent. Children who were rebellious and called "little Hitlers" were also warned that if they did not make good their parents would suffer a fate worse than under the Nazis. Children raised under such pressures gave evidence of great inner conflict and confusion.

In reliving Holocaust traumata, the parents needed to feel that even if they expressed rage repeatedly, it would not be lethal for their children. Outbreaks of rage appeared to be an active reliving of passively experienced hostile assaults suffered in a ghetto or camp. However, parents might also feel that the treatment they had suffered had been their own fault. They would then need to expiate their guilt so that superego pressures would relent, a need frequently expressed in treatment. Feelings aroused by victimization can be shed only by masochistic surrender, self-destruction, or special "tortures" or "labors" to be borne with the aim of being pronounced "not guilty." Under the impact of internal pressures that have led to traumatic reliving, the sadistic component of the superego becomes externalized and converted into acts of discharge against contemporaries through practices and rituals aimed at expiation. This becomes a moral code that is then transmitted to the survivor's child. The readiness to suffer passively when assaulted has a long tradition in Jewish history:

The Talmud began to develop in the first traumatic period of Jewish powerlessness, after the destruction of the Second Temple. The rabbis addressed themselves, not just to timeless pieties but by political indirection also to the political realities confronting them so as to evolve an appropriate posture and modus vivendi that would ensure Jewish survival. "Belong ever to the persecuted rather than to the persecutors," the Talmud taught. "God loves the person persecuted and hates the persecutors." To compensate for lost natural autonomy, the religious tradition, making a virtue of necessity, elevated powerlessness into a positive Jewish value (Davidowicz, 1975, p. 465).

When parents and child relived the parents' survival mechanisms, the child unconsciously hoped to save the parents through this participation. A restitutional fantasy, even if totally unrealizable, often acted as an organizer of the child's psychic motivational life—even in a child who alternated between rebellion and submission in an expression of inner conflict. The restitutional fantasy represented an unconscious wish to save the parents. Thus, the child was made a part of an expiation ritual which, it was hoped, would in turn ensure his or her own survival.

SHARED SUPEREGO PATHOLOGY

Concretization

Normal identification from the preoedipal and oedipal periods, formed from abandoned object cathexes (Freud, 1917), leads to internalization, desexualization, and deaggressivization of objects and to consolidation of the psychic structure and thereby to a more adaptive superego formation.

In survivors, however, a sudden assault on the personality from a force in the external world led to traumatization in which once stable internalizations were weakened or destroyed. Excessive hostile assaults on individuals created traumatic overstimulation. An unconscious link between external arousals and the individual's own unconscious sadistic fantasies promoted splitting mechanisms and heightened sexualization, preoedipal regressions, or perversions. Thus damaged, the superego became unable to protect the personality from within. As emphasized earlier in this chapter, it seemed that for survivor-parents the process of externalizing the past created a mechanism for preserving a needed link to their pretraumatic past. This need led to the expression of psychic conflicts and fantasies in a *concrete* mode.

It has been observed repeatedly that massive traumatization can weaken or destroy the capacity for fantasy formation. This may be the reason so many fantasies shared between survivor-parents and their children had to be concretized and lived out before an affective connection to their inner representations, one with symbolic meaning, could once again become part of the survivor's psychic reality, or be established in the survivor's child for the first time. When this succeeded, however, new internalization processes could gradually replace tendencies toward concretization and hostile enactment.

The behavioral phenomenon defined here as *concretization* refers to fantasies lived out, grafted onto the environment, and woven into current reality, rather than being verbalized. This action contains unconsciously expressed themes from the original trauma. Concretized fantasy enactments may symbolize *re*animation or *de*animation—bringing one back to life, or "making" someone dead. Kestenberg (personal communication, 1981) has commented that the superego has a "wooden quality" when the person is given to concretization. She described one case (Kestenberg, 1980) in which everything had to be analyzed from at least two points of view, with Holocaust fantasies more entrenched than other fantasies. She commented that because of their concreteness, sadistic attitudes tended to invade a patient's superego in a concrete fashion. *It is my hypothesis that concretization occurs when reality appears worse than fantasy; action, it is hoped, will ameliorate or undo a terrible reality, or help deny it.*

Concretizing an unbearable situation is an assertion of omnipotent control over what cannot be tolerated. This helps in denying hostility engendered by experiences of loss, by traumatizing exposure to sadistic experiences, or by the struggle against sadistic fantasies. Concrete action creates a situation that appears to be under the person's control and that, in its wishful aspects, suppresses rage and anxiety.

It is characteristic of concretizing activity that an important person is unconsciously assigned a role and that a particular response is solicited in interaction with that person (Sandler and Sandler, 1978). A current object relationship is used to relive traumatic aspects of an earlier one. A defensive externalization contains an unconscious dialogue with objects and carries an important affective message; sometimes a projection of inner feelings onto the environment, or an actual manipulation of the environment, serves to validate fantasy. There may be a loss of differentiation between death wishes and frightening external events; that is, between psychic and external reality.

When a hostile person becomes equated with a Nazi or with Hitler, internal conflict has lost its capacity to be expressed symbolically. Confusions between past and present, fantasy and reality, internal and external, abound; external reality becomes drive-laden and overstimulating. Under such conditions the protective and anticipatory functions of the superego become paralyzed. Reprojecting problems into the realm of external interaction with objects may permit some discharge of frightening affects and can substitute for the loss of more reliable internal defenses. Survivors' children often respond to the primal scene by having sadistic or perverse fantasies about past parental activity, including fantasies that their parents appeased the Nazis by having sexual relations with an overseer or guard, which accounted for their survival. Survivors' children may not recognize these as fantasies; rather, fantasies thus concretized, by their excessively frightening and over-stimulating nature, attain the status of a conviction. Concretization facilitated by the "pact of silence" prevented the parents' Holocaust past from being discussed with the children and thereby gave aspects of reality an unreal cast.

Mourning

Freud (1917) thought that in mourning one gradually detaches oneself from what is lost. When the work of mourning is done, life energy flows back into the self. It seems possible that in some cases survivors are so traumatized that their ability to detach themselves from external objects is lost and the mourning process therefore becomes impossible. Under normal conditions, the mourned external object becomes internalized; however, when the lost object is not mourned and its death is denied, other objects may be sought as substitutes. Restitutional behavior may then take the place of mourning (Loewald, 1962, p. 484).

Although survivors are often too traumatized to mourn lost loved ones, they engage in a variety of displacement mechanisms that might be called "substitute-for-mourning" mechanisms. Symbolic displaced actions, lived out with current real objects—their children—are unconsciously addressed to lost love objects. The survivor's child, when cast in the role of a deceased person, identifies with the parents' past, which the child shares in fantasy. In such a fantasy, expressed in symbolic acts, the child "resurrects" former objects in the service of mastering the parents' traumata. Mourning is thereby circumvented.

Concretization of the mourning process amalgamates past and present: the living out of roles assigned by parents to their children in external life situations in lieu of mourning lost loved ones, often represents a fantasy dialogue with an internal object who perished and has now been externalized. Externalization and concrete action ward off hostility against internal objects, particularly if such action has a symbolic content that in some way repeats traumatic events.

The concept of concretization used here includes actualization but is broader in scope. Although all persons may be inclined to act rather than verbalize in times of stress, traumatization gives the need for concretizing a particular urgency. Trauma lowers the capacity for cognitive and affective control; there is a regression in the capacity for symbolization and the use of words that favor action. A loss of cognitive capacity and an inability to express affect without reactivating a situation that contains the trauma in symbolic form may also occur. In their concretized form, traumatic themes may be expressed with excessive affect or no affect at all. Reality may be distorted as a means of expressing an inner need prompted by excessive internal pressure.

Paradoxically, a constant preoccupation with the deceased, with death and survival, makes the reality of actual death unreal as from day to day it becomes "a living reality" among members of the survivor's family. Excessive preoccupation with life and death may lead to magical acts that symbolize an undoing of what is most feared. When magical acts are expressed in concrete action, they disguise underlying anxieties. A patient who was attempting to help her parents work out what they had lost in the past, once said to her therapist, "My parents' history is more real to me than my own life."

When survivors' children mourn the sudden loss of their parents, internal representations of the parents become blurred or repressed. Since the traumatic losses parents transmitted to their children made internalization processes unstable, the mourning process may not occur. Instead, a search for the lost parental object may begin in the outside world. As this task proceeds, it replaces internal processes, particularly mourning and the stabilization of object ties. If guilt has been externalized, it perpetuates the fantasy that the dead person is alive, rendering mourning unnecessary.

As long as such fantasies are active, both parents and children can deny that family members were killed. When idealization of the dead takes the place of mourning, archaic fantasies related to the dead are taken into the superego and continue to influence affects and actions. Keeping the dead alive in fantasy necessitates concretizing action to "prove" they are still alive. Concretization, a kind of living in two realities, results in the splitting of ego and superego representations of both self and object.

Concretization has been found to be common among both traumatized survivors and their children. This mechanism seems to appear in the children as a result of the creation of shared fantasies with their parents. If fantasies are not shared with the parents, there may be an unconscious prohibition on fantasy formation within the child altogether.

SURVIVOR'S GUILT

Survivor's guilt, the leitmotif of continuity in these families, was transmitted to the children. In the literature on survivors, guilt feelings found universally to exist as a core affective state have been ascribed to identification with the aggressor (Krystal, 1978) and to ambivalence or death wishes toward siblings and parents. Survivor's guilt probably reactivates oedipal themes in a regressive form and absorbs some of the loving and hateful feelings survivors may have felt toward their parents when they were children.

There is an analogue between survivor's guilt and certain oedipal problems. The Oedipus complex is reawakened phase specifically during many periods of the life cycle (Loewald, 1962). It influences important life events, and causes psychic change throughout life. The Oedipus myth deals with themes of both love and death. A successful resolution of oedipal conflict during any period of a person's life includes an oedipal victory over the parents, accomplished by a lessening of the ambivalent conflicts toward them, permission from the superego to triumph over achievements without undue guilt, and desexualization of the parent–child relationship. Upon reaching maturity as a result of internal separation from the parents, the individual can more easily accept the inevitability of death. (Analysts are familiar with this sequence of inner events from the termination phase of analysis.)

However, survivors, once traumatized severely, try to stave off death through concrete acts and omnipotent fantasies in their myth making. Shared fantasies that interlock parent–child relationships sexualize this relationship unconsciously, cement this bond, and reaffirm a mutual dependency and denial of ambivalent feelings. The inability to express hostility openly without becoming "a little Hitler" may increase death anxiety and survivor's guilt in the child.

Aaron, who told his analyst that "for a man to become successful puts him on the side of the Nazis," was unable to free himself from the survivor's guilt shared with his parents by making good and thereby trying to change their past. He was equally unable, because his guilt feelings toward his parents were excessive, to reach a post-oedipal independence and start a new life.

Some children, however, are capable of reaching an independent oedipal equilibrium, despite their involvement with survivor-parents, particularly when freeing oneself from the parental past is not unconsciously associated with killing the parents. Such children have given evidence of empathy toward their parents, which can be expressed only when unconscious guilt is not excessive. These patients have demonstrated an increased capacity for play, fantasy, and sublimation, and a new ability to enjoy life.

After the Holocaust, uniqueness centered on survival itself, and in a majority of cases studied, marriage partners were selected on the basis of having experienced a comparable fate during the war years. Survivor's guilt, related though it was to actual events during the Hitler period, nevertheless provided a screen for earlier feelings of ambivalence and death wishes toward the survivor's parents.

From the very start of the Nazi assaults on the Jewish population, a constant, affect-laden psychic experience provided inner continuity and was unshakable: survivor's guilt. This guilt, which involves one's most guarded, secret, affectively overdetermined psychic experiences, tied the individual to those who had been lost. It also constituted an obstacle to integrating one's current life with the nontraumatic past. As guilt was overcome, the threads to the pre-Holocaust past could emerge.

Survivor's guilt became intimately related to a person's core identity: *it preserved the inner core of the superego.* As a psychic phenomenon, this guilt became a primary organizer that maintained an inner continuity with the self and object representations established before the Holocaust. It introduced a temporal dimension to the traumatized psychic structure, linking both the pre-Holocaust and Holocaust periods to the present. However, it also presented an obstacle to one's adaptation to a new world. It protected the victim from identification with the aggressor and thereby from potential psychopathic tendencies. As such, it is an example of emergency adaptive function. The tenacity of survivor's guilt seemed to say: there is one thing no one can take away from me, my guilt feelings toward those who have perished. I have found that this guilt could therefore under any conditions, remain *an internalized part of the psyche, protecting the core of psychic representations.*

The enormous burden of survivor's guilt was the most important and recurrent theme of the shared fantasies of survivors and their children. The children continued to be in the position of having to be "forgiven for something." By having taken a dead child into the self representation, they sought expiation of guilt on behalf of the parents, as well as narcissistic restoration of the self.

The impact of shared survivor's guilt resulted in the creation of a "double reality" in which the parents' past and the child's present needed to be amalgamated for purposes of adaptation to current life. By identifying with the parent as victim, the child too became a "survivor." The extent to which survivors' children took the burden of parental needs upon themselves varied, as did their need to concretize fantasies related to past traumata or current conflicts.

Many survivors' children who could not lead their own lives fully were inclined to think of themselves as failures. In some cases, survivor's guilt was exacerbated by hostility toward the parents, resulting in an inability to fulfill an assigned role. In view of the narcissistic problems that ensued in survivors' children, it apparently remained difficult for them to find a way toward independent self-expression. Thus, survivor's children often remained alienated from their own ego ideal, conflicted between wishing to play a role that met parental expectations and realizing their own needs and wishes.

Because of excessive guilt, survivors' children were often afraid to follow professions of their own choosing or to hold on to what they had achieved: good and bad, success and failure, became polarized. There was the added problem that being successful, so ardently pressed for by the parents, meant to the child becoming a Nazi, while failure was an attempt to express strivings for personal autonomy. The child became enmeshed in an externally imposed destiny that concentrated on life and death and on a personal mission to vindicate the parent; but it was not an autonomous choice based on personal freedom. The survivor's child had to make good or be told, "You are the death of me." This joint attempt to cope with survivor's guilt created within the family a concretized replication of an unconsciously repeated situation of being dominated, of inequality, of traumatic dangers, of archaic fantasies. This often brought about developmental fixations at the level of superego precursors, and the need for externalization of hostile fantasies and wishes became common.

Survivor's guilt assigned the child a restitutional role that became infused with earlier omnipotent fantasies. A split image of the self, whereby the child was at once linked both to the parents' past and to his or her own reality, was thus created. By being linked to the parents and by reliving their trauma, the child unconsciously took on a share of the parent's survivor's guilt. Phase-specific separation and individuation needs of the child, a wish to determine one's own destiny, would then threaten the parents and create a superego conflict in the survivor's child. Thus, the child was likely to remain tied to the parents via archaic narcissistic fantasies that would interfere with various aspects of development, particularly the achievement of oedipal victory.

The child's feeling of being "an exception" remained emphasized in lieu of the renunciations demanded by a successful resolution of the oedipal conflict.

Shared fantasies about the past were significant for superego formation. If these were formed as a result of cumulative traumata, they broke the barrier of superego censorship by permitting themes of excessive cruelty, perversions, or incestuous wishes toward important objects to become conscious.

The most feared unconscious fantasies are not as bad as the destructive forces the survivor-parent encountered in reality. Thus, reliving traumata in a concretized situation takes the place of discharge and attempt at mastery (Lipin, 1963; Krystal, 1978). There is a lifelong unconscious expectation that the trauma will recur unless new internalizations have reached a level comparable to a pre-Holocaust core of the individual's psychic structure. In the case of children, differentiation from the Holocaust past of the parents was possible after they had distinguished their current lives from those of the parents and after they had found new means for individuation and a new, separate identity.

Concretization is a phenomenon that serves the repetition compulsion (Freud, 1920). It is also an attempt at self-healing: it is the externalization of an inner meaning. This meaning, rescued from a traumatic constellation, becomes crystallized, first as *action*. The person has *"to do it"*: first, in order to experience it affectively, and then to understand the action and translate it into a cognitive mode. As soon as action becomes symbolized and intelligible, it may receive a new mental representation and become internalized. Awareness of the unconscious meaning of actions strengthens symbol formation and subsequently facilitates internalization.

The dialogue with an object previously lost may require the reestablishment of an inner representation before genuine mourning can begin. Mourning facilitates the resolution of traumata related to losses. In contrast, concretization, by virtue of leading to externalization and action, has the function of avoiding or postponing mourning and separation.

If new internalizations occur, admission of death takes on normal proportions: a unified picture of a coherent reality may permit completion of oedipal strivings, and, as a result of mastery of survivor's guilt, oedipal victory over the parents may be achieved.

Superego pathology has been traced within shared fantasies between survivors and their children. My hypothesis is that superego components, when externalized as a result of traumatic stress, can be preserved by being concretized and played out in the environment. Externalizing action in all probability contains the major traumatic themes in protosymbolic form. Reintegration of the psychic structure becomes a possibility when such action is understood and given psychic representation.

For the survivor, the tenacity and intensity of guilt toward those who have perished may have permitted survivors to establish an internal continuity with pre-Holocaust internal representations. Although these may have served as a core psychic organizer preventing destruction of the psychic structure under traumatic stress, the link to internal representations from times of peace became unavailable under emergency conditions in which every bit of strength, internal or external, was needed for survival.

Survivors' children can embrace a new life only insofar as they can free themselves from participation in the unconscious self-healing of the parents and from the burden of sharing survivor's guilt. Treatment aimed toward separation from a guilt-laden past, and from shared fantasies with parents, is indicated in such cases. Happily, when survivors' children are brought up to identify with wishes for self-healing and recovery, as they so often are, they may be better able to use treatment that facilitates their psychic reintegration.

8.

An Infantile Trauma and a Trauma during Analysis

The case described here involves a patient who suffered a trauma while in the final stages of a successful analysis. The trauma temporarily eclipsed many of the gains of the analysis. Surprisingly, however, the pervasive regression caused by this trauma led to a further lifting of repression. First, though, the regression necessitated a period of psychotherapy that lasted almost a year, until the patient asked to resume her analysis. The patient's regression resulted in new information, greater affective expression, and greater therapeutic gain than would otherwise have been possible.

In this patient a severe childhood trauma and the affects surrounding it had been repressed. Because the patient's mother needed to keep the father's psychotic illness a family secret, denial was encouraged, and her father's illness became the cause of Miriam's childhood trauma. Thus, when the patient entered analysis only scanty information about that trauma was available. Only when a trauma occurred during analysis did the childhood trauma emerge from repression. Both analyst and patient were then able to confront the earlier trauma and complete the analysis on a deeper level.

Trauma is usually experienced as a hostile blow from the outside world, evoking an immediate conscious feeling of being overwhelmed, helpless, disorganized, and narcissistically injured. Typically the trauma victim is unable to put what has happened into words.

Generally, intrapsychic reaction to severe trauma is character- ized by damage to ego functions. Capacities for cognition, fantasy formation, verbalization, and sublimation are reduced (Furst, 1967; Krystal, 1978, 1988; Bergmann and Jucovy, 1982). Defensive ego regression may lead to splitting in an attempt to disown the trauma, or to fusion with traumatizing objects in order to absorb the trauma. Erosion of certain parts of the psychic structure may result.

If, as is likely, interference with the functioning of the anxiety signal occurs (Freud, 1926), the capacity to protect oneself from danger by anticipating one's own needs and those of others may be impaired and lead to difficulties in maintaining normal communi- cation with objects. Further, a reliable differentiation between acute and potential dangers may be impaired, interfering with reality testing.

At times a childhood trauma heals with the help of fantasy for- mation leading to intrapsychic adaptation. If a trauma is absorbed in this manner, its impact may go unnoticed in analysis and deeper pathology connected to it may not surface. In the case of Miriam, a report of whose analysis follows, traumatic screen memories formed, resulting in a mixture of fact and fiction that made reconstruction of the childhood traumatic occurrences difficult.

Without Miriam's second trauma, a deep layer of psychic con- flict would have remained unanalyzed. This has important implica- tions. As a rule, only certain unconscious themes surface in analysis, while others remain dormant. When the "average expectable envi- ronment" changes radically, however, new layers of the unconscious become available, including new childhood memories. When a new traumatic experience causes a deep internal eruption, the analytic process may have to be interrupted for the upheaval's duration.

CASE HISTORY

Miriam came from a highly regarded professional family. Her mother, the more active parent, was often absent. Between the ages of 3 and 5 Miriam played peekaboo and other games with her father. Sometimes these games took place in bed, when he came unclothed from the shower. Miriam enjoyed and admired her father a great deal and felt enthusiastic about their games. Her mother was present at these games, but only as an onlooker. Miriam's memories indicated that her father excessively sexualized his relationship with his little girl, but it was also a rich and close relationship; they shared games, crafts, fantasies, and stories.

When Miriam was 5 years old, her father became manic-depressive with paranoid traits and underwent treatment. Miriam remembered that from then onward her father was very strange. Overly concerned with self-defense, he would throw knives alone in the backyard. He was moody and unpredictable, and Miriam never knew how she would find him when she came home from school. He was depressed, often "not himself," and accused Miriam of "not being herself." Such experiences were at variance with Miriam's perception of reality and confused her. She could not bring school friends home because her father hurt their feelings, but when she confronted him with this, he denied hurting anyone.

When Miriam was between 5 and 6, she learned how to soothe her father when he was frightened. She began to handle her own anxieties about his behavior by attempting to identify with his views, even if they contradicted her perceptions. Sometimes she wondered whether or not something she was experiencing was real.

The ability to soothe her father and to understand his language enhanced Miriam's feelings of omnipotence at home. She displaced her anxiety about her father onto other people, and her sense of helplessness against the outside world increased. She tended to think of other people in simple, sometimes stereotypical terms, focusing on what was most predictable about them.

Miriam's childhood trauma culminated with her father's hospitalization. When the second trauma occurred later in analysis, Miriam and I came to understand that during her father's first hospitalization she developed deep wishes for a wordless closeness to a needy or sick person. However, her sexualized relationship with her father prevailed. Thus, her oedipal development did not take an optimal turn and so did not lead to resolution. Before and after his acute illness, her father assumed a maternal role toward Miriam, another impediment to oedipal development, one that potentiated her turning her own maternal wishes toward her father.

It was difficult to obtain memories of Miriam's early relationship with her mother or to reconstruct their relationship before Miriam's latency period. Miriam recalled being her mother's favorite; her mother preferred her because she was more beautiful, livelier, and more intelligent than her siblings. When Miriam and her mother felt close, her mother spoke mostly about herself. As a latency child Miriam felt anxiety when she needed something, and felt also that her mother liked her best when she asked for nothing. When her mother was desperate and needed advice, she would wring her hands helplessly, in striking contrast to her usual aura of competence. As Miriam grew up, she tried to comfort her mother at such times. Miriam admired her mother's professional life and her prominent social role in the community. When the mother took trips away from home that she regarded as professionally necessary, the children stayed with their father and the housekeeper; it fell to Miriam to soothe and comfort her father when he was upset.

Thus, Miriam became a caregiver toward both parents, especially after the age of 6, when her father returned from the hospital. Miriam's mother felt that no one could calm or cheer him better than Miriam, and Miriam regarded this as her special role in the family.

Although Miriam's mother gave her daughter feminine things, she herself never attempted to look "pretty," and Miriam rarely experienced her as soft and feminine. In her professional life, she wore suits and hats; she was always practical and matter-of-fact. Miriam felt that in some respects her mother was "more of a man" than her father. Thus, it was difficult for Miriam to create a maternal feminine ideal. Her transference toward me was formed on the model of an omnipotent bisexual mother. The lines between femininity and masculinity were sometimes blurred, particularly regarding a woman's professional achievement.

Because she held these conflicting images of her parents, Miriam was unable to integrate feminine and masculine strivings within herself until an internal separation from these conflicting representations could be achieved in analysis. She therefore had conflicts about her gender identity and intermittent confusion regarding her gender role. She had lost her rational father to his illness and kept losing her mother to absences and professional pursuits; oedipal triangulation was at a minimum and oedipal victory assured on all fronts. Disappointment in each parent promoted distancing; taking a parental role toward each of them disturbed her sense of feminine identity and strengthened her omnipotent defenses.

She had bisexual fantasies in which I was either impersonating a woman—since I was a psychoanalyst, I really had to be a male—or in which, because I was indeed a woman, I was an impostor only pretending to be a psychoanalyst. She remembered that recognition of a person's true gender had become confusing during puberty, when she had felt alternately feminine or masculine. We reconstructed that her fear of men began around that time.

As a young woman, Miriam married a man who seemed extremely "normal" to her, with whom she was not in love, and for whom she had no strong enthusiasm. Her mother encouraged the marriage, and Miriam, though she had her doubts, did not dare break off the engagement. She had two children in the marriage. Her first was difficult from birth. Restless at the breast, he had sleeping disturbances and was hyperkinetic. Though he was highly intelligent, his attention span remained minimal. Miriam constantly tried to keep him entertained. She surrendered the child to her husband on demand and believed that were she a better mother her baby would not be so difficult to manage. She reproached her own mother for never having taught her how to be a mother. Her second child was normal and easy, which helped her realize that the older child had manifested abnormal reactions from birth that no one understood.

When her children reached adolescence, Miriam began to emancipate herself from her husband. Her marriage had been cold and distant; her husband was a voyeur who preferred looking at women to touching them.

Miriam had come to analysis to understand why she was afraid to separate from her husband and get a divorce. She reported periodic difficulties in verifying her reality perceptions of situations and people. She sometimes wondered in fantasy whether her father was as normal as other men during his calm periods. This helped her deny her anxiety about men. Miriam's relationship with her husband had not changed her image of men or added to her sense of security about being married. The ultimate estrangement from her husband had occurred two years earlier, when her mother died after a serious illness and her husband had not been supportive. It became apparent that remaining in the marriage had been part of her attachment to her mother.

Analysis revealed that Miriam's relationship to her father in his psychotic state was the most disturbing element in her development. Nonetheless, I considered her analyzable, as an essentially neurotic structure had remained intact. A more disturbed aspect of her psychic structure became apparent only when her psychic life was disorganized by a second trauma.

During the first part of Miriam's analysis, we analyzed her role reversal—her parenting of her parents (see chapter 1)—as well as her current relationship with her husband and children, and her bisexual fantasies that enabled us to analyze her Oedipus complex.

While in analysis, Miriam established herself professionally, got divorced, managed her home and children on her own, and ultimately found a man she could love and with whom she had a deeply personal and sexually gratifying relationship. Although there were problems and necessary adaptations in this relationship as well, Miriam felt happy and married him. Her treatment began to reach its termination phase. We agreed that Miriam's relationship with her older son, whose continuing difficulty in getting along with people and adapting to the demands of academic life she could not accept without anger, still had to be improved. Her newly acquired feminine identity also needed to become more firmly established. She wanted to master these problems and then terminate her analysis. At that point Miriam had been in analysis for six years, five times a week.

Then the second trauma struck. Miriam's older son, now an adolescent, was hospitalized as manic-depressive (possibly schizophrenic). The following day, Miriam called to say she would not come to her session. "You only have words for me," she said, "and words don't mean anything." She then continued her hour on the telephone, telling me that the words of her son's analyst had not protected him from illness; that nobody understood how a very disturbed person feels, which she knew from childhood; that only she could understand and comfort her son; and that she would like it best if she could take him into her innermost self, become one with him, body and soul, and give him the feeling that he was understood and not alone. She now suddenly remembered similar feelings toward her father, in spite of his strange and often uncommunicative language.

It had been extremely difficult to get precise data about Miriam's father before her son's breakdown. After this second trauma struck, however, the childhood trauma dramatically emerged from repression. Many details about Miriam's relationship to her father before, during, and after his acute mental illness were now recalled. She remembered how from early childhood on she had learned how to communicate with her father when he was in his psychotic world. This very capacity made her later doubt her perceptions of men. She sometimes fantasized that all men were crazy, thereby protecting the image of her father.

Miriam remembered that as a child she felt responsible for her father's illness, especially when she was playing and forgot to come home. A childhood superego precursor resulting in an exaggerated sense of responsibility contributed to Miriam's difficulty in separating from her father. She also recalled sometimes sleeping in her father's bed when she was sick or her mother was away. On those occasions she thought she had touched or held his penis, but was never certain whether these were memories or fantasies.

She remembered calming him when he thought people working nearby were after him. She would say, "It's all right, Dad; you're home now; we all love you; nothing is going to happen to you." She would stroke him, put her arms around him, and quiet him even when she was very little. As Miriam relived the ways she dealt with her sick father, we could see how, as a child, feelings of omnipotence had prevented her from experiencing excessive anxiety in his presence.

In all these recollections Miriam was alone with her father in a frightening, at times almost intolerable, situation. Miriam's mother was absent as a protector. A maternal aunt, however, was a great comfort to her. Miriam spent many hours in her home, cooking, laughing, and listening to stories. She also had a close friend whose parents were loving, supportive, and protective toward Miriam.

When Miriam's son became ill, she initially experienced him as if he were a sick part of herself. She felt that she alone could help him both because she was responsible for his illness and because she understood him better than did the doctors. As a result of what she had learned in relating to her father when he was ill, she was able to develop a way of communicating with her son that was, when she was at her best, extraordinary. She felt that she alone knew what he needed and tried to participate in plans for his care.

All her life Miriam had been able to deny or split off disturbing stimuli. After the onset of her son's psychosis she regressed to a symbiotic feeling state with him and simultaneously merged with her father, reinforced by emergent memories of his psychosis. This led to a regression that made Miriam unambitious, unfeeling toward herself, and withdrawn from the world. She was interested only in her son and stopped caring for herself. She became less analyzable for extended stretches of time and her inner life became temporarily frozen.

As the gains of her analysis became temporarily eclipsed, I found it necessary to interrupt the analysis and begin a phase of psychotherapy that became an extended and significant part of

Miriam's treatment. Before her son's breakdown, and as a result of previous analytic improvements, there had been an idealization of me and of the power of analysis, but now Miriam's transference had turned bitterly negative. She saw her son's psychosis as evidence that I had been powerless to protect her. Miriam deeply resented the fact that I had in addition referred her son to an analyst who had not protected him from his psychotic outbreak. Her perceived loss of my support left her feeling totally undermined and deepened her regression.

After the temporary merger with her father receded, transference fantasies again became analyzable. During her psychotherapy my function was to act as an intermediary between the outside world and her omnipotent wishes to rescue her child. I helped her establish a more realistic and less merged attitude in her relationship with her son. Subsequently, as his condition improved, so did her own.

Miriam's psychotherapy lasted almost a year, after which she asked to resume her analysis. In retrospect, I realized that her psychotherapy had manifested itself in three phases. In its first phase, during Miriam's most intense crisis, she had difficulty maintaining her boundaries in her relationship with both her son and her father. The sick father of childhood and the sick son now became part of herself.

Miriam did not identify with her son, but rather, *fused* with him. Thus, a reconstruction could be made that as a child she must periodically have fused with her father in his psychotic state. Before the son's trauma, Miriam's past had appeared in a different light: her disturbances appeared neurotic, and we had worked on her *identification* with her sick father. After the trauma of her son's illness, it became evident that her father's psychosis had resulted in greater psychic impairment than could have been recognized before.

During her initial libidinal and ego regression, Miriam cried a great deal. I postponed interpretations, sensing that she would have experienced them as unempathic, thereby increasing the distance between her victimized self and me, the unscathed helper. I did not interpret her destructive rage toward professional helpers, including myself, whom she did not trust, and toward her own sick child, in a thinly disguised manner, until much later. At this point interpretations would have been experienced as overstimulating intrusions.

During this first phase of Miriam's psychotherapy, I stressed the difference between the childhood trauma and the current one, in order to promote new boundary formation, a greater capacity for verbalization and cognition, and improved reality testing. Thus, the rebuilding of ego functions began. We discussed practical measures related to Miriam's daily life, which helped her gradually regain a capacity for anticipation. Miriam increasingly acted on her own behalf in ways that were less destructive.

When it became possible to interpret her regression, a second phase began. A further differentiation of father from son, of past from present, became possible. Through interpretation of her hostility, she was able to separate the representations of father and son. This new capacity slowly restored her sense of autonomy.

Miriam now experienced a deep sense of loss. No longer merged with her son, she felt she had lost him, as if her child had died. She would never again be the same person; she would never be able to trust anyone as she had before. Having lost her sense of omnipotence and given up the omnipotence she had projected onto me, Miriam now felt she could never be the person she had been before. She sheltered her son but became angry and ambivalent toward him. She recognized that he had exhausted her "time and inner resources."

As her son's condition improved, he accused her of being responsible for his illness. She felt she had always preferred her younger child, and that her divorce might have contributed to the breakdown. As she began to mourn what she had lost, a strong negative transference developed, exacerbated by the analysis of Miriam's earlier feelings of omnipotence. The negative transference was a defense against deep feelings of guilt. She admitted that her fantasies of responsibility for her son's illness related to how she had raised him, and perhaps to having transmitted a defective gene from her father.

As further differentiation became possible, in the third phase of Miriam's psychotherapy, Miriam discussed her son's illness with a great deal of affect. She remembered many details, previously repressed, of his early infancy. She spoke sadly of trying to soothe, interest, distract, and amuse her hyperkinetic, unresponsive baby. She described her anxiety about being an unsuccessful mother and her disconsolate feeling that she had not even been able to soothe her baby at the breast; he was restless and only nursed fitfully.

After almost a year of psychotherapy, Miriam discovered her inner life and asked to resume her analysis. Her sexual feelings, which had disappeared during her traumatic crisis, returned. It was now possible for her analysis to proceed to its conclusion, much enriched by the new information released by working through the two great traumas of her life.

When we began analysis again, the transition was initially difficult for her. Back on the couch, she felt "off-center" and "out of balance." Upon returning to analysis, Miriam struggled with her conflicts about her gender identity and object relationships, which were torn by conflicting affects. Miriam now understood that her mistrust of men had represented her warded-off desire for her "bad and dangerous" father. After analysis of her omnipotent fantasies, she gradually conceded that a psychoanalyst can protect a human being from psychotic breakdown only in a limited manner. Although Miriam was in acute pain, she demonstrated a new awareness about the realities of her life, a genuineness of affect, and a wish to help herself and her son in a dramatically new and forceful manner. This began the renewal of loving feelings toward herself and the others in her life.

DISCUSSION

Freud (1937) asked if it is possible to analyze latent trauma. Fenichel (1974) convinced us that we work with it constantly. In the case of my patient, I believe that had the adult trauma not occurred, transference alone would not have brought out her central trauma. Miriam would have remembered the initial trauma, but it would have lacked its full affective impact.

In some patients only certain aspects of object relationships and conflicts emerge in the transference, while others remain buried unless cataclysmic events occur in the outside world. Before her son's illness, Miriam never fully relived her infantile trauma or her feelings about her father's psychosis. Her early wishes to merge with her father, a sign of preoedipal pathology, were separate from her maternal transference, which surfaced in the pretraumatic period of her analysis, while her hostility toward her father entered the transference only afterward.

The encapsulated internalized relationship with her father came to the fore after the onset of her son's illness. Her relationship with her psychotic father flooded her psychic reality for a period during the acute phase of her son's illness. Her wish to merge with her father became conscious not in the transference but as a result of her son's psychosis. This wish therefore represented an extratransferential event of great psychic power.

In the transference, Miriam continued to experience me in the role of her mother, but I was no longer idealized. Instead I became the mother who does not understand the father-daughter unit. While her real mother *sent her* to help her irrational father, I became the mother who *rescued her* from her irrational father. This contributed greatly to her idealization of me and freed her from the need to save her father. Her image of her internal mother improved and her feminine identification became stronger, enabling Miriam to begin a more fulfilling relationship with a "normal man."

As a result of previous changes, we had both felt that her analysis was coming to a conclusion. When her second trauma then erupted during analysis, an unexpected layer of the unconscious became available, namely, Miriam's wishes to merge with her psychotic father. Until that time, neither of us knew how strong these wishes had been, or how afraid the patient was about letting them emerge. Some important aspects of psychic life do not enter the analysis via the transference neurosis, but can be understood only through external factors in the patient's life (Blum, 1986). Only after the trauma of her son's illness made reliving the father's illness possible could Miriam's analysis be completed, since this formerly isolated aspect of her psyche could now be analyzed. Apparently, only the more organized aspects of her psychic structure had entered the transference neurosis, whereas disorganizing influences that impinged upon the developing psyche either became repressed or were not relived in transference, and in either case were therefore more difficult to capture in analysis.

Traumatized patients frequently have difficulty knowing whether affects come from within or without. These patients therefore need to observe the effect of their actions in the outside world. They fear the return of the trauma, yet they tend to retraumatize themselves through repeated actions symbolizing aspects of the trauma. Similar observations were made in Holocaust survivors and their children (Bergmann and Jucovy, 1982).

I understood that Miriam's confused enactments and affects during the height of her traumatic state were due to her loss of self-protective capacity, which occurred after the healthier aspects of her personality were split off. Simultaneously, Miriam's capacity for insight and interpretation was reduced, and she needed my help to maintain her reality testing. Miriam used action and externalization to bring about situations that validated her fantasies. The concept of actualization, proposed by Sandler and Sandler (1978), is suggestive of this psychic need, as is what I have termed *concretization* (see chapter 7). This is a psychic state in which fantasies and wishes are discharged in the external world because they cannot be verbalized in treatment; action therefore becomes the arena for living out past and present internal conflicts related to trauma. Analyzing and healing depend primarily on the capacity to relive the trauma with its original affects (Krystal, 1988). It was the aim of the analysis that the patient internalize, interpret, and accept both the childhood and the adult trauma affectively and cognitively and come to terms with them.

Miriam's infantile trauma was reawakened by her adult trauma, an unforeseeable occurrence. One might speculate, however, that a repressed trauma with its strong affective cathexis "behaves" as if "searching" for a situation in which to reappear. A trauma, like other repressed events, remains cathected and "pushes upward" (Freud, 1915a) in a less threatening environment. Sometimes the analytic situation—and "acting in"—may provide such a shelter.

In later stages of treatment a person can simultaneously reenact being the active traumatizing agent, as well as the passive victim of the trauma. This frequently represents an attempt to deal, in small doses, with the hostility, sadomasochistic reactions, and narcissistic injuries engendered by the trauma. Miriam's fusion with her son and its antecedent, her identification and periodic fusion with her traumatizing father, could be characterized as "identification with the traumatizing object."

Such identification or fusion has a defensive function, as it prevents the surfacing of excessive anxiety and rage. As long as such emergency measures are successful, the trauma itself becomes the nucleus around which resistances to the analysis are organized. The defensive structure is maintained as a safeguard against the feared recurrence of the trauma. When the trauma is analyzed, however, the patient's characterological adaptation to the traumatic experience must be addressed. The ways in which the trauma is kept alive by defensive actions in current life need to be analyzed. Where it is possible to reactivate the feeling states of the original trauma, such reliving convinces the patient that the trauma indeed has already occurred, and that its more specific disturbing emanations in current life can be understood.

From the time of her father's first psychotic episode, Miriam's internalized image of him had not changed. Until she had relinquished this fixation on her father, her relationship with him had characterized her relationships with other men. After analysis of this fixation, she could intrapsychically differentiate these other men from her father. This newfound capacity consolidated her second marriage.

When introjected representations of parents have been only partially internalized, and oedipal conflicts only partially repressed, the real parents may remain alive in a special affective state. Internalized parental images may become distorted or idealized, but as a result of trauma their psychic representations may be insufficiently separated from the parents of the external world. Once a year Miriam went to the cemetery where her parents were buried, sat on a bench, and spoke to her parents as if they were still alive.

In the case of most neurotic patients, much effort is directed to bringing the repressed representations of the parents to life. When a certain temporal sense is lost as a result of trauma, the parents remain alive until analysis makes it possible for them to gradually become objects of the past. During analysis, and as a result of her treatment, Miriam moved from preoedipal to oedipal to postoedipal time (for a discussion of the traumatized person's denial of the irreversibility of death, see Blum [1986, p. 23]).

Two observations can be made from the outcome of Miriam's case. Chance events in the patient's current life can sometimes make it possible for us to penetrate more deeply into an analysand's unconscious. Alternatively, those external events may in fact be creating additional pressures, thereby freeing up unconscious material. In Miriam's case both inner psychic reality and external events influenced the analysis to an extent that could not have been foreseen.

It is generally assumed that the transference neurosis awakens the childhood neurosis in a more or less sequential form, and that the process of uncovering proceeds from within, independent of current life. Miriam's case suggests that reality continuously impinges on the psychic life of the patient and may bring to the fore new aspects of the patient's psychic life that would not otherwise have emerged. In Miriam's case her son's illness, a trauma analogous to one that occurred much earlier, reawakened for her an encapsulated traumatic state from her childhood.

9.

Retraumatization Anxiety and the Defensive Function of the Negative Therapeutic Reaction

In this chapter I deal with the fear of retraumatization, by which I mean a patient's fear of reliving an earlier trauma within the analytic transference. Two clinical examples are cited. In one, a powerful negative therapeutic reaction, brought on by failing defenses against attendant anxiety, was followed by retraumatization. When the full extent of the trauma was experienced by this patient, he was retraumatized in analysis. In the second case, a crisis necessitated the patient's return to treatment. During this brief return, the patient recovered a repressed memory and experienced the full impact of a childhood trauma. Both patients responded initially by discharging inner pressures via enactment and, subsequently, by experiencing anxiety about retraumatization.

When, following trauma, ego control is insufficient, there may be a phobic avoidance of situations that have become associated with the trauma, a tendency to relive traumatic themes affectively, or a fixation on trauma (Furst, 1978). Failure to master trauma creates a permanent organizing effect on the psyche and its

175

defenses. Traumata will thereafter alter the intrapsychic representation of self and object, unconscious fantasies, and character structure (Blum, 1996).

Another consequence of trauma is the fear of retraumatization, a state in which a trauma experienced in the past threatens to reemerge. This threat brings about an anxiety reaction that signals the need for defense against the recurrence of trauma. Though a past trauma may no longer be consciously experienced as such, the fear of retraumatization lies at its very core.

The concept of retraumatization has its roots in Freud's early analytic thinking. In "The Neuro-Psychoses of Defense," Freud (1894) maintains that a "reaction to traumatic stimuli . . . can . . . be resolved and cured by 'abreaction' . . . [unless] . . . the ego was faced with an experience . . . which aroused such a distressing affect that the subject . . . had no confidence in his power to resolve [it]" (p. 47). In his early psychoanalytic thinking Freud was aware that traumatic stimuli needed to be discharged in order to deal with anxiety about reliving the original trauma. It has been my clinical experience that patients search for a means of defense against having to deal once again with a traumatic occurrence.

To avoid retraumatization, some persons will henceforth avoid all experiences analogous to the situation that originally traumatized them: someone whose love relationships ended traumatically will make sure not to fall in love again. At the same time, a person may search for and often find a situation in which the trauma can be recapitulated (as in fate neurosis): as Freud (1939) noted, "A girl who was made the object of a sexual seduction in her early childhood may direct her later sexual life so as constantly to provoke similar attacks" (pp. 75–76). The trauma is then converted into a characterological pattern that becomes subordinated to the repetition compulsion (Fenichel, 1945; Blum, 1986).

As analysis deepens, the fear of retraumatization within the analytic situation itself becomes a growing source of anxiety and may result in symptom formation. For a patient in analysis, the potential impact of the return of the repressed evokes anxiety, and the patient may have to prove to the analyst how dangerous treatment is (Freud, 1914b). Every patient is afraid of reliving those aspects of the past that were traumatic.

The anxiety of reliving the trauma, of experiencing an invasive break in the protective barrier of defenses such as occurred at the time of the original trauma, may be especially strong when a trauma has been repressed. Since the meaning of the repetition of traumatic themes remains unconscious or becomes only partially conscious, the individual remains helpless to explain to himself (or herself) why he (or she) feels compelled to perform certain actions. The pressure to relive derivatives of the original trauma in enactments crosses boundaries of past and present and may contain fantasies about the future. The anxiety of being retraumatized can unconsciously be equated with a recurrence of the traumatic feeling state itself. No truly traumatic occurrence is ever completely assimilated without leaving traces of increased vulnerability (Greenacre, 1967).

In 1926 Freud integrated the theory of anxiety with the recurrence of trauma, which he had observed as early as the 1880s. In *Inhibitions, Symptoms and Anxiety* he emphasizes that anxiety is created as an affective state in accordance with an already existing mnemic image which has been incorporated in the mind as a precipitate of primeval traumatic experiences. When a similar situation occurs, the traumatic experiences are revived as mnemic symbols in memory (p. 93). When the psyche has mastered the capacity to anticipate danger, "it nevertheless *behaves as though all danger situations still exist and keep hold of the earlier determinants of anxiety*" (p. 147; emphasis added). Freud thought that even in an individual capable of the most mature levels of functioning, the anxiety signal is necessary for communicating impending danger situations and for regulating affects.

Freud indicated that past forms of anxiety are retained as psychic representations long after the danger has ceased to exist. Past forms of anxiety create an expectation of conflict, an assumption of the return of the trauma that creates new anxiety and a fear of retraumatization with its attendant fear of helplessness.

At times, unconsciously motivated enactments outside the analytic situation may usher in a resurgence of traumatic anxiety. When past traumatic experiences were severe, recurring enactments of the trauma in symbolic form may continue into the present and may be an instance of the repetition compulsion (Freud, 1920). A fear of retraumatization, coupled with an unconscious need to relive the trauma, appears to be a motivating force in the continuation of these enactments.

Freud assumed that recall is not equivalent to retraumatization, because the adult ego of the analysand can handle without repression ideas and affects that would overwhelm the ego of the child.

However, patients most afraid of retraumatization are those whose childhood traumata caused developmental fixation. Such patients are likely to cling to their defenses, as relinquishing them would endanger the self just as the original trauma did.

Sometimes the knowledge provided by a self-protective ego—as when one reminds oneself that a frightening movie or dream is not "real"—is not enough, and a person abdicates the reality testing function and yields to the disorganization of traumatic impact. When there is an absence of a mature observing ego that can maintain the difference between remembering and reexperiencing a traumatic event, the structure of the psyche cannot protect the individual, who will then become afraid of being retraumatized. In the therapeutic situations discussed here, the negative therapeutic reaction is seen as an *emergency* defensive reaction that occurs when a previous defense against retraumatization has failed.

When the patient's fear of reliving a trauma is uppermost, the negative therapeutic reaction may be resorted to as a form of emergency self-help obviating the need for engagement and more specific preventive measures. The negative reaction is behavioral and may be wordless. Just as the defensive system was overrun when the original trauma occurred, it is lacking once again in those areas that relate to the original traumatic situation. The negative therapeutic reaction may now appear as a rallying point against retraumatization.

When the defensive constellation against danger does not operate adequately, the fear of retraumatization may trigger the negative therapeutic reaction and make a patient inaccessible for analytic work. A "no" becomes attached to the therapeutic process (Olinick, 1964; Loewald, 1972). A sudden change in the patient's attitude toward treatment frequently coincides with a sudden break in the transference relationship. Once a patient manifests oppositional behavior, no manifest anxiety may be apparent. A behavioral change due to unconscious anxiety may occur, with or without verbal communication, or without a communicable affective response. A new vulnerability and a potential crisis may be created when the analyst comes to represent a menacing primary object (Limentani, 1981; Maldonado, 1983). When a threatening aspect of a psychic representation is projected onto the analyst, the patient's reactions toward the analyst predictably become negative. Subsequently, this projection results in a lack of communication motivated by an inability to put affective experiences into words.

The patient manifests increased hostility due to recurring traumatic anxiety which is in danger of not being mastered, and may cause regression and acting out. As a result of various forms of negative and self-destructive behavior, the anticipatory and self-protective functions become disorganized and no overt reaction against danger can occur. The fear of retraumatization is experienced, as was the original; trauma, as a danger for which there has been no preparation.

This may well account for the difficulties the analyst experiences when an anticipatory or defensive stance is absent in the patient. Neither analyst nor patient may know that trauma-related material is threatening reemergence; neither patient nor analyst is aware of the danger the patient experiences in anticipation of retraumatization. As a result, the origins and motivation of a global antitherapy response may be obscure and its presence therefore puzzling. The patient's anxiety is displaced or projected onto the analytic situation or the person of the analyst. The latter searches for mistakes he or she might have made, based on countertransference feelings or responses. The inception of this situation may be insidious and the reasons for it unconscious in both participants.

CLINICAL EXAMPLE: MR. M

In the following case, the analytic process was interrupted by a negative therapeutic reaction arising from fear of retraumatization. Subsequently, a traumatic feeling state occurred within the therapeutic setting. Derivatives of the trauma were expressed in a transitory symptom, and the transference neurosis became the arena for reliving early childhood traumata.

Mr. M was a middle-aged businessman who had been in treatment several times before with other psychoanalysts. He complained of a discrepancy between his intelligence and capabilities and his much lower level of performance. He consistently created situations that made things go wrong after he and I had worked to improve his life. He came from a large family which, though impoverished, placed a high value on education. Though he loved learning, he could not integrate his efforts because he erotized his professional activities. He was bulimic and had perverse, pedophilic fantasies. His need for these fantasies compelled him to interrupt his work for masturbation.

This behavior had its roots in his earliest history. Mr. M was his mother's menopausal child and her youngest. When he was a little boy, his siblings were already grown and, for the most part, out of the home. Mr. M experienced a double trauma in the earliest period of his life. His father was killed in a violent episode, so that he was left alone with his mother, and he was told by his mother that shortly after his birth that he had almost died from an allergic reaction to milk.

He had an organizing screen memory in which he is $2^1/2$ or 3 years old. His mother puts him on top of a dresser. He is fat, with round cheeks, and they smile at each other. She is feeding him. Both are laughing and are happy. In actuality, Mr. M's mother force-fed him for as long as he could remember. He was overweight and found her force-feeding increasingly intrusive, but he shared his mother's fantasy that he might die if he did not eat everything she served him. Because of this lifelong anxiety, he could not fend her off. A split representation of his mother as loving and nurturing on the one hand, and menacing and invasive, on the other, led to a life-long internal conflict. His pedophilic ideation developed out of a sexualized aspect of his relationship with his mother, whose feedings were experienced as a seductive union. In his sexual interest in little girls, he identified with his mother feeding him. In his fusion fantasies he unconsciously felt himself to be both the little girl and himself in the role of the aggressive, forcing mother who penetrates the child with her spoon. Although anxiety made him stop short of engaging in pedophilic activity, in his fantasies he wished to unite with a girl-child and present himself as a bisexual child to his mother. In these fantasies he excluded his father. He played out what he feared most, and what had become sexualized during his early years, probably from the time he was a toddler.

After several years of work, Mr. M accused me of still not helping him and of interpreting things he already knew. Subsequently, his analysis became stalemated by an overwhelming negative therapeutic reaction. He felt discouraged and angry, as all his previous treatments had been a failure. For a considerable length of time it seemed to both of us that our work would be subjected to the same fate.

However, the analytic situation changed dramatically when I focused our joint analytic attention on his father's absence, which subsequently moved to the center of analytic scrutiny. Following this, Mr. M developed nightmares. These were wordless, but he was left in a state of terror and felt utterly alone. When associations about his absent father were added, Mr. M developed insomnia. When he could not sleep he would raid the refrigerator, gain several pounds overnight, and try to jog them off the next day. He always enumerated what he had eaten. At times this included entire cakes and several quarts of ice cream.

One day he was suddenly afraid to lie on the couch and asked to sit up. It was clear that Mr. M needed to interrupt the manner of our analytic work and was terrified to continue. He said he was afraid that lying down would bring on his recurring nightmares. He sat up and held his head in his hands, feeling unable to look at me. He complained about the light in the room, and I realized he had developed a photophobia. Subsequently, I had to draw the blinds tightly. Mr. M could not talk and wore dark glasses to protect himself against the light. I had a sense that he was protecting himself against overstimulation in the analytic hour and that he was experiencing an hallucinatory reliving of his trauma in the transference neurosis. He asserted that he needed to sit up but he could not verbalize what put him into a state of utter terror. I sensed that his nonverbal behavior carried a message and felt that any word on my part would have been overstimulating. He sat at my desk, his head bent and supported by his arms and hands. He seemed to know when the time was up, and left punctually, without saying a word. When he entered my room wordlessly for his next hour, I greeted him with a serious nod and he followed me into the room. He never missed a session and came four times a week. At the end of the month he paid the correct amount. This went on for two months, perhaps a little longer. I sensed his suffering and his need for me to be in the role he had put me in, a silent witness of his tortured silence.

Eventually Mr. M began to talk of his own accord. He said he could not bear to be touched. I replied that I thought he reacted like a person who was beginning to remember having been overstimulated to the point of feeling that if intrusion continued, he would perish. Working on this theme helped him connect his fear of the light in the room with the fear of being intrusively force-fed by his mother, and with the fear that he would die if he did not eat. Unconsciously, dying meant that he would be killed like his father; a fantasy emerged that his mother had killed his father and that he would be next.

His associations made it clear that his photophobia had represented a displaced wish to shut out his intrusive mother, who was represented by the incoming light. As long as there was a "danger" that I would talk during his sessions, I could turn into his menacing mother. He asserted that his wish to eliminate visual perception almost completely was related to the wish to deny the terrors of his childhood. This included "seeing," i.e., admitting, that his father had died a violent death. He now associated that his nightmares had dealt with monsters who attacked him in the dark. This statement refers to some of the details of his father's actual death. As memories from childhood appeared, the nightmares became less frequent and the patient gradually gained control over both his eating habits and his perverse fantasies. As he struggled to gain autonomy and separate from his mother, his phallic and oedipal needs emerged in treatment: his preoedipal fixation receded in favor of a phallic oedipal self-image. Conflicts that had prevented productive work shifted gradually to the area of intrapsychic conflict, and the analytic work began to flourish.

After the revival of this trauma in analysis, Mr. M's vague memories of his father became centrally important. Eventually it became possible for him to replace his preoedipal identification with his mother with a masculine identification with his father, with the attendant features of oedipal anxiety and subsequent triumph. Mr. M's perverse fantasies began to recede at this time, and he was able to do his work without interruptions for the first time in his analytic experience. At this time he began to work increasingly within his actual capacities.

The case of Mr. M illustrates how the negative therapeutic reaction can appear in treatment as a sign of impending retraumatization anxiety. The reaction was first manifest in his assessment of his analysis as repetitive and stalemated. When his father moved to the center of analytic scrutiny, Mr. M had to sit up and become silent; he created a transference symptom, the photophobia, that represented a displacement from the mouth to the eyes. Through the hallucinatory reliving of his traumata in the transference, Mr. M created in "transference language," a symbolic link to his perverse fantasies. Through his reliving of his traumatic feeling states in the transference, his symptoms became intelligible and therefore analyzable.

Mr. M experienced a wordless reliving of early traumatization from the time when his mother was almost his only object, and, in his nightmares, the recreation of a traumatic feeling state. These experiences led to retraumatization within the analytic transference: the menacing mother had become associated with his internal representation of me, who would "force-feed" him by not allowing him to pace his analytic intake. This in turn would put him in the role of his victimized father, who would be attacked by his mother, now the analyst, and die a violent death. He had a fantasy that by becoming physically strong by overeating, he could stave off death and prevent himself from being killed like his father. His fantasized sexual intrusion on a young girl, who would then feel overfed, would also stave off his death. This fantasy constellation was based on his destructive wishes, particularly death wishes against his mother. Overwhelming feelings of guilt were associated with these destructive impulses, lived out in the bulimia and pedophilic fantasy, which were the magic that would keep him alive. The addictive aspects of bulimia and perverse sexual fantasy represented a fantasy shared with his force-feeding mother: bulimia and pedophilic fantasies had been a compromise compliance with the traumatizing mother. With these symptoms, Mr. M both destroyed and resurrected her. When during analysis the persecutory aspect of his internal parental objects began to haunt him, and his defenses against them became inadequate, retraumatization occurred. Mr. M then needed to interrupt the analytic process.

Mr. M, an abused child, became an adult haunted by abusive desires (Blum, 1996). Throughout his childhood his mother had been experienced as phallic, while he had felt castrated. He had made a pseudophallic adjustment. He then needed to destroy his threatening objects symbolically in order to survive the threat of annihilation. By altering the formal analytic setting, he was able to remain in treatment. Structuring our subsequent meetings as a "wordless dialogue," he assigned me the role of a quiet, listening presence. This was his self-protection against overstimulation, the hallucinatory reliving of which had created an impasse in his capacity to symbolize. Through this enactment, he regained the capacity to talk. Because I did not talk or "feed him" against his will, he reacquired the capacity to symbolize and thereupon regained the ability to put his feelings into words. Mr. M's all-intrusive maternal representation had not permitted the symbolization of the maternal image. As Green (1975) has written, "the object which is always intrusively present, permanently occupying the personal psychic space, mobilizes a permanent countercathexis in order to combat this break-in . . . [to] get rid of its burden by expulsive projection. *Never being absent, it cannot be thought*" (p. 8; emphasis added). Mr. M, however, was able to give communicative signals, most likely in an attempt to reconstitute connections that were disrupted internally. Thus had his lack of differentiation from his mother interfered with independent thought.

Mr. M's problems had begun as an early feeding trauma. As he was then too young to symbolize, the trauma could not be consolidated as a psychic phenomenon. I assume that when I sat with him in silence, he came to experience that I was not his overfeeding mother. His transference enactments had indeed begun as a concretization in which he could say no to her. Our joint enactment acquired symbolic meaning only afterward, when he realized the difference between his mother and me as his analyst. This finally allowed for the internal representation—and eventually the analysis—of what had occurred in his childhood.

Valenstein (1973) suggested that a person who demonstrates an affinity for painful affect, which by reconstruction may be related to an early developmental defect stemming from a preverbal relationship with the mother, will relive this pain in the form of a negative therapeutic reaction. I believe that in his tortured, wordless silence Mr. M may have relived a similar attachment to his traumatizing mother, which started most likely in infancy and continued throughout life.

CLINICAL EXAMPLE: NAOMI

Naomi, a Holocaust survivor, was also the child of a survivor. Now a marriage counselor, she had undergone psychoanalytically oriented psychotherapy with me for several years and had emerged, in her own words, "a new person." For several years she wrote me on holidays, sending pictures of her children, with reports that her marriage was happy and her life fulfilling. One day, however, she telephoned, extremely agitated, and demanded to see me as soon as possible. Arriving in a disorganized anxiety state, she told me that a young man who wanted a divorce and whom she counseled was about to sue her. A few days earlier she had received a call from a relative of his informing her that this young man had a gun in his hand and was threatening to kill himself because of his failed marriage. He had demanded to see her at once. Uncharacteristically, since she was an extremely caring person, Naomi said that she would not see the young man immediately, even though he was threatening suicide. At that point the relative summoned a person close to the family, who tore the gun away from the young man's hands, in the process falling and breaking an ankle. Subsequently the entire family became furious and concentrated their rage on Naomi, the unhelpful counselor who had refused to intervene.

Naomi said she was unable to think. She would be summoned by an ethics committee and could lose her license. Everything she had built up would be ruined. She felt paralyzed. I said it was understandable that it was difficult for her to come to the rescue of a man who was holding a gun, but why was she paralyzed? She did not know. Naomi experienced abdominal pain that was so acute I wondered whether she might need to be hospitalized. I said that whatever she was feeling, and whatever her unconscious conflicts were, it seemed that her difficulties were "lodged in her abdomen."

In our third meeting, Naomi recounted a memory that she had not previously recalled in treatment. She was between 5 and 6 years old when her mother was taken away to a concentration camp, and she had been left in a ghetto with two older siblings. A new memory now emerged. One day everyone was herded into a courtyard to be executed. Her siblings protectively put her in the middle because she was the youngest. Across from them, on a balcony, was a stormtrooper ready to shoot. They were told to lift both arms. She remembered thinking that she would be shot in the stomach, but as the man lifted his gun and aimed at the group, an air-raid alarm sounded, causing him to flee.

I said the young man who threatened to sue her and who carried a gun was now her executioner. For the first time Naomi was able to laugh. In her fourth and last session she reported that she had written up her defense and sent it in. The ethics committee had canceled the meeting. She had contacted her young client, and he and his family had dropped the suit. She was safe. She said the young man with the gun was a confused, vindictive boy, not a stormtrooper. She realized that her life was not in danger. Naomi ended her hour happily. She had worked her way out of a *double reality*: her Holocaust reality and her current somatic symptom and displaced fantasies.

Although it is impossible to ascertain the exactness of Naomi's memory, there is no doubt that she had believed that the entire ghetto population would be shot in the stomach and die. We knew from her previous treatment that her relationship with her next older sister had always been problematic; as her mother had explained, the sister had been "a problem" from the time of

Naomi's birth. She was jealous because Naomi had become her mother's favorite. When their mother was forcibly torn away from them, Naomi was left with one loving and one jealous sister as her only protectors. Thus, being shot in the stomach became an organizing fantasy laden with guilt toward her older sister, as well as with survivors' guilt.

In the current incident Naomi unconsciously felt she was in danger. When she learned that the young man had a gun, she unconsciously feared nothing less than execution. She therefore did not see her client immediately. Initially, however, there was no recall of the traumatic incident. It took the external crisis and my question about her abdominal pain to bring Naomi's childhood memory into consciousness and to explain her somatic concretization.

Twice in Naomi's life a "man with a gun" had threatened her life. Temporal distinctions were obliterated, as the "man with the gun" from past and present were conflated into one. Her psychosomatic symptom and her "paralysis" represented this threat, which became a concretized theme related both to her early childhood and to her current situation. Naomi was retraumatized by the current external event, while the memory of the ghetto experience remained unconscious. It is safe to assume that she would not have become paralyzed and would have seen her disturbed client sooner had the incident not reawakened the unconscious connection to a "man with a gun."

She recognized with relief that the current situation was not nearly as bad or as dangerous as the original trauma. Her paralysis was related to the scene in the ghetto courtyard, but in her current situation she was able to act and to protect herself. As an adult Naomi experienced near-death anxiety and paralysis that she had not fully realized as a child. Her affective reliving occurred before her memory became conscious. Somatization had taken the place of action. The unconscious connection between the idea of being shot in the stomach and her mother's pregnancy, which had filled her older sister with jealousy, had remained repressed. In her previous treatment, Naomi had not relived and mourned her separation from her mother. An intense conflict related to survivors' guilt and death anxiety thus accounted for the derivatives of her reawakened trauma. Naomi's functioning was fully restored once this was understood.

Apparently, without the crisis of the external event, this unconscious link would not have become conscious. Naomi had to reenact derivatives of her childhood trauma in order for it to become conscious with the help of treatment. As a result of analytic work, two events once equated became distinct: the threatened attack by the Nazi and the attack in unconscious fantasy on her mother's stomach. The condensation of these two events had created Naomi's inability to create anticipatory anxiety, protect herself, and act realistically. Analytic work was necessary here because condensation is not easily penetrated: under such conditions, enactment must stand in for verbal interpretation until internalization and symbolization are established. Naomi had experienced a cognitive and affective regression, which had led to retraumatization.

DISCUSSION

Psychic trauma, originally a real-life experience, becomes a reservoir of intrapsychic representations and fantasies. Under optimal conditions the ego is strong enough to exert its protective function so that a patient can remember a trauma and work it through as one would any other disturbing material. More frequently, however, when a severe trauma has occurred, a patient is unable to raise adequate defenses against the anxiety of experiencing the affect of the original trauma. Recollection of the trauma, if impelled from within and relived in transference, may therefore be experienced with a surprising intensity, reminiscent of the original event. A person with a history of trauma can be expected to employ defenses against retraumatization as soon the trauma or its derivatives threaten to emerge, and may withdraw from treatment altogether unless retraumatization anxieties can be analyzed. A negative therapeutic reaction, should one occur in this context, may be viewed as a sign that the patient is in the grip of unconscious retraumatization anxiety.

In the analytic situation, we *implicitly* ask the patient to tolerate painful affect, emphasizing a need to relive trauma affectively, with maximum verbalization and a minimum of acting out. Only when affect is experienced as real and the trauma is acknowledged, can the latter be worked through and begin to heal. At the same time, we want patients to be aware that reliving within the transference neurosis, even with all the concomitant affects of the trauma, is not the original trauma itself. Recognizing this difference while dealing simultaneously with the affect of the trauma and the manifestation of the trauma in transference may be a tall order, because it contains an inherent contradiction from the patient's point of view. While the anxiety signal may continue to operate in real life, in treatment we wish patients to put feelings of danger into words. Yet patients are invariably, and quite naturally, afraid to do this, particularly those who have suffered severe traumatization in the past. Although verbalization, interpretation, and explanation by the analyst may be experienced as supportive, it may also be felt as a move toward separation, and may therefore interfere with the perception of the analyst as a protective, sustaining presence who will prevent retraumatization from occurring.

In the discussion of the negative therapeutic reaction in Mr. M's case, the overwhelming emphasis has been the transformation of aggressive drive derivatives into hostility. Although I am dealing here with the negative therapeutic reaction as an emergency reaction against retraumatization, I have emphasized that a patient may use a hostile and self destructive stance to avoid facing the original trauma. Mr. M submitted masochistically to his mother. His sadomasochistic and self-destructive relationships became ongoing, were sexualized in fantasy, and led to a negative therapeutic reaction when analyzed. When a psychic constellation is reactive to an unprotective, traumatizing milieu that has led to chaotic internal images with split self and object representations, it creates devaluing, denigrating, or sadistic enactments that are aimed at an internal object, turned against the self, or projected onto the analyst (Kernberg, 1992, pp. 257–262). The individual's incapacity to cope creates an imbalance between hostility and libidinal forces that may be trauma producing as such, causing a state of internal disharmony that interferes with defense against retraumatization.

When a repressed memory is first evoked in treatment, it may not be connected to an observable affect or ideation. Later, when an upsurge from repression occurs by virtue of transference reliving or an event in the outside world, an unconscious memory related to it may be released.

By its very nature, a trauma is never completely assimilated and is rarely successfully adapted to without analysis. Trauma is actualized via myriad enactments. Both avoidance and repetition affect character structure and its defenses. If a trauma has been repressed, it may be retrieved retroactively in an unconscious fantasy, or a screen memory, or through an external event, and may become an example of return from repression. If the trauma cannot be mastered, it remains what I would call "a heavy sediment at the bottom," concretized in enactment. As it has been absorbed by the psyche as a trauma, it is not inert. Derivatives emerge in the analytic process and when they create a new trauma the patient experiences what I call "retraumatization" in this discussion. A successful analysis permits the trauma to be subjected to more abstract symbolization in language and frees the patient for the first time from the burden of the original trauma.

In his sessions Mr. M recreated an event and symbolized it in transference language. In order to understand what happened between himself and his mother he had to create the necessary distance from her. He experienced the shock of his force-feeding mother for the first time in analysis. Subsequently, the trauma occurred in analyzable form within the transference relationship. Prior to analysis, enactment functioned as a concrete and primitive form of symbolization. An event that is pressing on the psychic system and cannot be symbolized will often result in enactment or somatization, as in the case of Naomi's stomach pain.

Mr. M's photophobia replaced the perception of the true danger, his self-destructive rage against his internal objects. Both his disruption of the analytic process and his photophobia occurred in the absence of signal anxiety, the capacity for which had been lost during his massive traumatization in childhood.

When a parent instills a fear of death in a child, as in the case of Mr. M, adequate defenses against internal danger may be impossible for the ego to develop or, if established, may be lost. A perverse organization, which may replace it, eliminates a fear of death (Chasseguet-Smirgel, 1985). As long as Mr. M engaged in bulimic and pedophilic fantasies, he forever remained a child, more girl than boy, and death could not touch him. Analyzing his fear of death by analyzing the defenses against it would therefore lead predictably to the emergence of retraumatization anxiety in the transference. Freud believed, from the very inception of his psychoanalytic studies in his work on hysteria in the 1880s, that overstimulation early in life causes traumatization. I believe that Mr. M's case may serve as an example of overstimulation as a trauma-producing phenomenon.

Naomi required an event outside the treatment to mobilize past trauma. Initially the man with the gun in her childhood registered as "a man with a gun will probably shoot me in the stomach." This was repressed within the childhood context of the event. Because she unconsciously feared execution, she was unable to use an anticipatory danger signal as a self-protective function. Instead she created a symptom that condensed a new event in her life and a past traumatic event of major proportions. In Naomi's case a psychosomatic symptom replaced the danger signal and she suffered a total inability to act self-protectively.

When the anxiety signal does not function protectively, the connection of things that belong together is altered and a thought disorder may result. When thought and affect cannot be combined, a disturbance in the capacity to symbolize occurs. The impact of trauma on the capacity to symbolize is complex. In some cases an event once symbolized abstractly may be concretely reenacted. In Naomi's case, a psychosomatic symptom took the place of what had never been symbolized. The analytic aim is to help the patient become capable of symbolization so that actions, affects, and conflicts may receive psychic representation.

These two patients manifested two different ways of actualizing and concretizing past traumata. It is noteworthy that neither patient was traumatized by discovery of the traumatic *content*, and that neither patient relived the past traumata directly. Nor did either verbalize a fear of retraumatization. In both cases, an important segment of repression remained active until analytic work led to an understanding of the crisis.

In chapter 8 I described a case of retraumatization during the analysis of a patient, who had a psychotic father and whose son suffered a psychotic episode while she was in analysis. Although the crisis with her son occurred outside the analysis, my patient held me responsible and her total disillusionment with my trustworthiness and my capacities as an analyst manifested itself in a manner typical of the negative therapeutic reaction as we have traditionally understood it. Unable to continue her analysis, she remained with me in psychotherapy for a year and then asked to return to the couch. In addition to the trauma of her son's psychotic breakdown, Miriam was retraumatized by memories of her psychotic father which emerged, stimulated by the crisis with her son. She became temporarily disorganized, engaged in a fantasy of fusion with her psychotic son, and shut out the world of reality as much as she could. When she could resume her analysis, she was able to remember a wealth of new facts and fantasies about her relationship with her father and how as a child she had dealt with his psychosis. These now became analyzable and would not have emerged from repression without her reaction to the psychotic breakdown of her son.

The three cases of retraumatization I have discussed demonstrate that each person's internal representation of traumata is unique. In every therapeutic situation, past traumata will be relived in the analytic situation, though how this will occur is by no means predictable, nor the extent to which retraumatization will take place.

Affective experiences that surge up from repression create an affective memory. Reliving previous traumatic situations in analysis is a *refinding* of affect experienced in the original trauma. Under favorable conditions the relationship to the analyst has to be a sufficiently trusting one to make such reliving possible without excessive fear of retraumatization. However, where past object relations have been inadequately sustaining, and have led to developmental deficits, internal pressure engendered by the danger of retraumatization is all the greater. When a severe trauma occurs, the protective functions of parental representations are disrupted and the reworking of traumatic events in analysis means replacing an absent protective object, or one considered life-threatening, with a more realistic internal representation (Laub and Auerhahn, 1993).

When protective internal images become unavailable verbal communication is impaired. Subsequently, when experiences are not properly assimilated, symbols may not be formed because the symbolizing function is interrupted. It is quite typical that affect cannot be put into words and is instead acted out in concretizing traumatic themes. The analyst is then supposed to decipher this action and facilitate its verbalization, thus reestablishing ego functions and the return of a greater capacity for verbalization.

Clinical experience indicates that certain traumatic events are so powerful that the capacity to symbolize abstractly and represent events in language has never developed or has been extinguished. Symbolization may become concretized in action marked by a concomitant diminution in the ability to experience the action as symbolic.

I believe that a trauma can also create a situation in which an intrapsychic representation of the event cannot be formed. However, with the aid of an increased verbal capacity which facilitates abstract symbolization, developed via the analytic process, such an event can acquire a meaning that can be internalized and will henceforth always be recalled within that meaning.

When the trauma cannot be repeated in analysis in "mitigated form" (Freud, 1926), the fear of retraumatization will forever be present. Despite this danger of retraumatization in analysis, many authors hold that analytic work can be successful if the patient's communications can be understood and that a therapeutic alliance can if necessary, as in Mr. M's case, be maintained in a nonverbal mode. With patients who experience states of panic, preservation of the analytic dialogue, even a wordless one, becomes paramount (Maldonado, 1983).

It is the ultimate aim of analysis to create a new psychic equilibrium that will contain a defensive system that is self-protective. In therapeutic work, psychoanalysts need to attempt to differentiate themselves from an internal threatening object in order to deal more effectively with retraumatization anxiety. If analysis is successful, the negative therapeutic reaction is transformed into an anticipatory danger signal indicating a *now conscious* fear of retraumatization. Traumatic themes from the past gradually come to be viewed as if from a distance, as distinct from the patient's current life, a process comparable to the mourning process at the end of an analysis.

Part IV

Creativity and Work Inhibition

10.

Creative Work, Work Inhibitions, and Their Relation to Internal Objects

Between the conception
And the creation
Between the emotion
And the response
Falls the Shadow
  [T. S. Eliot, 1925]

Artists engaged in their endeavors may find their work overshadowed by a dialogue with internalized parental objects that interfere with their freedom to create. I have found that if parental objects have been internalized as love giving, a "libidinal dialogue" with a "good enough" object is possible and creative work, narcissistically valued by its creator, is safeguarded from within. If a creative person suffers from work inhibition, however, it is often the result of an unconscious hostile dialogue with internalized parental images perceived as punitive and as disregarding of that person's creative efforts. I have observed this to be the case with artists who come to me because they have experienced their creativity as having been hampered predominantly by internal struggles emanating from a deeply felt hostile relationship with their internalized parental objects. This in turn has given rise to severe conflicts that interfere with creative freedom. Internalized relationships with parental images, whether unconscious or expressed as a conscious fantasy, may lead to inhibition or even paralysis of the creative function.

In the external world artists create things that people use. From an intrapsychic point of view, however, creative work can be conceptualized as an unconscious communication addressed to an internalized object. Such communication is a psychic reality, "not a fantasy that is taken for the real truth, for an actual event, but the 'real' recollection of a psychic event with its mixture of fact and fantasy" (Arlow, 1969, p. 43). Intrapsychic interaction is characteristic of the relationship of the self and its objects in the internal world (Sandler and Rosenblatt, 1962, pp. 132–133). Such interaction results in an internal structure replicating "in the intrapsychic world both real and fantasied relationships with significant others" (Kernberg, 1991).

When internal parental images are implicated in the creative process, artists often have difficulty separating the act of creation and its product from their "internal dialogue" with their parents. Creating a product that is valued as distinctly one's own and separate from this self-defeating hostile dialogue may not be achievable without analytic help.

Creative impairment can be experienced either as total incapacity to work or as inability to work at one's highest level. Inhibited artists feel a sense of urgency about incomplete work. Although this creates anxiety, it may not be the patient's original motivation for seeking treatment. Initially patients may not wish to explore their intrapsychic conflicts, but at the same time they hunger unconsciously for a new object who can be trusted to remain libidinally invested and support their creative efforts until an artistic product is completed.

At times certain events emanating from psychic conflict impair the creative process and lead to work inhibition. As internal representations of parental objects become structured, and as internalized self and object relationships appear in the interaction between a patient's internal wishes and their prohibition, a permanent inhibition of creativity may result. The accessibility of these internalized objects in the analytic process varies from patient to patient and also varies depending on whether the patient exhibits neurotic or borderline pathology. Conflict may be deeply repressed in neurotic pathology but is more easily accessible in borderline pathology, where object relations have not readily yielded to the formation of intrapsychic structures. In neurotic patients, inter- and intrapsychic conflicts usually have been superseded by object relations that have been repressed, so that at first only more accessible intrapsychic conflicts are apparent. As analysis proceeds and regression occurs, object relationship conflicts within psychic structures become more evident. In borderline cases, internalized object relations have not lost their voices.

A complex correlation exists between psychic disturbance and creative inhibition. Some severely disturbed people are highly productive, whereas others use their creativity as a way of managing intrapsychic conflicts and therefore become less productive. The creator's relationship to the created product is symbol forming and communicative. While artists may have no difficulty creating symbols initially, they may nonetheless need major encouragement to preserve their products: their symbolizing capacity tends to break down under excessive pressure of hostile affect toward their internalized objects.

Psychoanalytic writers have drawn attention to the hostile attitude artists sometimes hold toward their creative products. As a rule, the artistic product is a symbolic object, but in severe pathology the symbolic function may be lost. An example is given by Gross and Rubin (1973), who report that Edvard Munch, after a psychotic break, treated his paintings like internal objects, "stacking them upright on the grounds surrounding his house and claiming their exposure to every kind of weather was a 'horse doctor's cure' which would do them good" (p. 351). De Tolnay (1960) describes how when a day after Michelangelo's death, "an inventory of Michelangelo's belongings was taken . . . much less was found in [his] house than had been thought to be there. The artist had had many of his drawings burned. As for works of art, [there were] . . . three unfinished marble statues . . . one of them . . . identified as the Pietà Rondanini . . ." (p. 16). That Pietà was a young Madonna and dying Christ that Vasari reported as "obviously" having been created by Michelangelo for his own grave. Liebert (1983) stresses that the Pietà Rondanini is unique in that it is the only work that Michelangelo actually tried to destroy and then abandoned: "After years of work he mutilated the group . . . " (p. 398). Liebert believes that a psychoanalytic inquiry into Michelangelo's destruction of that Pietà needs to focus first on why the mutilation occurred at that time, and on how to regard Michelangelo's own explanation for the destruction, "that he was so vexed by Urbino's nagging that he attempted to destroy a group for his own tomb" (p. 402). Liebert quotes Steinberg's (1983) explanation that "the...[Christ figure's] slung leg was to be recognized as an unmistakable symbol of sexual aggression or compliance." Steinberg believed that Michelangelo "destroyed it in despair" when he found that he had pushed "the rhetoric of carnal gesture beyond the limit of acceptable expression . . ." (p. 399).

As in the more famous Pietà in St. Peter's basilica, the Madonna sculpted by Michelangelo is remarkably young and beautiful, a reference most likely to Michelangelo's mother, who died when she was very young. As Freud suggested in "The Theme of the Three Caskets" (1913), in death we try to rejoin our mothers who nurtured us when we were born. Because Michelangelo's own mother had left him when he was so young, he was unable to portray her as giving him comfort in his death. The unconscious hostility engendered in him by the early loss of his mother is likely what kept him from completing the Rondanini Pietà.

While such destructive impulses may occur only episodically, an analyst treating creative patients may be called on to protect the patient's product from its creator's fury. In the examples that follow, work inhibition reproduced conflictual relationships with internal objects. To overcome the creative impasses that resulted, these patients needed help in realizing that they wanted me to protect their artistic product from their aggression. My perceived failure to do so resulted in a negative therapeutic reaction and difficulty in differentiating the analyst from the internalized object toward whom hostility was unconsciously directed. This hostility was externalized in the wish to destroy what had been created. Such destructive episodes give analyst and patient a chance to arrive at a more dynamic understanding of creative inhibition and of the creative process per se.

Many pathological solutions are beyond the scope of this chapter, which presents only cases in which analysis facilitated productivity by illuminating how internalized pathological object relations and ensuing unconscious conflicts contributed to creative inhibition. In such cases a therapeutic alliance is fostered when the analyst is differentiated from ambivalently cathected internalized imagos. The therapeutic alliance plays a crucial role in helping the patient form a bridge of communication with the creative aspects of the self. The patient can then gain some distance from the conflict-laden dialogue with internalized parental imagos; this intrapsychic separation leads to a decrease of creative inhibition in the patient and may be the first breakthrough of autonomous creative experience.

In my experience with such patients, the transference relationship involves a triple-faceted relatedness: the analyst is expected to relate not only to the patient's intrapsychic problem, but also to both the ongoing work process and the product as external events. During periods of positive transference the patient believes that the analyst furthers creative capacity, accepts the creative product as valuable, and agrees that its completion is a primary life goal. In the examples that follow I hope to show how my external, at times "extra-analytic" activity, related to my patients' creative process and products, facilitated creative development and the overcoming of creative inhibition.

CLINICAL EXAMPLES

Laura

A sculptor in her forties, Laura came to analysis because she was "stuck." The assemblage and construction of her work required much more than a single burst of energy to complete, and she had become incapable of sustained effort. Indeed, she felt compelled to disassemble her work-in-progress and return it each time to its unworked elements. She then became anxious that she would never be able to make her work whole again. Often she brought reports and actual work of these incomplete attempts to her sessions, and upon associating to her work would find its completion easier.

When Laura first came to see me she was overweight. A chain smoker and heavy coffee drinker, she also frequently consumed alcohol to the point of stupor. She was easily aroused sexually but after marriage did not experience orgasm. She had a disturbed sense of self. She would "forget to work" but pretend to others that she had completed a project. In states of greater reality testing, she would wonder, "Where have I been all this time?" It appeared that Laura's forgetting to work occurred in fuguelike states.

In childhood Laura took care of a cranky brother three years her junior, whom her mother could not handle. She recalled never being thanked for her efforts, even though they restored peace in the family. When Laura was between 9 and 10 years old, she had major surgery requiring general anesthesia. During her prolonged hospitalization her mother stayed in an adjoining room, where she and Laura's father spent many hours behind closed doors. Her father visited Laura daily and brought her the comics, but always remained in the doorway. He never entered her room to kiss or touch her, though she was not contagious. Although we later reconstructed that her father had a germ phobia, at the time Laura thought he did not want to touch her because she was ugly and crippled, a self-image she maintained from then on.

Following her recovery, Laura began to masturbate compulsively. She fantasized that she was spreading germs to everyone, particularly her phobic father. Germs were equated with semen and impregnation, and she fantasized producing a defective baby with him. Masturbation and overeating made her feel whole again, undoing feelings of genital mutilation. The underlying fantasies contained death wishes toward the oedipal father and revenge themes for having been rejected. Laura also needed to fend off her cannibalistic wishes. She was physically attracted to her mother, who constantly offered overgratification and had devouring impulses. Laura felt drawn to her mother's overweight body; its layers of fat fascinated her. In recurring dreams she wished her mother's fat would engulf and protect her. Both parents overgratified Laura with material things but failed to make her feel lovable. When Laura was 21, her parents died a short time apart, leaving her traumatized and desolate. She fantasized at times that her mother was alive inside her and at other times that she carried her as a dead anal baby inside her stomach.

At a certain point in her analysis Laura wrote down her thoughts rather than save them for her analytic hour:

I begin every day with convictions and end in doubts—coffee, cigarettes, vodka, and wastebaskets filled with the day's fresh start. These line up in my studio like sentinels of a beheading. Every day I murder a few hours before I start my work and then run from it in guilt, only to return the next day to retrieve what I had lost, thereupon doubling my losses. The third triples, the fourth quadruples, and so on into the following day's loss. What is strange is that like a true gambler, I return each time with a fresh hope that I have found some winning combination. My fantasy is that the work will arrive whole, magically, out of one sitting. It is a childish, passive fantasy.

Luck or nature or God or hired hands [the analyst] will do the work for me . . . I feel I belong nowhere . . . I cannot get to my destination, nor can I go back to where I started. I'm lost and my time is running out . . . In my fantasies I think that success could kill me, a heart attack or cancer. Meanwhile I'm eating up my savings. Worse, I'm eating up my heart. Who wants to die like that? In my fantasy, it's better to die with a little posthumous work and, if you'll forgive the pun, it could be inscribed on my tombstone, I met my last deadline. The biggest risk you take is that it may be said of you that your little operation was a success and wasn't it too bad the patient died?

Laura's ritualistic behavior involved symbolic actions designed to resurrect her parents and subsequently kill them again, underscoring the prominence of the murder theme in her written piece. At the beginning of her day Laura did chores her late mother would have done for her, then proceeded to "make herself beautiful" or "hide her ugliness" from her father. After these ritualistic restitutional reenactments, she felt ready to start working, but usually by then the day was nearly over.

These rituals also served to protect her creative work from wishes to hurt her fantasized bad internalized objects. She manifested separation anxiety related to completing her work, as completion would amount unconsciously to triple murder—parents and her brother. Thus, her work inhibition was "an act of kindness." A fear of revenge by parents or sibling made oedipal victory a threatening prospect, comparable to Loewald's concept of parricide (1979).

Laura was frightened when she felt close to me or had homosexual dreams in which she was nursing at my breasts or making love to me. She feared finishing her sculptures because she expected to be faced with an ugly baby her parents would hate, created either by us or by her and her father. This fantasy sometimes had the status of a genuine belief.

Laura's work inhibition was overdetermined and female genital anxiety conflicts over gender identity were prominent. She was enraged that her parents had "subjected" her to surgery as a child. She fantasized that it had left her ugly and deformed. In her art work she repeatedly recreated a crippled body, a fantasy image connected to her surgery. Her traumatized body image also expressed itself in disassembling her sculpture and fearing she would never be able to make it whole again. Her tendency to self-denigration made her doubt her work was good enough to preserve and "keep alive." At other times Laura successfully completed her projects. This gave her a sense of autonomy from parents and siblings and was followed by a marked decrease in hostility. She often mentioned that in her innermost soul she was really working for her father's enthusiastic response and approving smile. These paternal gestures would signify she was whole as a female and did not have to feel ugly.

When in a state of narcissistic self-denigration Laura could not sustain object love, a situation that placed her work in danger of destruction. At a particularly difficult juncture in a project, she was impelled to flee; she could not rely on creativity to sustain her. The analytic gain of lengthening her creative attention span from twenty minutes to several hours corresponded to a newfound ability to form an internal self-image as a creative artist.

Laura remained dependent on the outside world for affirmation of her self-worth. The traumatic impact of her body image confusion following surgery had coalesced into a fantasy that to be successful she would have to be male like her brother or beautifully "feminine" like her mother. This fantasy continued into adulthood and expressed her narcissistic injuries, which impeded her work as a sculptor. Narcissistic and oedipally competitive fantasies retained a sense of "actuality" sustained by projective identification whenever hostility or depression temporarily got the upper hand.

After Laura's omnipotent fantasies and murderous wishes were analyzed, and she was able to create an autonomous, feminine self-image, distinct from her childhood wishes of love from her mother and approval from her father for her creative work, she became a happier and more creative person capable of completing projects. These artistic successes gave her satisfaction, pride, and greater stability in the real world.

Ellen

Ellen came to treatment in her twenties, deeply depressed. Her marriage had been loveless and unhappy, and her husband had recently died. Ellen came from a poor farm family in the dust bowl. As a child she had been close to her father, a revered but isolated professional in a small town. Ellen felt ambivalent toward her mother, whom she thought preferred her little brother. She fantasized that her mother loved her only because she performed endless, onerous household chores. Ellen had noticed early in life that she could conceal her real feelings and feign other emotions; she could "act" and get away with it. Ellen always worked, putting herself through college and then tentatively embarking on an acting career. Her family had discouraged emotional freedom, however, leaving her unable to trust her abilities as an actress.

Ellen's first role was a small character part in which she chose to appear so heavily costumed, to the point of being disguised; altering her voice, she became even more unrecognizable. She fantasized that revealing herself on stage might disclose her hostile fantasies about her mother and brother, of whose relationship she was intensely jealous. Initially we worked on differentiating her hostile conflicts about family members from those of the characters she portrayed.

Early in analysis she got her first important acting part, but experienced such a crisis, such an inability to animate certain lines, that she was in danger of losing the role. When prolonged analysis did not reveal the cause of her increasing inhibition, she became frantic, deeply depressed, and less and less verbal. Finally she asked whether I would attend a rehearsal and observe her as she tried to speak the lines that so paralyzed her. Having agreed to this "extra-analytic" foray, I slipped into the darkened theater and recognized immediately that Ellen's affect became flat and unconvincing when she had to express the hostility of an evil and powerful female character. She failed as an actress when her lines expressed themes related to her own sadomasochistic and murderous fantasies about her mother, which her strict superego would not permit her to acknowledge.

Sandler (1990) discussed underlying internal obstacles in a psychic constellation similar to those that accounted for Ellen's behavior: "if one *identified* with some aspect of the parent, then one would duplicate that perceived aspect in oneself and become more like that parent. If one *introjected* the parent, then the introject would not modify one's self-representation but would become an internal companion, a sort of back-seat driver. Of course one can . . . identify with the introject just as we might identify with an object perceived in the external world" (p. 865). In Ellen's case the introjected mother was not sufficiently differentiated from the real mother, and neither was sufficiently differentiated from the character Ellen was portraying. The introjected mother thus served as Sandler's "back-seat driver" when Ellen was on stage, forbidding the vocalization of hostility.

After I saw Ellen rehearse, I was able to tell her what I had observed, and she was subsequently able to verbalize her hostility toward her mother, which threatened to emerge when she had to speak the lines that gave her such difficulty. She understood why her affect became forced, and we could now explore her hostile introject. My participation helped form a boundary between herself, her mother, and the character she was creating.

Aided by this liberated verbal capacity, Ellen became able to analyze conflicts related to her internal objects. This enhanced her creativity. Subsequently, she drew on her creative capacities to externalize bad objects, including the analyst in the negative transference. She used her treatment to transpose affects based on libidinal and hostile fantasies to create the characters *she* was playing. When she became able to dip freely and without anxiety into her personal experiences, she created a role in which she combined the excessive punctiliousness and cleanliness of her mother with her own love of "the beautiful objects" she saw in my office. This enabled her to sublimate hostile themes in an exquisitely integrated characterization of a woman who cared more about things than about people.

When Ellen discovered that I was pregnant, it evoked her hostility toward mother and brother with renewed ferociousness. She had a masturbation fantasy in which she visualized a woman looking like Diana of Ephesus with many ever lactating breasts. The woman permitted Ellen to nurse forever, like a mother who never left. These libidinal fantasies did not disappear, even after oedipal wishes became prominent. Because Ellen had already reached the point in analysis where she was able to separate internal conflicts from her creative work, this temporary regression did not cause a resurgence of her work inhibition.

After I gave birth, she sent me flowers and a note that said "I forgive you." Her own feminine wishes subsequently emerged. Ellen remarried and had several children. A few years after ending her treatment, she brought her children for a visit so I could participate in her joy in being a mother. Her femininity and creativity liberated, she was able to go on to achieve fame in her work.

Anita

Anita came to analysis in her late twenties. The oldest of three children, she was a musician and singer of popular songs. When I met her, she had moved far away from home, putting almost the entire width of the United States between herself and her family. Since her separation from home, she had been extremely upset, lonely, and afraid to perform her songs. Her artistic work had become sporadic, and she had developed a tendency to spoil her opportunities to perform. She impressed me as a fragile little bird, highly intelligent, probably talented, erratic, and painfully thin. Her motions were anxious and her speech clipped, as if she were uncertain whether I would help or hurt her.

During Anita's childhood, her mother, who had been a performer in a related field, had little time to spend with her children. Anita had the impression that her mother had been competitive with her. The mother also planned and arranged everything for her children, instead of giving them the opportunity to choose what they wished to do. Anita felt that she had grown up in a straitjacket.

Her mother was very concerned with Anita's toilet functions when she was 2 and 3. Anita had been constipated in childhood and spent long periods on the toilet, reading as soon as she was able. When she did not produce stools, her mother forced her to have enemas, a practice that continued well into the oedipal phase. Reading the "grown-up" books and magazines she found in the bathroom came to represent forbidden pleasures, and during analysis she realized that she had always feared she would be punished for seeking independent knowledge. During the preoedipal and oedipal phases, the enema ritual had become sexualized; while her mother administered the enema, Anita had the fantasy that she was united with both mother and father. As she lay on her belly receiving the enema, her clitoris was apparently stimulated; she developed a masturbation fantasy in which she became an indispensable link responsible for the happiness of her parents. This fantasy produced feelings of omnipotence and probably contributed to her ability to tolerate the pain and rage caused by the procedure. She also was force-fed from early on. Later she often allowed her food to get cold; if she ate it all, she frequently vomited afterward. She survived by stealing food from the refrigerator—a surprisingly nourishing combination of edibles—and devouring it furtively.

Throughout her growing years, Anita was periodically anorexic. Though she was sent for psychotherapy for brief periods, her parents would interrupt her treatment as soon as she showed signs of improvement. During the sixties and early seventies, she became a very poor student, abused drugs, and hung out with friends who were an affront to her parents' sense of social status. She developed food fads, continued to be constipated, and went to myriad "healers" and nutritionists who tried, not very successfully, to deal with her many allergies and physical aches and pains. The physical intrusions into her body, the enemas and force-feeding, from early childhood on had physically overstimulated and frightened her. She could consult a regular physician and have her body examined only after she came to trust me. In adulthood, working became equated with being forced and she held jobs only sporadically. Her parents paid for her treatment, but by way of protesting their lack of recognition of her needs, she lived in great poverty, eating only one meal a day.

After she had progressed in the analysis toward greater individuation and a less passive, masochistic, and self-destructive stance toward her forcing mother and indifferent father, Anita was less frightened, fell in love, and after further analytic work was able to enter an excellent marriage. She began to cook and enjoy food for the first time in her life. She gained a great deal of weight, which she had difficulty taking off again. As she developed an image of her body as belonging to her, as less an object to be intruded on and beaten down, she became less fragile, her allergies lessened, and her hysterical reactions decreased. But, while the physical symptoms abated, the work inhibition remained. It belonged to a deeper, traumatic layer of early childhood that was uncovered later in analysis.

Anita continued to fear exposing her talent in public. She likened performing to exposing herself naked. A paranoid fantasy of being exposed and having to avoid having her products forcibly removed interfered with her work and creativity. She did not believe that her talent belonged to her. Differentiation from her parents had remained partial. Unconsciously, the narcissistically protected, sexualized bodily products had remained the joint property of herself and her parents. Only as long as she could keep her work secret could she believe that it belonged to her.

During this period, Anita was presented with an opportunity to produce a musical composition of potentially great importance to her career. At first it was difficult to know what aspects of her traumatic childhood experiences most paralyzed her creativity. Her composition demanded that she establish within the music an organized hierarchical structure that followed a certain logical sequence. However, her notations showed inconsistency, and both compositional structure and sequence were confused. Incapable of synthesizing her work, she felt powerless and driven. Paralyzed with anxiety, she considered giving up the project. A thinking disorder had become evident.

Anita then decided to bring her work to her analytic sessions. The first clue was her saying that when she attempted to establish a sequential order it felt as if everything was "rushing in on [her] simultaneously." She remembered how her body felt when the water from the enema bag rushed into her and she was so frightened that she could not hold it inside herself long enough. As long as everything rushed in at the same time, she could not synthesize or structure her work. Separation from the mother had initially been achieved by a regression from cleanliness to being messy. Unconsciously her work had to be messy and to remain in "bits and pieces": what was messy belonged to her and what was orderly belonged to her mother. All that was clean had to be given up. Secondary process thinking represented closeness to her father, from whom she felt barred; such "good" thinking had also to be handed over to her mother. Thus, her artistic creations, like her eating during childhood, had to remain secret. Once this connection was worked through, her sense of autonomy improved and she was able to produce an original piece of work without having to hide it. She gradually overcame her cognitive inhibition and thinking disorder. Subsequently, she resumed performing in public.

The patient's thinking disorder, which had created the work inhibition, was based on reliving a traumatic state (from the oral and anal periods) that surfaced whenever she attempted to work. Her mother's forcing had become sexualized and had made it impossible for her as an adult to claim as her own the products of her work. Once she achieved autonomy over her thinking, a spurt in oedipal development followed. Anita's success helped her to separate from her forcing mother and give up the fantasy of being (via the enema fantasy) a part of her parents' sexual union. Consequent on this was an improvement in her adult love life with her husband.

DISCUSSION

Many analysts who study the relation of creative persons to their products are influenced by Winnicott (1953, 1965, 1971), who believed that artistic work takes place in the "transitional space" between mother and child and reorganizes that space. In this "transitional space" there may be communication with more than one object. Elements of love and aggression motivate efforts to facilitate communication with an idealizable mother who understands the message and therefore the child. The "other" (the "not-me") may be not the mother but instead may represent the transformation of the primary object for the sake of experimentation by the infant—and later the adult—in the environment with things outside the self, and without participation of the object. Endowing the transitional object with fantasy, the infant becomes progressively more individuated, finding its way in the external world, increasingly separated from the mother whom the patient internalizes as a safe object. The extent to which this development is relevant for the adult creator varies, but I believe there is always a need for personal space and for empathic communication with an object related to the artistic process, and a need to express idealization of, and restitution toward, an internalized object representation. With the achievement of autonomy, pathological aspects of the dialogue with the internal object no longer interfere with productivity.

Oremland (1989) characterizes creativity as a form of object relatedness that begins early on and continues throughout life (p. 29). He has observed that the artist demands that the analyst relate to the artistic product as both part and not part of the patient's self.

Rose (1987) points out that the creative function may be blocked at a very early developmental level. The capacity for the timing of work may be disrupted as well. Relatedness disrupted by a serious, at times traumatic, break between object and growing child may lead to severe work inhibition.

When narcissistically invested primary objects fail to give sufficient recognition to independent efforts in the child that may lead to mature achievements, the child as an adult may have a tendency to submit masochistically to a task (Novick and Novick, 1991). Sexualized and sadomasochistic fantasies also contribute to work inhibition. Severe fluctuations in self-esteem may produce obsessive doubt about one's capacity for creative work or lead to work paralysis. Gedo (1983) discusses this creative paralysis and work inhibition in relation to trauma. Ambivalence or splitting, originally object-directed, may subsequently be displaced or projected onto the creative product, leading to paralysis or to destruction of the product.

All the patients discussed here manifested bisexual wishes and sadomasochistic impulses that endangered the self or the creative product. Laura experienced conflicts related to early traumatization by premature separation from primary objects. This influenced libidinal and psychosexual development, which in turn led to problems in body image formation. All three patients had been put in the position early in life of being caregivers to their mothers (see chapter 1). The creative process gave an impetus to their desire to free themselves from this role.

In the cases discussed, masturbation fantasies served as compromise formations; they simultaneously expressed a need for the object and a denial of that need. Fantasies also expressed a sadomasochistic bond with internal objects and the narcissistic wounds inflicted by them. Analysis of masturbation fantasies frequently released creativity.

As a result of analysis, internal objects became less threatening, superego conflicts more benign, and lasting gains in creativity were achieved. Laura's creations, for instance, had centered on a restitutional narcissistic fantasy designed to alleviate psychic pain. Analysis enabled her to give up her addictive predispositions and her compulsive behavior—drinking, her overeating, excessive withdrawal into fantasy, compulsive masturbation, fantasies of being her parents' unloved child, and most of all her need to disassemble her creative work. Her attention span increased, her sleep disturbance abated, and she was able to form more successful relationships, which released her creative capacities.

The creatively inhibited patient is usually unable to invest creative work with an adequate amount of healthy narcissism. To the extent that the patient's narcissistic fantasy is rooted in an unrealistic appraisal of his or her ability, it is destined to interfere with creative activity in pathological ways. Some creative patients surrender personal narcissism in favor of their product in the service of an aspect of their ego ideal: they will sacrifice momentary gains for the sake of creative work. What they produce may tyrannize them until they become satisfied with their product, which becomes a triumph of creative self-expression.

Patients with creative disorders, such as Laura, Ellen, and Anita, need the therapeutic support of an analyst against forces that threaten to destroy the creative process or the creative product. In these three instances I found that my activity related to these patients' triple-faceted transference, facilitated a previously unexperienced communication and a new awareness of the value of the creative product.

Freud's analysis of Hilda Doolittle, as described by Richards (1992), cured her inhibited creativity. His technique provided understanding of her narcissistic injuries from early childhood, her bisexuality in her personal life, and its role in her creativity. He demonstrated "the capacity to understand fantasy as unreal while at the same time treating it and experiencing it as real and crucial" (p. 26). Doolittle thus was able to use this liberating communication with Freud to identify with him, leading to new compromise formations that rescued and enhanced her creativity. As Freud provided her a capacity to identify with him as a new internalized object, her creative inhibition disappeared.

My "extra-analytic" activities involved either seeing or hearing something *concrete* produced by the patient that was in "creative trouble" or crisis. Meeting the patient's need to be seen or heard within the working frame of analysis—even when, as with Ellen's rehearsal, this involved my leaving the office—protected the artistic products from destruction and overcame the work inhibition. One is tempted to speculate that, just as the earliest dialogue between mother and child relates to recognizing her face and hearing her voice, so my active intervention may have provided an affective experience crucial for creativity that was either absent during early development or needed affirmation anew because of the patient's internal deficits.

Neubauer (1987) reports several cases in which he was able to correlate disturbances in perception and memory with difficulties in object relatedness and the capacity for internalization. "Is visual perception," he asks, "necessary for 'knowing' about the object, that is, for the object-self differentiation and internalization?" (p. 345). He further questions whether such a "representational fault" interferes with autonomous ego development and reality relationships. Neubauer's patients needed to use the analyst's presence to enhance the ego functions of perception and memory. In my cases of work inhibition, where my "seeing or hearing something" alleviated the work crisis and promoted internalization, I felt I was augmenting early primitive affect and the perception of a product related to a self representation not yet fully formed.

At the time of my "concrete" activities, the creative products were cathected by the patients and myself in a precariously shared "narcissistic alliance" that I considered necessary to support the patient against destructive, regressive rages. It was as if I were being tested as to whether I was different from the parent in my ability to accept, symbolically, anal or urethral products or vomit. Equal in importance to early psychosexual reliving was the surfacing of narcissistic injuries related to bodily products, body image, and a conflicted sexual identity. Paranoidally tinged anxiety and fantasies emerged that hostile internal objects would demand death as punishment for success.

Thus, my concrete extra-analytic actions helped my patients improve the "dialogue" with their internal objects, from whom positive feelings had previously been withdrawn. Internalization was in each of these cases the felicitous result.

An analysis can be regarded as the mutual creation of patient and analyst. These particular patients sought help because they could not complete a creative work. However, though seeking the analyst's help, the patient does not want to share his or her creation with the analyst: it must be the patient's alone. In reliving childhood conflicts, the patient projects jealousy and hate onto transference, and the creative process is once again inhibited. The analyst must then demonstrate that in spite of these feelings the patient is permitted to be the sole creator of his or her work without having to fear its destruction by a jealous parent. As children, these patients had regarded the creation of products as jealously guarded by parents; they frequently experienced parental prohibition of their free self-expression, while simultaneously being excluded from the parents' creations, such as the primal scene, the oedipal experience, and the creation of babies. Such exclusions are reexperienced in treatment; the patient does not feel entitled to have a "baby" without sharing it with the analyst.

Not until the analytic relationship is built on a sense of trust and the patient believes in his or her autonomous capacities can the patient acquire the ability to separate the actual creative product from a fantasized product in constant danger of reclamation by the parent. The creative product, proceeding from the patient's acknowledged self-expression, can, for the first time, belong to its creator alone.

References

Abelin, E. L. (1971), The role of the father in the separation-individuation process. In: *Separation-Individuation: Essays in Honor of Margaret S. Mahler,* ed. I. B. McDevitt & C. G. Settlage. New York: International Universities Press, pp. 229–252.

———— (1980), Triangulation. In: *Rapprochement,* ed. R. Lax, S. Bach, & E. J. Burland. New York: Jason Aronson, pp. 151–166.

Arlow, J. (1963), Conflict, regression, and symptom formation. *Internat. J. Psycho-Anal.,* 44:12–22.

———— (1969), Unconscious fantasy and disturbances of conscious experience. *Psychoanal. Quart.,* 38:1–27.

———— (1991), Character perversion. In: *Psychoanalysis, Clinical Theory and Practice.* Madison, CT: International Universities Press, 1991, pp. 177–194.

Bach, S. (1980), Self-love and object-love. In: *Rapprochement,* ed. R. Lax, S. Bach, & E. J. Burland. New York: Jason Aronson, pp. 171–196.

———— (1994), *The Language of Perversion and the Language of Love.* London and Northvale, NJ: Jason Aronson.

Bak, R. C. (1968), The phallic woman: The ubiquitous fantasy in perversions. *The Psychoanalytic Study of the Child,* 23:15–36. New York: International Universities Press.

———— (1971), Object-relationships in schizophrenia and perversion. *Internat. J. Psycho-Anal.,* 52:235–242.

⟶ ———— (1973), Being in love and object loss. *Internat. J. Psycho-Anal.*, 54:1–8.

————(1974), Distortions of the concept of fetishism. *The Psychoanalytic Study of the Child*, 29:191–214. New Haven, CT: Yale University Press.

Barnett, M. C. (1966), Vaginal awareness in the infancy and childhood of girls. *J. Amer. Psychoanal. Assn.*, 14:129–141.

Benedek, T. (1973), Parenthood as a developmental phase. In: *Psychoanalytic Investigations*. New York: Quadrangle/The New York Times Book Co., pp. 378–407.

Bergmann, M. S. (1971), Psychoanalytic observations on the capacity to love. In: *Separation Individuation: Essays in Honor of Margaret S. Mahler*, ed. J. B. McDevitt & C. G. Settlage. New York: International Universities Press, pp. 15–40.

———— (1987), *The Anatomy of Loving: The Story of Man's Quest to Know What Love Is*. New York: Columbia University Press.

————Jucovy, M., Eds. (1982), *Generations of the Holocaust*. New York: Basic Books.

Bergmann, M. V. (1988), Masochistic character formation and the re-emergence of traumatic feeling states. In: *New Concepts in Psychoanalytic Psychotherapy*, ed. J. M. Ross & W. A. Myers. Washington, DC: American Psychiatric Press.

———— (1995), Observations on the female negative oedipal phase and its significance in the analytic transference. *J. Clin. Psychoanal.*, 4:283–295.

Blos, P. (1967), The second individuation process of adolescence. *The Psychoanalytic Study of the Child*, 22:162–186. New York: International Universities Press.

———— (1974), The genealogy of the ego ideal. *The Psychoanalytic Study of the Child*, 29:43–88. New Haven, CT: Yale University Press.

———— (1980), Modifications and traditional psychoanalytic theory of female adolescent development. Lecture delivered at the New York Psychoanalytic Institute, November 11.

Blum, H. P. (1973), The concept of erotized transference. *J. Amer. Psychoanal. Assn.*, 21:61–76.

———— (1974), The borderline childhood of the Wolf Man. *J. Amer. Psychoanal. Assn.*, 22:721–742.

Blum, H. P. (1977a), Masochism, the ego ideal, and the psychology of women. In: *Female Psychology: Contemporary Psychoanalytic Views*, ed. H. P. Blum. New York: International Universities Press, pp.

———— (1977b), The prototype of preoedipal reconstruction. *J. Amer. Psychoanal. Assn.*, 25:757–783.

———— (1986), The concept of reconstruction of trauma. In: *The Reconstruction of Trauma*, ed. A. Rothstein. Madison, CT: International Universities Press, pp. 7–27.

———— (1996), Seduction trauma: Representation, deferred action, and pathogenic development. *J. Amer. Psychoanal. Assn.*, 44:1147–1164.

Boesky, D. (1982), Acting out: A reconsideration of the concept. *Internat. J. Psycho-Anal.*, 63:39–55.

Bonaparte, M. (1953), Disturbing factors in feminine development. In: *Female Sexuality*. New York: International Universities Press, pp. 46–61.

Bourdier, P. (1972), La prématurité des enfants de parents psychotiques. *Revue Français de Psychoanalyse*, 36:19–42.

Brenner, C. (1975), Position statement made at the International Congress of Psychoanalysis, London.

———— (1979), Depressive affect, anxiety, and psychic conflict in the phallic-oedipal phase. *Psychoanal. Quart.*, 48:177–197.

Brodey, W. M. (1965), On the dynamics of narcissism. *The Psychoanalytic Study of the Child*, 20:165–193. New York: International Universities Press.

Brunswick, R. M. (1940), The preoedipal phase of the libido development. In: *The Psychoanalytic Reader*, ed. R. Fliess. New York: International Universities Press, 1948, pp. 261–287.

Burlingham, D. T. (1935), Empathy between infant and mother. In: *Psychoanalytic Studies of the Sighted and the Blind*. New York: International Universities Press, 1972, pp. 52–70.

Chasseguet-Smirgel, J. (1970), Feminine guilt and the Oedipus complex. In: *Female Sexuality: New Psychoanalytic Views*. Ann Arbor: University of Michigan Press, pp. 94–134.

———— (1984), The femininity of the analyst in professional practice. *Internat. J. Psycho-Anal.*, 65:169–178.

———— (1985), *Creativity and Perversion*. New York & London: W. W. Norton.

———— (1986), *Sexuality and Mind*. New York: New York University Press.

Chused, J. F. (1991), The evocative power of enactments. *J. Amer. Psychoanal. Assn.*, 39:615–639.

Clower, V. (1977), Theoretical implications in current views of masturbation in latency girls. In: *Female Psychology*, ed. H. P. Blum. New York: International Universities Press, pp. 109–125.

Coleman, R., Kris, E., & Provence, S. (1953), The study of variations of early parental attitudes: A preliminary report. *The Psychoanalytic Study of the Child,* 8:20–47. New York: International Universities Press.

Condorcet, J. A. (1933), *Esquisse d'un tableau historique des progres de l'esprit humain.* Paris: Boivin et cie.

Cooper, A. M. (1991), The unconscious core of perversion. In: *Perversions & Near-Perversions in Clinical Practice, New Psychoanalytic Perspectives,* ed. G. I. Fogel & W. A. Myers. New Haven and London: Yale University Press, pp. 17–35.

Davidowicz, L. (1975), *The War Against the Jews, 1933–1945.* New York: Holt, Rinehart & Winston.

Deutsch, H. (1930), Hysterical fate neurosis. In: *Neuroses and Character Types.* New York: International Universities Press, 1965, pp. 14–28.

DeWind, E. (1968), The confrontation with death: Symposium on psychic traumatization through social catastrophe. *Internat. J. Psycho-Anal.,* 49:302–305.

Edgcumbe, R., & Burgner, M. (1975), The phallic-narcissistic phase: A differentiation between preoedipal and oedipal aspects of phallic development. *The Psychoanalytic Study of the Child,* 30:161–180. New Haven, CT: Yale University Press.

Eliot, T. S. (1925), The hollow men. In: *Collected Poems, 1909–1935.* New York: Harcourt Brace, 1936, p. 104.

Elise, D. (1998), The absence of the paternal penis. *J. Amer. Psychoanal. Assn.,* 46:413–442.

Escoll, P. (1983), The changing vistas of transference. *J. Amer. Psychoanal. Assn.,* 31:699–711.

Esman, A. (1973), The primal scene: A review and a reconsideration. *The Psychoanalytic Study of the Child,* 29:49–83. New Haven, CT: Yale University Press.

Fast, I. (1984), *Gender Identity: A Differentiation Model: Advances in Psychoanalysis, Theory, Research, and Practice,* Vol. 2. Hillsdale, NJ: Analytic Press.

———— (1990), Aspects of early gender development: Toward a reformulation. *Psychoanal. Psychol.,* 7 (Suppl.):105–117.

Fenichel, O. (1927), The economic function of screen memories. In: *The Collected Papers of Otto Fenichel: First Series.* New York: W. W. Norton, 1953, pp. 113–116.

———— (1945), *The Psychoanalytic Theory of Neurosis.* New York: W. W. Norton.

——— (1974), Review of Freud's "Analysis terminable and interminable." *Internat. Rev. Psycho-Anal.*, 1:109–116.

Fleming, J. (1975), Some observations on object constancy in the psycho-analysis of adults. *J. Amer. Psychoanal. Assn.*, 23:743–759.

Freud. A. (1936), *The Ego and the Mechanisms of Defense.* London: Hogarth Press, 1937.

——— (1963), The concept of developmental lines. *The Psychoanalytic Study of the Child,* 18:245–265. New York: International Universities Press.

——— (1965), *Normality and Pathology in Childhood.* New York: International Universities Press.

——— (1971), The infantile neurosis: Genetic and dynamic considerations. *The Psychoanalytic Study of the Child,* 26:79–90. New York: International Universities Press.

Freud, S. (1887–1902), *The Origins of Psychoanalysis. Letters to Wilhelm Fliess, Drafts and Notes,* ed. M. Bonaparte, A. Freud, & E. Kris. New York: Basic Books, 1954.

——— (1894), The neuro-psychoses of defence. *Standard Edition,* 3:45–61. London: Hogarth Press, 1962.

——— (1897), Extracts from the Fliess papers. *Standard Edition,* 1:173–280. London: Hogarth Press, 1966.

——— (1900), The Interpretation of Dreams. *Standard Edition,* 4. London: Hogarth Press, 1953.

——— (1905), Three Essays on the Theory of Sexuality. *Standard Edition,* 7:123–243. London: Hogarth Press, 1953.

——— (1909), Analysis of a phobia in a five-year-old boy. *Standard Edition,* 10:1–147. London: Hogarth Press, 1955.

——— (1910), A special type of choice of object made by men (contributions to the psychology of love, I), *Standard Edition,* 11:163–175. London: Hogarth Press, 1957.

——— (1913), The theme of the three caskets. *Standard Edition,* 12:289–301. London: Hogarth Press, 1958.

——— (1914a), On narcissism. *Standard Edition,* 14:67–102. London: Hogarth Press, 1957.

——— (1914b), Remembering, repeating and working through. *Standard Edition,* 12:145–156. London: Hogarth Press, 1958.

——— (1915a), Instincts and their vicissitudes. *Standard Edition,* 14:109–140. London: Hogarth Press, 1957.

——— (1915b), Observations on transference-love. *Standard Edition,* 12:157–171. London: Hogarth Press, 1958.

———— (1917), Mourning and melancholia. *Standard Edition*, 14:237–258. London: Hogarth Press, 1957.

———— (1919), A child is being beaten. *Standard Edition*, 17:175–204. London: Hogarth Press, 1955.

———— (1920), Beyond the pleasure principle. *Standard Edition*, 18:1–64. London: Hogarth Press, 1955.

———— (1921), Group Psychology and the Analysis of the Ego. *Standard Edition*, 18:65–143. London: Hogarth Press, 1955.

———— (1923), The Ego and the Id. *Standard Edition*, 19:1–59. London: Hogarth Press, 1961.

———— (1924a), The dissolution of the Oedipus complex. *Standard Edition*, 19:171–179. London: Hogarth Press, 1961.

———— (1924b), The economic problem of masochism. *Standard Edition*, 19:155–170. London: Hogarth Press, 1961.

———— (1925a), The Future of an Illusion. *Standard Edition*, 21:1–56. London: Hogarth Press, 1961.

———— (1925b), Some psychical consequences of the anatomical difference between the sexes. *Standard Edition*, 19:243–258. London: Hogarth Press, 1961.

———— (1926), Inhibitions, Symptoms and Anxiety. *Standard Edition*, 20:75–172. London: Hogarth Press, 1959.

———— (1931), Female sexuality. *Standard Edition*, 21:221–243. London: Hogarth Press, 1961.

———— (1933), New Introductory Lectures on Psycho-Analysis. *Standard Edition*, 22:1–182. London: Hogarth Press, 1964.

———— (1937), Analysis terminable and interminable. *Standard Edition*, 23:209–253. London: Hogarth Press, 1964.

———— (1939), Moses and monotheism. *Standard Edition*, 23:1–137. London: Hogarth Press, 1964.

Furst, S., Ed. (1967), *Psychic Trauma*. New York: Basic Books.

———— (1978), The stimulus barrier and the pathogenicity of trauma. *Internat. J. Psycho-Anal.*, 59:345–352.

Gedo, J. (1983), *Portraits of the Artist*. New York: Guilford Press.

———— Goldberg, A. (1973), *Models of the Mind*. Chicago: University of Chicago Press.

Green, A. (1975), The analyst, symbolization and absence in the analytic setting (on changes in analytic practice and analytic experience). *Internat. J. Psycho-Anal.*, 56:1–22.

———— (1980), *On Private Madness*. New York: International Universities Press.

Greenacre, P. (1950), General problems of acting out. *Psychoanal. Quart.*, 19:455–467.

——— (1953), Penis awe and its relation to penis envy. In: *Drives, Affects, and Behavior*, ed. R. M. Loewenstein. New York: International Universities Press, pp. 176–190.

——— (1966), Problems of overidealization of the analyst and of analysis: Their manifestations in the transference and counter-transference relationship. In: *Emotional Growth*, Vol. 2. New York: International Universities Press, 1971, pp. 743–761.

——— (1967), The influence of infantile trauma on genetic patterns. In: *Emotional Growth*, Vol. 1. New York: International Universities Press, pp. 260–299, 1971.

——— (1970), The transitional object and the fetish: With special reference to the role of illusion. In: *Emotional Growth*, Vol. 1. New York: International Universities Press, pp. 335–352, 1971.

——— (1975), On reconstruction. *J. Amer. Psychoanal. Assn.*, 23:693–712.

Greenson, R. R. (1958), On screen defenses, screen hunger, and screen identity. *J. Amer. Psychoanal. Assn.*, 6:242–262.

Gross, G. E., & Rubin, I. A. (1973), Sublimation: The study of an instinctual vicissitude. *The Psychoanalytic Study of the Child*, 27:334–359. New Haven, CT: Yale University Press.

Grossman, L. (1992), An example of "character perversion" in a woman. *Psychoanal. Quart.*, 61:581–589.

Grossman, W., & Stewart, W. (1976), Penis envy: From childhood wish to developmental metaphor. In: *Female Psychology*, ed. H. P. Blum. New York: International Universities Press, pp. 193–212.

Grubrich-Simitis, I. (1979), Extremtraumatisierung als kumulatives Trauma. *Psyche*, 33:991–1023.

Halberstadt-Freud, H. C. (1998), Electra versus Oedipus: Femininity reconsidered. *Internat. J. Psycho-Anal.*, 79:41–56.

Hartmann, H. (1939), *Ego Psychology and the Problem of Adaptation*. New York: International Universities Press, 1958.

Herzog, J. (1982), World beyond metaphor: Thoughts on the transmission of trauma. In: *Generations of the Holocaust*, ed. M. S. Bergmann & M. E. Jucovy. New York: Columbia University Press, pp. 103–119.

Hoffer, W. (1949), Mouth, hand, and ego-integration. *The Psychoanalytic Study of the Child*, 3:49–56. New York: International Universities Press.

———— (1950), Development of the body ego. *The Psychoanalytic Study of the Child*, 5:18–24. New York: International Universities Press.

Horney, K. (1926), The flight from womanhood. *Internat. J. Psycho-Anal.*, 7:324–339.

———— (1932), The dread of women. *Internat. J. Psycho-Anal.*, 13:348–360.

———— (1933), The denial of the vagina. *Internat. J. Psycho-Anal.*, 14:57–70.

Jacobson, E. (1937), The effect of disappointment on ego and superego formation in normal and depressive development. *Psychoanal. Rev.*, 33:129–147.

———— (1959), The exceptions. *The Psychoanalytic Study of the Child*, 14:135–154. New York: International Universities Press.

———— (1964), *The Self and the Object World*. New York: International Universities Press.

Jones, E. (1911), *Papers on Psycho-Analysis*. London: Bailliere, Tindall & Cox, 1948.

———— (1933), The phallic phase. *Internat. J. Psycho-Anal.*, 14:1–33.

———— (1935), Early female sexuality. In: *Papers on Psycho-Analysis*. London: Balliere, Tindall & Cox, 1948, pp. 485–495.

Keiser, S. (1967), Freud's concept of trauma and a specific ego function. *J. Amer. Psychoanal. Assn.*, 15:781–794.

Kernberg, O. (1967), Borderline personality organization. *J. Amer. Psychoanal. Assn.*, 15:641–685.

———— (1975), *Borderline Conditions and Pathological Narcissism*. New York: Jason Aronson.

———— (1977), Boundaries and structure in love relations. *J. Amer. Psychoanal. Assn.*, 25:81–114.

———— (1991), Aggression and love in the relationship of the couple. In: *Perversions & Near-Perversions in Clinical Practice: New Psychoanalytic Perspectives*, ed. G. I. Fogel & W. A. Myers. New Haven, CT: Yale University Press, pp. 153–174.

———— (1992), *Aggression and Personality Disorders and Perversions*. New Haven, CT: Yale University Press.

Kestenberg, J. (1956), Vicissitudes of female sexuality. *J. Amer. Psychoanal. Assn.*, 4:453–476.

———— (1968), Outside and inside, male and female. *J. Amer. Psychoanal. Assn.*, 16:457–520.

———— (1971), From organ-object imagery to self and object representations. In: *Separation-Individuation*, ed. J. B. McDevitt & C.

G. Settlage. New York: International Universities Press, pp. 75–99.

———— (1980), The three faces of femininity. *Psychoanal. Rev.*, 67:313–335.

———— (1982), Rachel M's metapsychological assessment. In: *Generations of the Holocaust*, ed. M. S. Bergmann & M. E. Jucovy. New York: Columbia University Press, pp. 145–158.

Kleeman, J. (1976), Freud's views on early female sexuality in the light of direct child observation. In: *Female Psychology: Contemporary Psychoanalytic Views*, ed. H. P. Blum. New York: International Universities Press, pp. 3–28.

Klein, H. (1981), Presentation to Yale Symposium on the Holocaust, September 26.

Klein, M. (1928), *The Psycho-Analysis of Children*. New York: W. W. Norton, 1932.

Kohut, H. (1971), *The Analysis of the Self*. New York: International Universities Press.

———— (1972), Thoughts on narcissism and narcissistic rage. *The Psychoanalytic Study of the Child*, 27:360–400. New Haven, CT: Yale University Press.

Kris, E. (1951), Some comments and observations on early auto-erotic activities. *The Psychoanalytic Study of the Child*, 6:9–17, 47. New York: International Universities Press.

———— (1956), The recovery of childhood memories in psychoanalysis. *The Psychoanalytic Study of the Child*, 11:54–88. New York: International Universities Press.

Krystal, H., Ed. (1968), *Massive Psychic Trauma*. New York: International Universities Press.

———— (1978), Trauma and affect. *The Psychoanalytic Study of the Child*, 23:81–116. New York: International Universities Press.

———— (1988), *Integration and Self-Healing*. Hillsdale, NJ: Analytic Press.

———— Niederland, W. G. (1971), *Psychic Traumatization: After Effects in Individuals and Communities*. Boston: Little, Brown.

Lampl-De Groot, J. (1965), *The Development of the Mind*. New York: International Universities Press.

Laub, D., & Auerhahn, N. (1993), Knowing and not knowing massive psychic trauma: Forms of traumatic memory. *Internat. J. Psycho-Anal.*, 74:287–302.

Laufer, M. (1993), The female Oedipus complex and the relationship to the body. In: *The Gender Conundrum*, ed. D. Breen. London and New York: Routledge, pp. 67–81.

Lax, R. (1994), Aspects of primary and secondary genital feelings and anxieties in girls during the preoedipal and early oedipal phases. *Psychoanal. Quart.*, 63:271–296.

——— (1997), *Becoming and Being a Woman*. Northvale, NJ: Jason Aronson.

Lewin, B. D. (1933), The body as phallus. *Psychoanal. Quart.*, 1:22–47.

Lichtenberg, J. (1978), The testing of reality from the standpoint of the body self. *J. Amer. Psychoanal. Assn.*, 26:357–385.

Liebert, R. S. (1983), *Michelangelo: A Psychoanalytic Study of His Life and Images*. New Haven, CT: Yale University Press.

Limentani, A. (1981), On some positive aspects of the negative therapeutic reaction. *Internat. J. Psycho-Anal.*, 62:379–390.

Lipin, T. (1963), The repetition compulsion and maturational drive representatives. *Internat. J. Psycho-Anal.*, 44:389–406.

Loewald, H. (1960), On the therapeutic action of psychoanalysis, *Internat. J. Psycho-Anal.*, 41:16–33.

——— (1962), Internalization, separation, mourning, and the superego. *Psychoanal. Quart.*, 31:483–504.

——— (1972), Freud's conception of the negative therapeutic reaction. *J. Amer. Psychoanal. Assn.*, 20:235–242.

——— (1973), On internalization. *Internat. J. Psycho-Anal.*, 54:9–17.

——— (1979), The waning of the Oedipus complex. In: *Papers on Psychoanalysis*. New Haven, CT: Yale University Press, 1980, pp. 384–404.

McDevitt, J. (1971), Preoedipal determinants of an infantile neurosis. In: *Separation-Individuation: Essays in Honor of Margaret S. Mahler*, ed. J. McDevitt & C. Settlage. New York: International Universities Press, pp. 201–228.

McDougall, J. (1972), Primal scene and sexual perversion. *Internat. J. Psycho-Anal.*, 53:371–384.

——— (1985), *Theatres of the Mind*. New York: Basic Books, p. 279.

——— (1995), *The Many Faces of Eros: A Psychoanalytic Exploration of Human Sexuality*. London and New York: W. W. Norton.

Mahler, M. (1966), Notes on the development of basic moods: The depressive affect. In: *Psychoanalysis—A General Psychology: Essays in Honor of Heinz Hartmann*, ed. R. M. Loewenstein, L. Newman, M. Schur, & A. J. Solnit. New York: International Universities Press, pp. 152–168.

——— in collaboration with M. Furer (1968), *On Human Symbiosis and the Vicissitudes of Individuation*, Vol. 1. New York: International Universities Press.

——— (1971), A study of the separation-individuation process and its possible application to borderline phenomena in the psychoanalytic situation. *The Psychoanalytic Study of the Child*, 26:403–424. Chicago: Quadrangle.

——— (1975a), Separation-individuation and object constancy. *J. Amer. Psychoanal. Assn.*, 23:713–739.

——— (1975b), On the current status of the infantile neurosis. *J. Amer. Psychoanal. Assn.*, 23:323–333.

——— Gosliner, B. J. (1955), On symbiotic child psychosis. *The Psychoanalytic Study of the Child*, 10:195–212. New York: International Universities Press.

——— McDevitt, J. (1968), Observations on adaptation and defense *in statu nascendi:* Developmental precursors in the first two years of life. *Psychoanal. Quart.*, 37:1–21.

——— Pine, F., & Bergman, A. (1975), *The Psychological Birth of the Human Infant: Symbiosis and Individuation*. New York: Basic Books.

Maldonado, J. (1983), Analyst involvement in the psychoanalytic impasse. *Internat. J. Psycho-Anal.*, 65:263–271.

Mayer, E. L. (1985), Everybody must be just like me: Observations on female castration anxiety. *Internat. J. Psycho-Anal.*, 66:331–347.

Milrod, D. (1977), The wished for self-image. Lecture presented at Loewenstein Memorial Meeting, New York Academy of Medicine, New York, November.

Neubauer, P. (1987), Disturbances in object representation. *The Psychoanalytic Study of the Child*, 42:335–351. New Haven, CT: Yale University Press.

Novick, J., & Novick, K. K. (1991), Some comments on masochism and the delusion of omnipotence from a developmental perspective. *J. Amer. Psychoanal. Assn.*, 39:307–331.

Olinick, S. (1964), The negative therapeutic reaction. *Internat. J. Psycho-Anal.*, 45:540–548.

Oremland, J. (1989), *Michelangelo's Sistine Ceiling: A Psychoanalytic Study of Creativity*. Madison, CT: International Universities Press.

Panel (1958), Problems of identity. D. Rubinfine, reporter. *J. Amer. Psychoanal. Assn.*, 6:131–142.

———— (1976), The psychology of women. E. Galenson, reporter. *J. Amer. Psychoanal. Assn.*, 24:105–108.

Piaget, J. (1932), *The Moral Judgment of the Child.* Glencoe, IL: Free Press.

Rangell, L. (1972), Aggression, Oedipus and historical perspective. *Internat. J. Psycho-Anal.*, 53:3–11.

Raphling, D. L. (1989), Fetishism in a woman. *J. Amer. Psychoanal. Assn.*, 37:465–491.

Richards, A. K. (1992), Hilda Doolittle and creativity: Freud's gift. *The Psychoanalytic Study of the Child*, 47:391–406. New Haven, CT: Yale University Press.

———— (1996), Primary femininity and female genital anxiety. *J. Amer. Psychoanal. Assn.*, 44 (Suppl.):261–281.

Roiphe, H., & Galenson, E. (1971), The impact of early sexual discovery on mood, defensive organization, and symbolization. *The Psychoanalytic Study of the Child*, 26:195–216. Chicago: Quadrangle.

———— ————(1973), The infantile fetish. *The Psychoanalytic Study of the Child*, 28:147–165. New Haven: Yale University Press.

Rose, G. (1987), *Trauma and Mastery in Life and Art.* New Haven, CT: Yale University Press.

Sandler, J. (1967), Trauma, strain and development. In: *Psychic Trauma*, ed. S. S. Furst. New York and London: Basic Books, pp. 154–174.

———— (1990), On internal object relations. *J. Amer. Psychoanal. Assn.*, 38:859–880.

———— Rosenblatt, B. (1962), The concept of the representational world. *The Psychoanalytic Study of the Child*, 17:128–145. New York: International Universities Press.

———— Sandler, A.-M. (1978), On the development of object relationships and affects. *Internat. J. Psycho-Anal.*, 59:285–293.

Schur, M. (1953), The ego in anxiety. In: *Drives, Affects and Behavior*, ed. R. M. Loewenstein. New York: International Universities Press, pp. 67–103.

———— (1955), Comments on the study of metapsychology of somatization. *The Psychoanalytic Study of the Child*, 10:119–164. New York: International Universities Press.

———— (1963), Mctapsychological aspects of phobias in adults. In: *The Unconscious Today: Essays in Honor of Max Schur,* ed. M. Kanzer. New York: International Universities Press, pp. 97–118.

———— (1966), Correlation of childhood with adult neurosis; Transition from phobic to obsessive-compulsive symptom formation. In: *The Unconscious Today: Essays in Honor of Max Schur,* ed. M. Kanzer. New York: International Universities Press, pp. 119–124.

Shapiro, T. (1977), Oedipal distortions in severe character pathologies: Developmental and theoretical considerations. *Psychoanal. Quart.,* 46:559–579.

Silverman, M. A., Rees, K., & Neubauer, P. B. (1975), On a central psychic constellation. *The Psychoanalytic Study of the Child,* 30: 127–157. New Haven, CT: Yale University Press.

Solnit, A. J. (1982), Early psychic development as reflected in the psychoanalytic process. *Internat. J. Psycho-Anal.,* 63:23–37.

Spitz, R. A. (1955), The primal cavity: A contribution to the genesis of perception and its role for psychoanalytic theory. *The Psychoanalytic Study of the Child,* 10:215–240. New York: International Universitics Press.

——— (1957), *No and Yes: On the Genesis of Human Connection.* New York: International Universities Press.

——— (1965), *The First Year of Life.* New York: International Universities Press.

Stein, M. (1966), Self-observation, reality, and the superego. In: *Psychoanalysis—A General Psychology: Essays in Honor of Heinz Hartmann,* ed. R. M. Loewenstein, L. Newman, M. Schur, & A. J. Solnit. New York: International Universities Press, pp. 275–314.

Steinberg, L. (1983), *The Sexuality of Christ in Renaissance Art and in Modern Oblivion.* New York: Pantheon.

Stern, M. (1959), Anxiety, trauma and shock. *Psychoanal. Quart.,* 34:202–218.

Stoller, R. (1968), *Sex and Gender.* New York: Science House.

——— (1975), *Perversion.* New York: Pantheon.

——— (1977), Primary femininity. In: *Female Psychology: Contemporary Psychoanalytic Views,* ed. H. P. Blum. New York: International Universities Press, pp. 59–78.

Ticho, G. (1977), Female autonomy and young adult women. In: *Female Psychology: Contemporary Psychoanalytic Views,* ed. H. P. Blum. New York: International Universities Press, pp. 139–155.

Tolnay, C. de (1960), *Michelangelo,* Vol. 5. Princeton, NJ: Princeton University Press.

Tolpin, M. (1971), On the beginnings of a cohesive self. *The Psychoanalytic Study of the Child,* 26:316–353. Chicago: Quadrangle.

Valenstein, A. (1973), On attachment to painful feelings and the negative therapeutic reaction. *The Psychoanalytic Study of the Child*, 28:365–392. New Haven, CT: Yale University Press.

Wangh, M. (1959), Structural determinants of phobia: A clinical study. *J. Amer. Psychoanal. Assn.*, 7:675–695.

Winnicott, D. (1953), Transitional objects and transitional phenomena. *Internat. J. Psycho-Anal.*, 24:89–97.

——— (1960), Ego distortion in terms of true and false self. In: *The Maturational Processes and the Facilitating Environment*. New York: International Universities Press, 1965, pp. 140–152.

——— (1965), *The Maturational Processes and the Facilitating Environment*. New York: International Universities Press.

——— (1971), *Playing and Reality*. London: Tavistock.

Zavitzianos, G. (1982), The perversion of fetishism in women. *Psychoanal. Quart.*, 51:405–425.

Name Index

Abelin, E. L., 12, 17, 75
Arlow, J., 55–56, 106, 115, 196
Auerhahn, N., 191

Bach, S., 16, 131
Bak, R. C., 22, 61, 116
Barnett, M. C., 73
Benedek, T., 75
Bergman, A., 108, 109
Bergmann, M. S., 5–6, 81, 131, 162, 171
Bergmann, M. V., xi, xii, 81–82
Blos, P., 19, 25–26, 89, 100
Blum, H. P., 9, 15–16, 23, 28, 74, 84,
    93–94, 173, 176, 183
Boesky, D., 129
Bonaparte, M., 73
Bourdier, P., xii–xiii
Brenner, C., 82, 94
Brodey, W. M., 14, 16
Brunswick, R. M., 33, 80
Burgner, M., 77, 78
Burlingham, D. T., 14

Chasseguet-Smirgel, J., 88, 114n, 128,
    130, 189
Clower, V., 79
Coleman, R., 75

Condorcet, J. A., 3
Cooper, A. M., 130–131

Davidowicz, L., 150
Deutsch, H., 28
DeWind, E., 140

Edelheit, H., 105n
Edgcumbe, R., 77, 78
Eliot, T. S., 195
Elise, D., 74
Escoll, P., 11
Esman, A., 86, 103n

Fast, I., 74
Fenichel, O., 103n, 176
Ferenczi, S., 85
Fleming, J., 15
Fliess, J., 68
Freud, A., 11, 14, 61, 77, 82, 84, 109
Freud, S., 1–4, 11, 28, 30, 67, 68–71, 72,
    76, 79, 81, 82, 85, 86, 87, 93,
    109, 110, 122, 138, 144, 145,
    151, 153, 158, 162, 170, 172,
    176, 177, 189, 191, 198, 209–210
Furst, S., 162, 175

Galenson, E., 74, 75

Gedo, J., 85, 208
Goldberg, A., 85
Gosliner, B. J., 12
Green, A., 4, 29–33, 35–36, 38–39, 183
Greenacre, P., 73, 86, 93, 101, 103, 177
Greenson, R. R., 148
Gross, G. E., 197
Grossman, L., 115
Grossman, W., 77, 111n
Grubrich-Simitis, I., 139, 140

Halberstadt-Freud, H. C., 81–82, 89
Hartmann, H., 2, 71–72, 88
Herzog, J., 149
Hoffer, W., 72
Horney, K., 70–71

Jacobson, E., 16, 22, 88, 89, 109–110,
      138, 144, 146
Jones, E., 71, 72
Jucovy, M., 5–6, 162, 171

Keiser, S., 139
Kernberg, O., xii, 16, 79, 88, 96, 110,
      111, 115, 188, 196
Kestenberg, J., 15, 72–73, 74–75, 89,
      147, 151
Kleeman, J., 73
Klein, H., 137
Klein, M., 70–71
Kohut, H., xii, 96, 111
Kris, E., 72, 75, 136
Krystal, H., 139, 140, 154, 158, 162, 172

Lampl-De Groot, J., 81–82
Laub, D., 191
Laufer, M., 74, 91
Lax, R., 20, 26, 74, 86, 91
Lewin, B. D., 25, 78, 105
Lichtenberg, J., 71
Liebert, R. S., 197–198
Limentani, A., 178
Lipin, T., 158
Loewald, H., 21, 81, 109, 129, 153, 155,
      178, 201

Mahler, M., 5, 12, 17, 19, 48, 74, 76, 84,
      93–94, 95, 108, 109
Maldonado, J., 178, 192
Mayer, E. L., 74

McDevitt, J., 74, 108, 111
McDougall, J., 125, 128, 129
Mendell, D., 4–5
Milrod, D., 109–110

Neubauer, P. B., 11, 210
Niederland, W. G., 139
Novick, J., 208
Novick, K. K., 208

Olinick, S., 178
Oremland, J., 208

Piaget, J., 142
Pine, F., 108, 109
Provence, S., 75

Racamier, P.-C., xii
Rangell, L., 84
Raphling, D. L., 104, 116, 128
Rees, K., 11
Richards, A. K., 20, 26, 209–210
Roiphe, H., 74, 75
Rose, G., 208
Rosenblatt, B., 196
Rubin, I. A., 197

Sandler, A.-M., 129, 152, 171
Sandler, J., 129, 139, 152, 171, 196, 203
Schur, M., 109
Shapiro, T., 82, 110
Silverman, M. A., 11
Solnit, A. J., 11
Spitz, R. A., 72, 94–95, 100
Stein, M., 89, 138
Steinberg, L., 198
Stern, M., 139
Stewart, W., 77
Stoller, R., 73, 74, 95, 130

Ticho, G., 84
Tolnay, C. De, 197
Tolpin, M., 71

Valenstein, A., 184

Wangh, M., 109
Winnicott, D. W., 96, 108, 135, 207

Zavitzianos, G., 104, 128

Subject Index

Abandonment
  fear of, 14–15, 26–27, 63
  issues of, xii
Actualization, 171–172
Adaptability
  in children of Holocaust survivors,
    145
  to concentration camp life, 141
Adolescence, mother-daughter
    problems in, 21–22
Adult love relations, core infantile
    conflict and, 23–24
Affect, superseding reason, 3
Affective memory, 191
Aggressive drive derivatives, 188
Aggressor, identification with, 149,
    154–155
Ambivalence, 82
  toward artistic work, 208
Anal autonomy, 95
Anal sensations, 72
Analysis
  as mutual creation, 211
  trauma during, 161–173
Analyst, idealization of, 97
Analytic neutrality, 121
Androgynous character pattern, 49–50

Animal phobia, 100–102
Anorexia, 205–206
  with depression and role reversal,
    41–42
Anxiety
  recurrent trauma and, 177
  retraumatization, 175–192
Anxiety signal
  interference with, 162
  nonfunctioning, 190
Artists
  hostile attitudes of, 197–198
  work inhibition in, 197–207
Autarkic solutions, xiii
Average expectable environment,
    change in, 162

Baby, wish for, 50–51
Bad mother, 108
Beating fantasy, 86
Bisexual fantasies, 164–165
Bisexual fantasy self, 118
Bisexuality, 62–63, 76–77, 106–107
  in creativity, 209–210
  fantasies of, 122
  female, 5
  potential for, 70

229

Bleeding ulcers, 114
Body cathexis, primary, 72–75
Body feelings, female narcissistic, 76–77
Body image confusion, 115–116,
    208–209
Body self, integration of, 71–72
Borderline pathology, xii
    conflict in, 197
Boundaries, difficulty maintaining, 168
Bulimia, 49–50
    with depression and role reversal,
        41–42
    traumatizing mother and, 183
Bulimia-anorexia cycle, 51
    working through, 52–54

Career, versus motherhood, 46–47
Caregiving
    by mother and father, 110
    to parents, 164
Caregiving fantasies, 12–13
Castrating woman, 77
Castration anxiety, 69
    in girls, 70–71
Central psychic constellation, 10–11
Character formation, narcissistic and
        phobic, 93–112
Character perversion, 5, 55–56
Characterological hunger, 62
Child-mother, 13
Childhood trauma
    versus current trauma, 168–169
    developmental fixations with, 178
    encapsulated, 173
    intrapsychic adaptation to, 162
    repression of, 162–173
Children
    identification with parental suffering
        and losses, 147–149
    as victimizers of parents, 149–150
Christ, identification with, in Holocaust
        survivors' children, 144
Cohesive self, lack of, 125
Compromise formations, 209, 210
Concentration camps, capacity to adapt
        to, 141. See also Holocaust
        survivors
Concretization, 149, 171–172, 210–211
    in Holocaust survivors, 151–152

of mourning process, 153–154
    repetition compulsion and, 158
    somatic, 186, 190
    by trauma survivors, 137
    of traumatic themes, 191
Concretized fantasy enactments, 151–152
Core affect, 94
Core feelings
    bisexuality in, 76–77
    pleasurable sexual sensations in, 73
Core identity, 156
Core infantile conflict, 23–24
Countertransference, 52–54
Creativity
    inhibitions of, 195–199, 208–211
    nature of, 6
    as object relatedness, 208
    in relationships and work, 57–60
    as substitute for procreativity, 55–57
    in transitional space between mother
        and child, 207–208
    treatment of inhibitions of, 199–207

Dead, beloved child, 147–149
Dead mother
    concept of, 29–30
    wish to repair, 30, 31–39
Death
    anxiety over, 140–141
    fear of, 127, 189–190
    inevitability of, 155
    as reunion with nurturing mother, 198
Delayed gratification, 87
Depersonalization, xii, 105, 125–126
    with body image confusion, 115–116
Depression, 4
    dead mother concept and, 29–39
    family conflicts and, 202–203
    mother-daughter role reversal and, 41
    role reversal and, 61
    severe female superego in, 87–88
Detachment, 96–97
Development
    Oedipus complex influencing, 85–87
    phase-specific oedipal issues of, 83
    precursors of oedipal complex in,
        71–72
Developmental arrests, 94
Developmental fixations, 178

Disillusionment, premature, 35, 37–38
Dissociation, 131
Dissolution, 81
Doll play, 74–75
  interference with, 15–16
Dolls, destruction of, 101–102
Doolittle case, 209–210
Double reality, 185

Eating disorders, xii, 47, 49–50. *See also*
  Anorexia; Bulimia
  with depression and role reversal,
    41–42
  working through, 52–54
Ego control, 175–176
Ego function
  diminished in trauma survivors,
    139–142
  oedipal development in, 83
  Oedipus complex and, 85–86
  sense of self in, 95
  superego and, 89
Ego ideal
  failure to develop, 109–110
  Oedipus complex in, 88
Ego psychology, developmental
  hypotheses of, 5
Ego regression, 168
Emergency defensive reaction, 178
Emergency morality, 141–142
Emotional disconfirmation, 13, 35–36
Emptiness, 98–99
Enactments, of early trauma, 176–177,
  186–187, 188–189
Enema ritual, 205–206, 207
Engulfing mother, fear if, 76
Engulfing mother, fear of, 12, 48–49, 64
  role reversal and, 61
Externalization
  in children of Holocaust survivors,
    143
  defensive, 152
  by trauma survivors, 137
  traumatic themes in, 158–159
  to validate fantasies, 171–172

False self, 96
Family
  in psychic recovery from trauma, 136

unconscious need to repeat
  constellation of, 25–27
Fantasies
  capacity for, in trauma survivors,
    139–140
  externalization of, 171–172
Fate neurosis, 28
Father
  collusion to exclude, 102–103
  daughter's envy of, 78
  daughter's identification with, 62–63
  in feminine development, 75
  fixation on, 114–115, 172
  identification with, 168
  interest in daughter's sexuality,
    21–22
  longing for, 102
  mental illness in, 163, 166 167, 190
  merger with, 167, 168, 171
  in mother-daughter role reversal,
    17–19
  overstimulation by, 101–102, 124–125
  as protector against intrusive mother,
    110
  relationship with, 34
  taking penis of, 124–125, 128–129
  violent death of, 180, 182
Father-daughter intimacies, 44–45
  exclusion from, 12
  precocious oedipalized, 20–21
  sexualized, 17–19
Father-daughter relationship
  attempts to repeat, 9–10
  caretaking, 34
Father figure, desexualized, 125
Feeding trauma, 180–184
Female development, 5
  growing awareness of, 4
Female Oedipus complex, 5, 67–68,
  90–91
  concurrent developments influenced
    by, 85–87
  contemporary view of, 80–85
  developmental precursors, 71–72
  female sexuality and, 68–71
  negative oedipal phase in, 76–80
  oral phase as primary body cathexis,
    72–75
  pathological, 113–131

rapprochement subphase of, 75–76
superego development in, 87–90
unconscious organization of, 82
Female perversion, 5
Female sexual identity
conflict over, 115–117
lowered self-esteem interfering with,
78
sacrifice of, 61–62
Female sexuality
Freudian view of, 68–71
penis envy in, 76–77
Feminine self-image, 4
Femininity
history of, 67–68
primary, 73
problems with, xii
Force-feeding, 102, 183, 205–206
hostility to, 98–99, 100, 104–105,
112
intrusive, 180
resistance to, 182–183
Freudian concepts, relevance of, 1–2
Frigidity, 97, 104
in marital relationship, 123–124
oral traumata and, 99
phobic roots of, 105–106
Fusion fantasy, 168, 179–180
with traumatizing object, 172

Gender differentiation, lack of, 56–57
Gender identity. *See also* Female sexual
identity; Sexual identity
core, 74
fluctuating, 62–63
self-perception in, 75
uncertainty about, xii
Generations of the Holocaust (Bergmann
and Jucovy), 5–6
Genital mutilation, feelings of, 200
Genital theft fantasy, 124–125, 128–129
Genitalia, female, cathexis of, 72–75
Genocidal events, survivors of, 136–137
Good enough mothering, 108*n*
Good enough object, 195
Good mother
internalization of, 77, 108
symbiotic, 24, 76, 104–105, 112
Grandiosity fantasies, 122

Gratification
delayed, 87
pursuit of, through hostility and
vengeance, 130
Guilt feelings
with childhood trauma, 183
defense against, 169
survivor's, 154–159

Heterosexuality, flight into, 89
Holding environment, 135
Holocaust Study Group, 6
Holocaust survivors
children of, 5–6, 143–146
identifying children as aggressors,
149–150
massive traumatization effects on
psychic structure of, 139–142
pact of silence in, 138, 152
reality testing problems in, 137–138
retraumatization anxiety in, 184–187
superego pathology in, 135–159
survivor's guilt in, 154–159
Holocaust traumata, reliving of, 150
Hostility
binding, 111
defense against, 96
Human behavior, overdetermined, 3
Human psyche, growing understanding
of, 3
Hyper-maturity, xiii

Ideal children, of Holocaust survivors,
143–144
Idealism, post-Enlightenment, 2–3
Idealization
of children, 143–144
of parents, 89
Identification
conflicting, 89–90
with parents, 89
with traumatizing object, 172
Impulse control, mother's difficulty
with, 13
Incest, xii
Incest taboo, 69
Incestuous conflict, 114–115, 118
Incestuous oedipal wishes, 23–24
Incestuous tie, unconscious, 21–22

Individuation, from parental
    representations, 84. *See also*
    Separation-individuation
Infantile amnesia, 6
    lifting of, 100
Infantile trauma
    magical denial of, 130–131
    trauma during analysis and, 161–173
Inhibitions, Symptoms and Anxiety
    (Freud), 177
Internal objects
    conflictual relationships with, 198
    work inhibition and, 195–211
Internalization, 211
    difficulties with, 210
    incomplete, 89–90
    normal, 108
    split in, 89
    of traumata, 191
Internalized relationships,
    encapsulated, 170
Intrapsychic conflict, interfering with
    creativity, 195–196
Introjected parent, 203

Latency, mother-daughter problems in,
    21–22
Libidinal dialogue, 195
Libidinal regression, 168
"Little Hitler" image, 149–150

Madonna, Michelangelo's, 198
Magic phallus, 103
Marriage, fear of, 24–25
Masculinity complex, 76
Masochism, 86
    female, 90
    narcissistic rage and, 87
Masturbation
    in feminine development, 73–74
    guilt over, 80
    in oedipal girl, 79–80
    during psychosexual period, 79–80
    to restore feeling of wholeness, 200
Masturbation enactments, 119
Masturbation fantasies
    bisexual and omnipotent narcissism
        in, 106
    as compromise formations, 209

Maternal father, 110
Maternal identification, split, 89, 90
Maternal image, desexualized, 117
Maternal trauma, internalization of,
    29–39
Maternity
    conflicting with sexuality and
        marriage, 10
    fear of, 24–25
    mother-daughter role reversal and,
        25–27
    rejection of, 43–44
Meaning, loss of, 35
Messianic delusions, 147
Messiness, 207
Michelangelo, destruction of works by,
    197–198
Mistress fantasy, 18–19, 27–28, 31, 44
Mood swings, 41
Moral absolutism, 142
Mother. *See also* Dead mother; Engulfing
        mother, fear of; Good mother
    ambivalence toward, 82
    child as caregiver to, 12–13, 209
    clinging to, 123
    conflict over rejection by, 51–52
    depressed, 29–39, 41
    disturbed identification with, 78–79,
        89–90
    emotionally unavailable, 29–30
    engulfing, 64
    fear of abandonment by, 63
    fear of reengulfment by, 12, 48–49
    hatred of, 125–126, 127
    idealization of, 103
    identification with, 79, 83
    inconsistent protectiveness by, 17
    introjected, 203
    intrusive, 180–183, 205
    nonnurturing, 114
    phobic, 109, 110
    preverbal relationship with, 184
    separation-individuation from,
        75–76, 207
    traumatizing, 180–184
    unexpressed hostility toward,
        203–204
    wish for reunion with, 107–108
    wish to reanimate, 29–30, 31–32

Mother-child dyad
  failure of, 98
  unmet needs of, 77
Mother-child interaction
  paradigm of, 93–94
  reconstruction of, 93
  symbolization in, 75
  transitional space in, 207–208
Mother-child relatedness
  disturbances of, 15–16
  loss of, 13–14
Mother-daughter interaction, lack of
      love in, 43
Mother-daughter role reversal, xii–xiii,
      4, 9–12, 27–28, 165–166
  adulthood and, 23–24
  analytic process with, 46–47
  case psychoanalysis of, 41–64
  creativity and, 55–57
  dead mother and, 29–39
  father's role in, 17–19
  as genetic turning point, 12–17
  latency and adolescence problems
      in, 21–22
  life history of, 42–46
  love relations, work and creativity in,
      57–60
  marriage and, 24–25
  maternity and, 25–27
  negative oedipal constellation in,
      19–21
  reflections on analysis of, 61–64
  termination phase with, 60–61
  transference in, 48–52
  working through and
      countertransference with, 52–54
Motherhood
  career conflict with, 46–47
  disturbed motivation for, 90–91
Motility, cathexis of, 85–86
Mourning
  blockage of, 140
  concretization of, 153–154
  process of, 153
Munch, Edvard, hostile attitude of,
      toward paintings, 197
Murderous fantasies, 202, 203
Mythmaking, by trauma survivors,
      136–137

Narcissistic alliance, 109, 210–211
Narcissistic character formation, case
      analysis of, 93–112
Narcissistic injury, 37
  denial of, 115
  superego development and, 88
Narcissistic pathology, xii
  phobic character formation and, 95
Narcissistic rage, 31
  masochism and, 87
  unmet needs in, 77
Narcissistic self-denigration, 200, 202
Narcissitic-phallic fantasy, 101
Negative oedipal phase
  constellation of, 19–21
  in female oedipal complex, 76–80
  mastery of, 79
Negative therapeutic reaction, 5, 6,
      33
  defensive function of, 175–192
  as emergency self-defense, 178
Neurosis
  Oedipus complex as nucleus of, 81
  repressed conflict in, 196–197
Not good enough mother, 108

Object constancy, 22, 95
Object loss, 32
  fear of, 111–112
  in separation-individuation, 75–76
Object relatedness
  creativity as, 208
  difficulties with, 210
Object relationships
  disturbed, 10
  from dyadic to triangular, 90–91
  oedipal, 82
  Oedipus complex and, 84
  sadomasochistic, 31
Oedipal conflicts
  in adult love relations, 23–24
  in all developmental phases, 83
  alternating currents of, 28
  partially repressed, 173
Oedipal constellation, pathological,
      113–131
Oedipal fantasies, fate of, 81
Oedipal guilt, heightened, 34
Oedipal objects, ability to cathect, 85

Oedipal phase
    development failure in, 89–90
    paternal overstimulation during, 101
Oedipal precocity, 17–18
Oedipal wishes, universal, 69
Oedipalization, 79, 89
Oedipus complex, 68
    contemporary view of, 80–85
    in developmental continuum, 11
    female, 67–91
    in neurosis, 81
    survivor's guilt and, 155
    unresolved, 85
Oedipus myth, 155
Omnipotence fantasies, 83, 202, 205
    survivor's guilt and, 157
Omnipotent narcissistic wishes,
        106–107
Oral phase
    as primary body cathexis, 72–75
    traumatic, 98–99
Organizers, 94–95
Overeating, 49–51. See also Bulimia;
        Eating disorders
    with depression and role reversal,
        41–42
    to restore feeling of wholeness, 200
Overstimulation, 101–102, 124–125,
        127
    protection against, 181
Overstuffed sensation, 49–51, 53

Pain, sexualization of, 86–87
Painful affect
    affinity for, 184
    need to tolerate, 187–188
Parent-child relationship
    mutually idealizing, 109
    in self-healing of survivors, 137
    traumatic, 136–137
Parent-child role reversal, 165–167. See
        also Mother-daughter role
        reversal
Parental lovemaking, exposure to, 119
Parental representations
    conflicting identifications with,
        89–90
    difficulties in internalization of, 87
    individuation from, 84

partially internalized, 172–173
Parents. See also Father; Mother
    dependence on, 96–98
    differentiation from, 48
    disappointment with, 163–164
    internal dialogue with, 196
    partial differentiation from, 206
    ritualistic resurrection and rekilling
        of, 200–201
Paternal phallus, child identified as, 26
Pathological oedipal constellation,
        female, 113–131
Pavor nocturnus, 86
Pedophilic fantasies, 179–180, 183
Penis
    fantasy of theft of, 124–125, 128–129
    phobia of, 101–102
Penis envy, 69, 70–71, 74
    as bedrock of feminine sexuality,
        76–77
    phase-specific, 17, 19
    phase-specific transition of, 77
Perception
    cathexis of, 85–86
    disturbances in, 210
Perfectionism, 100
Perverse character pathology, 115
Perverse oedipal fantasies, core of,
        125–126
Perverse trends, xii
Perversion, 5
    gratification through hostility in,
        130–131
    preoedipal fixation and, 113
    repressed, 113
Phallic-exhibitionistic self-expression,
        19–20
Phallic-narcissistic phase, 77
Phallic-oedipal phase, 77
Phobia
    in phallic stage, 100–102
    proneness to, 109–110
Phobic character formation, 93–112
Phobic reactions, emergence of, 95
Photophobia, 181–182, 189
Pietà Rondanini, 197–198
Pregnancy fantasy, 105n
Preoedipal fixations, 79
    in perversion, 113

Preoedipal phase
  influence on Oedipus complex,
    81–82
  paternal overstimulation during, 101
Primal scene
  fantasies and adaptive capacities
    related to, 86
  reconstruction of, 103–104
  wish to masturbate during, 106
Primal scene fantasies, 22
Primary objects, premature separation
  from, 208–209
On Private Madness (Green), 4
Promiscuity, 114, 130
  phase of, 104
Prostitute fantasy, 114
Psychic body experience, 72–75
Psychic conflict, interfering with
  creativity, 195–197
Psychic reintegration, 158–159
Psychic representations, core of, 156
Psychic sexual identity, 70
Psychic structures
  formation of, 87
  massive traumatization effects on,
    139–142
  Oedipus complex as organizer of,
    80–81
  phase-specific changes in, 91
Psychoanalysis
  evolution of concepts of, xi
  for traumatic crisis, 167–169
Psychoanalytic techniques, history of,
  xi–xii
Psychological trauma, xii
Psychosomatic symptoms, 190

Quasi-parental precocity, 14

Rapprochement crisis, resolution of, 95
Rapprochement subphase
  in female Oedipus complex, 75–76
  prevention of, 109
  resolution of, 87
Reality testing
  distorted, 116
  in Holocaust survivors, 137–138
  object constancy and, 22
  superego and, 89

Reason, power of, 3
Reconstruction, 93, 98–100
  of phallic phase memories, 101–103
  phase- and subphase-specific, 93–94
  of primal scene episodes, 103–104
Reengulfment
  bad mother of, 76
  fear of, 12, 48–49
Regression, interpretation of, 168–169
Reintegration, of psychic structure,
  158–159
Remembering, versus reexperiencing,
  177–178
Repetition compulsion
  concretization and, 158
  with unmastered trauma, 176–177
Repressed conflict, 196–197
Repressed memory, 175
  affective experience and, 191
  evoking in treatment, 188
Repression, 81
  analysis for, 161
  of early trauma, 176–177
Restitution fantasy, 150
Retraumatization
  emergency reaction against, 188
  fear of, 176
Retraumatization anxiety
  defense against, 175–192
  negative therapeutic reaction to,
    179–184
Ritualistic behavior, 200–201
Ritualistic restitutional reenactments,
  201
Role reversal
  case of, 4
  depression and, 29–39
  mother-child, 4
  parent-child, 165–166
  in transference, 35–39

Sadistic wishes, 139
Sadomasochistic fantasies, 86–87
  in work inhibition, 208
Screen memory, 99–100, 180
Self-cathexis, maintaining, 15–16
Self-cohesiveness, 13–14
Self-healing, 136
  parent-child interactions in, 137

Self-identity, role reversal and, 61
Self-image, first, 71–72
Self-protective capacity, loss of, 171–172
Self-renunciation, 141
Self representation, faulty, 109
Self-sufficiency, xiii
Selfhood, sense of, 114
Separation, 100
    premature, 208–209
    prevention of, 109–110
Separation anxiety, 76
    phobia and, 112
Separation-individuation, 75–76, 83
    in children of Holocaust survivors, 157
    problems of, in children of Holocaust survivors, 146
Sexual identity. See also Female sexual identity
    formation of, 70
    marriage and motherhood in, 11
Sexual overstimulation, 101–102, 124–125, 127
    protection against, 181
Sexual phantasy, 68–69
Sexual secrets, 119–120
Sexual vagina, 89
Sexuality
    conflicting with maternity, 10
    female, 68–71
Shared fantasies, in Holocaust survivors and children, 144–145
Somatic concretization, 186, 190
Somatic stress responses, 109
Specialness, sense of, 96
Splitting, 108n
    in work inhibition, 208
Sterilization
    parent-child relations and, 46
    rejection by mother and, 51
    role reversal and, 63
    sacrificing femininity, 61–62
Stress, maladaptations to, 94
Sublimation, 37, 56–57
Substitute-for-mourning mechanisms, 153
Superego
    development of, 87–90
    in males and females, 87–88

pathology of, in survivors, 135–159
    postoedipal, 88–89
    pressures of, in children of Holocaust survivors, 145–146
    traumatization impact on, 138–139
Superego pathology
    in postwar families of Holocaust survivors, 142–143
    shared between Holocaust survivors and their children, 151–154
    survivor's guilt and, 158–159
Superwoman fantasy, 116, 117–118
Survivors
    children of, 136–159
    superego pathology in, 135–159
Survivor's guilt, 154–159, 186
Symbiosis, good mother of, 24, 76, 104–105, 112
Symbiotic feeling states, 167
Symbiotic period, 72
Symbiotic relationship, wish for, 11–12
Symbolic actions, 200–201
Symbolization
    capacity for, in trauma survivors, 139–140, 141, 152
    enactment as, 189
    gender identity and, 75
    impaired, 152, 191
    reacquired capacity for, 183–184
    of repressed trauma, 186–187
    temporary loss of capacity for, 149

Therapeutic alliance, 198–199
Thinking disorder, 207
Toilet training, coercive, 99
Torture fantasies, 22
Transference
    break in relationship of, 178–179
    erotized, 9–10
    hostility to force-feeding in, 100
    idealizing, 111, 170–171
    maladaptations and arrests in, 94
    with mother-daughter role reversal, 48–52
    negative, 168, 169
    oedipal material in, 111
    reconstruction and, 93
    role reversal in, 14–15, 35–39
    sexualization of, 36–37

sustaining, 63–64
triple-faceted, 209
Transference fantasy, femininity
   conflict in, 116–117
Transference-fusion fantasy, 117
Transference neurosis
   idealization and disillusionment in, 22
   trauma reliving in, 181, 182,
      187–188
Transitional object, 208
Transitional space, artistic work in,
   207–208
Trauma, 5–6
   during analysis, 161–173
   anxiety of reliving, 176–192
   enactment of, 188–189
   failure to master, 175–176
   intrapsychic reaction to, 162
   latent, 170–171
   repressed, 176–177
   superego pathology in survivors of,
      135–159
   unmastered, 188–189
Traumatic freezing, 25
Traumatic reliving, 157–158
   hallucinatory, 181, 182
   in Holocaust survivors, 150
   in transference neurosis, 187–188
   in work inhibition, 207

Traumatization
   effects on psychic structure of
      Holocaust survivors, 139–142
   superego function affected by,
      138–139
Traumatized patients, xii
Traumatizing object, identification
   with, 172
Triangular relationships, 90–91
Triangulation, 82, 85
Tubal ligation, parents' involvement in,
   46

Vaginal sensations
   cathexis of, 112
   in feminine development, 75
   in oral phase, 72
   repressed, 71, 73
Vaginal tensions, discharging and
   mastering, 74–75
Value systems, preserving, 137
Verbal communication
   capacity for, in trauma survivors,
      140–141
   impaired, 191

Work inhibition, 54
   internal objects and, 195–211
Working through, eating disorder, 52–54

About the Author

Maria V. Bergmann is a practicing psychoanalyst in New York. She is a training and supervising analyst of the New York Freudian Society and the International Psychoanalytical Association; faculty and member of the Institute for Psychoanalytic Training and Research; and member of the American Psychological Association, Division of Psychoanalysis, and the American Psychoanalytic Association.

Her psychoanalytic papers and teaching activities in this country and abroad have centered on issues of feminine development, creativity, trauma, the Holocaust, problems of technique, and the treatment of perversions.